The Witches of Warboys

'*The Witches of Warboys* is a fascinating but neglected episode in the history of English witch-trials. Using contemporary texts and parish records, Philip C. Almond pieces together the story with scholarly diligence, investigative determination, and the imagination of a dramatist. The result is an engrossing, frame-by-frame tale of fear, prejudice and persecution in a rural parish, with intriguing ramifications for the social and intellectual history of Elizabethan England. There are ghosts, devils and demoniacs, bizarre dreams, afflictions and accusations, harsh interrogations and sordid executions. Professor Almond is a trustworthy guide into this lost world of belief and brutality, stripping bare the alien cosmology and mentality of our tense and troubled ancestors.'
Malcolm Gaskill, Fellow and Director of Studies in History, Churchill College, Cambridge, and author of *Hellish Nell: Last of Britain's Witches* **and** *Witchfinders: A Seventeenth-Century English Tragedy*

'This is a splendid case-study, of the classic kind that tells a gripping story in order to illuminate major historical themes. The whole of Elizabethan witchcraft is concentrated into a vivid consideration of one Huntingdonshire trial and the events that led up to it. As the story unfolds, we are confronted with the horrific double problem of how people can come to believe in a monstrous untruth, and how they can persuade others to believe in it as well. Psychology, history and literary criticism all meet in these pages, and sixteenth-century demonology comes face to face with modern issues surrounding the ability of interrogation methods to reveal or distort truths. This is at once a compelling study of the thought world of Reformation-period Protestantism and one of the timeless psychopathology of confession. Philip Almond takes us quite literally to realms beyond reason, where the only alternatives confronting an enquirer are demonic possession, paranormal human powers or mental illness. Even if the truth of what happened probably lies beyond any person now living, what this book does establish, convincingly and disturbingly, is the universe of belief within which such a tragedy can occur.'
Ronald Hutton, Professor of History, University of Bristol and author of *Witches, Druids and King Arthur* **and** *The Triumph of the Moon: A History of Modern Pagan Witchcraft*

'*The Witches of Warboys* is one of those rare scholarly works that press impeccable research into the service of a thumping good read. Eschewing the usual ornate postmodern theories of Renaissance daemonomania, Philip C. Almond articulates the Warboys tragedy with passion, compassion, and exquisite erudition. The result is the single best witch-craze narrative to appear in over a generation.'
James Morrow, author of *The Last Witchfinder*

The WITCHES _of_ WARBOYS

An Extraordinary Story of Sorcery, Sadism and Satanic Possession

PHILIP C. ALMOND

I.B. TAURIS

LONDON · NEW YORK

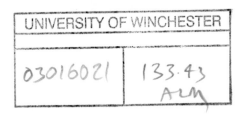
Published in 2008 by I.B.Tauris & Co. Ltd
6 Salem Road, London W2 4BU
175 Fifth Avenue, New York NY 10010
www.ibtauris.com

In the United States and Canada distributed by Palgrave Macmillan,
a division of St. Martin's Press, 175 Fifth Avenue, New York NY 10010

ISBN: 978 1 84511 508 1

A full CIP record for this book is available from the British Library
A full CIP record for this book is available from the Library of Congress
Library of Congress catalog card: available

Typeset in Minion by Dexter Haven Associates Ltd, London
Printed and bound in Great Britain by TJ International, Padstow Cornwall

To Father Des Brockhoff,
Mentor and Friend

Contents

Acknowledgements

This book would never have been completed in anything like a timely fashion if it had not been for the assistance of many others. I am grateful to the archivists at the Huntingdonshire, Bedfordshire, and Northamptonshire Record Offices for their kind assistance. I owe a debt of gratitude too to the librarians at the Cambridge University Library, the Bodleian at Oxford, the British Library in London, and the Norris Museum in St Ives. I am also grateful to Tyndale House, Cambridge, for providing delightful surroundings in which to pursue much of the research. I want also to thank Ms Diana Lucas, current owner of the manor house in Warboys for showing me through her home. I am grateful too to Mr Alex Wright of I.B.Tauris for his excellent advice and editorial skills, and to my colleague Dr Helen Farley for proof-reading the final manuscript.

The archival work was undertaken by means of a travel grant from the Centre for the History of European Discourses at the University of Queensland. This centre and this university continue as congenial places to do research on materials distant not only in time but also in space. I am fortunate to have had the support and friendship over many years of colleagues at this university. I thank my partner, Patricia Lee, who has patiently endured my reading the text to her as it was being written and has provided helpful criticism.

For ease of reading, early modern spelling and grammar have been modernised where and as appropriate.

Plates

10. Detail from frontispiece to Richard Boulton, *A Compleat History of Magick, Sorcery, and Witchcraft*, vol.1 (London, 1715). By permission of Monash University Library.

11. The title page of *The most wonderfull and true Storie, of a certaine Witch named Alse Gooderidge* (London, 1597). By permission of the Lambeth Palace Library.

12. Swimming the witch. Detail from title page of *Witches apprehended, examined and executed* (London, 1613). By permission of the Huntington Library.

13. The title page of *A most certain, strange, and true Discovery of a Witch* (n.p., 1643). By permission of Glasgow University Library, Department of Special Collections.

14. Frontispiece to Matthew Hopkins' *The Discovery of Witches* (London, 1647). By permission of the British Library.

15. The title page of *The Apprehension and Confession of three notorious Witches* (London, 1589). By permission of the Lambeth Palace Library.

16. The pond in Warboys.

17. Orchard Lane, Huntingdon.

18. The Huntingdon Gaol cellar.

19. The field outside Huntingdon which held the gallows.

20. Detail of Huntingdon from John Speed's *The Theatre of the Empire of Great Britaine* (London, 1611). By permission of the Fryer Library, University of Queensland.

Characters

The Parents
Robert Throckmorton
Elizabeth Throckmorton
Gabriel Throckmorton, Robert's father
Emma Throckmorton, Robert's mother

The Children
Jane Throckmorton
Elizabeth Throckmorton
Mary Throckmorton
Grace Throckmorton
Joan Throckmorton
Robert Throckmorton

The Neighbours
John Samuel
Alice Samuel
Agnes Samuel, daughter of Alice and John
Cicely Burder, a friend of Alice
The Chappels

The Relatives
Francis Dorington, the vicar of Warboys, brother-in-law of Elizabeth Throckmorton
Mary Dorington, wife of Francis Dorington, sister of Robert Throckmorton
Gilbert Pickering, witch-hunter, brother of Elizabeth Throckmorton
Dorothy Pickering, wife of Gilbert Pickering
Henry Pickering, brother of Elizabeth Throckmorton, grandfather of John Dryden
John Lawrence, a distant cousin
Robert Throckmorton of Brampton, cousin of Robert Throckmorton

Edward Pickering, brother of Elizabeth Throckmorton
John Pickering, cousin of Elizabeth Pickering
Elizabeth Cervington, cousin-in-law of Elizabeth Throckmorton, the last to be possessed
Gilbert Pickering, son of John Pickering, Elizabeth's cousin, and Elizabeth Cervington

The Friends
Mistress Andley of St Ives
Master Whittle of St Ives
Lady Susan Cromwell, wife of Sir Henry Cromwell, Oliver Cromwell's grandfather
Sir Henry Cromwell, Master of Hinchinbrook and Ramsey Abbey
John Dorington, Justice of the Peace, brother of Francis Dorington, friend of Robert Throckmorton
Cromwell Henry, son of Sir Henry Cromwell
Robert Poulter, vicar of Brampton

The Doctors
Philip Barrow of Cambridge
William Butler, Clare College, Cambridge

The Judges
William Wickham, the Bishop of Lincoln
Francis Cromwell, Justice of the Peace, and brother of Henry Cromwell
Richard Tryce, Justice of the Peace
Edward Fenner, assizes judge
Master Doctor Chamberlin, the chaplain to the condemned

The Devils
Pluck
Catch
White
Blue
Smack
Hardname
Smack, Smack's cousin
Smack, another of Smack's cousins
Callico

And why on me? Why should the envious world
Throw all their scandalous malice upon me?
'Cause I am poor, deformed and ignorant,
And like a bow buckled and bent together,
By some more strong in mischiefs than myself?
Must I for that be made a common sink,
For all the filth and rubbish of men's tongues
To fall and run into? Some call me witch;
And being ignorant of myself, they go
About to teach me how to be one: urging
That my bad tongue (by their bad usage made so)
Forespeaks their cattle, doth bewitch their corn,
Themselves, their servants and their babes at nurse.
Thus they enforce upon me. And in part
Make me to credit it.

The Witch of Edmonton (1621)

Act 2, Scene 1, 1–15a

Prologue

i.

A Neighbourly Visit

On Sunday 12 November 1589, Alice Samuel paid a visit to her next-door neighbours, the Throckmortons. They had recently taken up residence in the manor house in Warboys in Cambridgeshire. Then, as now, it was a small, bucolic village situated about sixteen miles north-west of Cambridge, and some seven miles north of Huntingdon (see Plate 1). For the last several days, Jane, the nine-year-old daughter of Robert and Elizabeth Throckmorton, had been sick. And Alice, acting on the principles of good neighbourliness, had come to enquire about the welfare of the child.

Alice settled herself into a seat in the large ingle-nooked fireplace. She had not had time to get comfortable before the child's condition appeared to worsen. Quite suddenly, Jane shouted aloud, gesticulating wildly at Alice, 'Look where the old witch sits. Did you ever see one more like a witch than she is?' (*The Witches of Warboys* sig.A.3.r).

With those fateful words, Jane set in motion a train of dramatic and dreadful events, which was to culminate over three years later in Alice Samuel, her husband and daughter appearing in court charged with the horrific crimes of witchcraft and murder.

Early in 1593 the Samuels faced serious charges under the Elizabethan witchcraft statute of 1563 'against Conjurations, Enchantments, and Witchcrafts'. The penalty for damage caused to persons or their property by witchcraft was one year's imprisonment and being pilloried for six hours once in every quarter of that year for the first offence. For any subsequent infraction an offender faced the death sentence.

The penalty was more forbidding for murder by means of witchcraft: 'If any person or persons after the first day of June next coming, use, practise or exercise any invocations or conjurations of evil and wicked spirits, to or for any intent or purpose; or else if any person or persons after the said first day of June shall use, practise or exercise any witchcraft, enchantment, charm or sorcery, whereby any person shall happen to be killed or destroyed...shall suffer pains of death as a felon or felons.'[1] And it was under this section of the Act that the Samuels were later brought to trial.

How could that single act of kindness by one neighbour to another in a quiet rural backwater near Cambridge result in one of the most infamous, horrifying, and celebrated cases of witchcraft persecution to take place in early modern England? This is the central question that I set out to answer when I began to write the story of the Witches of Warboys.

ii.

The Text, Fact and Fiction

The only account we have of the Warboys story is contained in a work entitled *The most strange and admirable Discoverie of the three Witches of Warboys, arraigned, convicted, and executed at the last Assises at Huntington, for the bewitching of the five daughters of Robert Throckmorton Esquire, and divers other persons, with sundrie Divellish and grievous torments: And also for the bewitching to death of the Lady Crumwell, the like hath not been heard of in this age* (see Plate 2).

The book was published by Thomas Man in 1593 under the patronage of Judge Edward Fenner. He it was who had presided over the trial of the Samuels. Twice a year, two judges were sent out from London to try criminal cases at the assizes courts in the counties. Granting that, the reference to '*the last Assises*' in the title suggests that the work was published within the six months after the death of the Samuels, somewhere between April and September 1593. We can narrow this down a little further. On 30 June 1593, a work entitled *Th[e] arraignement Judgement and execucon of three wytches of Huntingdonshire* was entered in the Registers of the Company of Stationers of London under the names of Thomas Newman and John Wynnyngton.

The title registered is only approximate to that of the Warboys account and it is attributed to Thomas Newman rather than Thomas Man. But it appears more than likely that this is the same text. The entry in the Registers indicates that the truth of it was vouched for by Edward Fenner 'under his handwriting shown in a Court or assembly held this Day according to the ordinances of the company', and that 'The note under master Justice Fenner's is Layd up in the wardens cupboard'.[2]

The version registered on 30 June 1593 may in fact be the second edition, since there is another version of the text, 'Printed by the Widdowe Orwin, for Thomas Man, and John Winnington'. For various stylistic reasons, this latter version is arguably earlier.

So it seems reasonable to deduce that – at the latest – within three months of the deaths of the Samuels their story entered the public domain, and may have appeared even earlier.

Compared to other texts about witchcraft and possession, the Warboys account is long, comprising around 50,000 words. Both versions run to over 110 pages of tightly packed script in the 'Gothic' style. Copies of the text survive in the British Library in London, the Bodleian Museum in Oxford, the Norris Museum Library in St Ives, Cambridgeshire, the Folger Shakespeare Library in Washington, DC, and the University of Glasgow Library.[3] All other accounts of the story are ultimately reliant on one or other of the two 1593 versions.

Apart from this text, we have no records at all of the case. No judicial or other documents have endured. The only other reference to the story from the period is the record of a ballad, entered in the Stationers' Registers on 4 December 1593, and entitled *A Lamentable Songe of Three Wytches of Warbos*. The ballad has not survived to be read. But its historical existence attests to the vivid impact that the story of the witches of Warboys had on the public imagination of the day.

But how do we know that the story of the witches of Warboys is not mere fiction? In the first place, the existence of many of the characters in the story can be verified independently of the text itself through contemporary records. Second, there is a verisimilitude implicit in the narrative itself. We don't know who wrote it; or rather, we don't know who finally put the text together in the form in which we now have it for the printer in 1593. However, what we can see is that there is a diversity of authorial voices within the text: Robert Throckmorton, the girls' father; Francis Dorington, the Warboys vicar; Gilbert and Henry Pickering, the children's uncles; Thomas Nut, vicar of Ellington; and so on. And the text draws upon a variety of oral and written reports: diaries kept at the time, records of confessions, and evidence from witnesses. The detailed chronology of events – times, places, dates – is intended to reinforce the accuracy of the reports, as is the juridical framework which holds much of the text together. In short, the story reads like a record of real events and actual conversations.[4]

Judge Edward Fenner seems to have had a role in producing the final version of the text. He took, we are told, 'extraordinary pains in perfecting this work for the printing' (sig.A.2.r). Fenner was doubtless concerned that his actions be presented in as positive a light as possible. However, it seems most likely, on balance, that the text was edited into its current form by Robert Throckmorton, father of the bewitched children.

Whatever its origin, the book was clearly intended to prove that the Samuels were guilty, that they really were the cause of the sufferings which beset the children, and the cause of the demise of Lady Cromwell. It served above all as a proof that the deaths of the Samuels were abundantly merited. It was the Throckmortons who had the latter brought to trial, and the dominant concern of the text is to justify their actions. And the whole drama was, at root, a class conflict between the socially superior gentry family of the Throckmortons and their relatives, and a yeoman family, lower down the pecking order, the Samuels. No one from Warboys appears as a witness, either for the Throckmortons, or the Samuels. All are relatives or allies of the Throckmortons.

Not long after the trial had ended, rumours began to circulate that an injustice had been perpetrated. We read that there were some in the county, among those who thought themselves wise, who said 'that this Mother Samuel now in question, was an old simple woman, and that one might make her by (fair) words confess what they would' (sig.H.1.v). Robert Throckmorton's reputation was brought into question. And the publication of the story was intended to reaffirm his standing in the community.

It was a commonly held belief that the power of witches could not be perpetuated beyond their own deaths, and that they had no capacity to harm others from beyond the grave. Those possessed returned to rude health once a witch was dead (or on occasion even when imprisoned). The recovery of the Throckmorton children reaffirmed the mendaciousness of the Samuels. And the Warboys book concludes with a report to this effect on the vitality of the children: 'If any desire to know the present state of these children, how they are and have been since the death of these parties, you will understand that, since their day of execution, not any of them have had any fit at all, neither yet grudging or complaining of any such thing, but have all of them been in as good estate and as perfect health as ever from their birth' (sig.O.4.r).

So, we must expect the text to present the Throckmortons in as flattering a light as is possible, and the Samuels in a correspondingly poor one. And the only voices we hear clearly are those of the persecutors and the prosecutors. But, even though they are faint, we can still hear the voices of the Samuels through a glass darkly, as it were, refracted through the shriller tones of those who recorded theirs: those who wrote not to suggest their innocence but to demonstrate their guilt, and damn them for all eternity.

iii.

A World of Sorcery

The Warboys story was no doubt of intense interest to contemporaries of the Samuels and of the Throckmortons. For, in the world which they inhabited, the story could easily have been a record of fact. In a culture which accepted as a given the reality of sorcerers and witches, bewitchment, and possession by wicked spirits, the critical question was: were the Throckmorton children really possessed and were the Samuels guilty of bewitching them and bringing about the death of Lady Cromwell?

To me, I must confess, the story is of interest not because it reflects a view of the world which could possibly be true but because, at the most fundamental level, it embodies assumptions about the world which could *not* possibly be so. The appeal of the story lies, in part, in its very 'otherness', in its powerful invocation of a world quite alien to our own. We do *not*, by and large, inhabit a world in which witchcraft is an accepted reality, or a world in which it is feasible to bewitch others to death and send evil spirits into children. And, if it is the case that witchcraft is not a possibility, then Alice Samuel, her husband, and her daughter must have been innocent. And her confessions of guilt could not have been true.

But, in spite of its quite different world view, it is also a story which seems familiar to us. For it is a narrative of unforeseen accidents and illness, of unexplained deaths, of conflict between neighbours, of accusations by children against adults, of the power and influence of the wealthy and the 'well-connected', and of the vulnerability to false accusations of the powerless in society. Although we no longer look to witchcraft as the cause, all too often we too are confronted by the inexplicable, the accidental, and the serendipitous.

This is not to suggest that there was no scepticism about witchcraft in sixteenth- and seventeenth-century England. Reginald Scot's *The Discoverie of Witchcraft* (1584) emphatically denied the veracity of sorcery and the power of the Devil. And Samuel Harsnett's

A Declaration of Egregious Popish Impostures (1603) debunked demonic possession and exorcism as so much theatrical mummery.[5] Elsewhere, Samuel Harsnett described *The Witches of Warboys* as 'a very ridiculous book, concerning one *M. Throgmortons* children, (supposed to have been bewitched by a woman of *Warbois*)'.[6]

But Scot's and Harsnett's views remained minority ones. And the denial of the demonic was generally seen as the thin end of a wedge, which would result in a dangerous revocation not only of bishops and kings but of God.

However, putting aside this philosophical issue for the moment, let us ask a different question: in a world in which it is considered empirically possible to do such things, to bewitch others to death, to despatch spirits into children to torment them dreadfully, did Mother Samuel, or John, or Agnes *try to do so*? Were they witches in the sense of considering themselves to have witches' powers? And, if not, why did Mother Samuel confess to sorcery? Why would someone not only confess to it if they were innocent, but elaborate their guilt, as we will see, into a complex tale of compacts with the Devil, of familiar spirits, of demonic torments and murder?

One thing we can rule out as the cause of her admissions is torture, or at least institutionalised, physical torture. As a means of extracting a witchcraft confession from a woman within the context of legal proceedings, torture seems never to have been utilised in England. In any case, the infliction of pain as a means of ensuring true speech from an accused would have been unnecessary in the case of Alice Samuel. As we shall see, she regularly confessed to her supposed crimes without that kind of physical torment being brought to bear (although she just as regularly withdrew her confessions). Why her confessions were false and her claims of innocence true is what I want to try to uncover in this book.

For Alice Samuel, like her husband John and her daughter Agnes, was cruelly and devastatingly framed.

Part One

Bewitched and Bewitching:

November 1589 to December 1590

i.

A Witch in the Manor House

The horror began in the autumn of the year 1589, just a week before the thirty-second anniversary of the reign of Queen Elizabeth I. On Friday 10 November 1589, Jane Throckmorton, one of the daughters of Robert Throckmorton, suddenly fell sick.[1] Jane was the second youngest of the five daughters of Robert, and the third youngest of his children. The Warboys text puts her age at nearly ten. The Parish Registers of the village record her christening on Thursday 21 August 1580 (see Plate 3).

In keeping with its Reformation sympathies and its Calvinist theology, the Anglican Prayer Book of 1552 had excised exorcism from the service of Baptism of Infants. But a widespread belief that children were the Devil's cesspools survived this removal, and daughters and sons were baptised soon after birth.[2] So Jane was probably around nine years and three months old when she 'fell into a strange kind of sickness and distemperature of body' (sig.A.3.r, and see Plate 4).

Jane's early symptoms would certainly have prompted consternation and fear. She was said to have sneezed very loudly and heavily for periods of a half an hour. While lying on her back, her stomach would lift up above the rest of her such that none could press her down flat. Sometimes she would shake one of her legs, sometimes the other. At other times one of her arms would jerk, then the other, and then her head.

The Throckmortons had only recently arrived in Warboys. According to the Warboys text, they were 'but newly come to the town to live' (sig.A.4.v), having arrived only at Michaelmas – that is, at the end of September 1589 – and only some six weeks before Jane fell ill. But they had had a long association with the village. The Warboys Parish Registers record the christening of all Robert Throckmorton's eight children in the parish church of St Mary Magdalene except one.[3] And he himself had been baptised in the same church on 1 October 1551, no doubt in the early thirteenth-century font which still stands at the back of the church, with its cover locked to keep the people from stealing the font water for magical purposes (see Plate 5).

The children were baptised by Francis Dorington, who had come to Warboys as the parish rector in 1565 and who was to remain there, meticulously keeping his parish records, until his death in 1611. He stood in a long line of thirty-five rectors of the parish which reached back to Alfricus in the early twelfth century. Dorington was the children's uncle by marriage, for on 23 October 1567 he had married Robert Throckmorton's sister, Mary. The Samuels could look to little comfort from him. This was just as well, for that was the measure of what they received.

The Throckmortons lived within earshot of the five bells in the steeple of St Mary Magdalene's (the sixth having been lost at sea). A church had stood on this site since the eleventh century, though its most significant features – its tower and spire – were built in the thirteenth (see Plate 6). Three hundred years later, Virginia Woolf was to spend a childhood summer living in the rectory opposite the church. She found the surrounding countryside 'melancholy'. The churchyard, she wrote, 'is full of sombre tombstones, with queer carvings & angel heads sprawling over date & name and all. There are many graves that are nameless; & I was startled to think that I was walking over some ancient dust forgotten & undistinguished from the hillocks of the field. The graves rising in swelling mounds side by side all along the bottom of the churchyard'[4] (see Plate 7).

In the throes of their bewitchment, it was the bells of St Mary Magdalene's calling the faithful to prayer that seemed to precipitate the children's fits. The bells had only just been mended – Leonard Poulter of Warboys having left three shillings and fourpence for their repair in his will, proved on 10 October 1589.[5] They tolled loudly, since the manor house of the Throckmortons stood immediately next to the church, as it still does. There are Jacobean and Victorian additions to the Elizabethan original (see Plate 8). But the original Elizabethan house can still be seen from the northern side (see Plate 9).

The house itself had been acquired by Robert Throckmorton's father, Gabriel, in 1540. And he had leased it from Richard Cromwell, who was nephew to the wife of Thomas Cromwell, Henry VIII's minister. He in turn had purchased the Huntingdonshire estates of Ramsey Abbey, which included the manor house in Warboys, in that same year, 1540, subsequent to the dissolution of the monasteries by Henry VIII in the second half of the 1530s.[6]

Gabriel Throckmorton was to die in Warboys in January 1553, leaving behind his wife Emma and his son Robert. However, there is a strong likelihood that Robert Throckmorton may have been raised elsewhere, at nearby Ellington or Brampton.[7] There is no need to reject the text's claim that he and his family were only recent arrivals at the manor house. But we know from the Parish Registers that, although he might not have lived there permanently until the autumn of 1589, at least by the time of the birth of his own children, in the 1570s and 1580s, he had re-established his connections with the village, not least because of the presence within it of his sister and her husband Francis, the vicar of Warboys.

It was two or three days after the onset of Jane's illness, around 12 or 13 November, that, among others, Alice Samuel came to visit the sick child. Alice and her family lived next door, on the north side of the manor house. It was the neighbourly thing to do, especially to new arrivals in the village. To love one's neighbour was not only a core element of Christian ethics. To live in love and charity with one's new companions was an early modern ideal. As the parish clerk of St Botolph's, Billingsgate, wrote:

> Even as sticks may easily be broken
> So when neighbours agree not then there is a confusion
> But a great many of sticks bound in one bundle will hardly be broken
> So neighbours being joined in love together can never be severed.[8]

Robert Throckmorton's wife, Elizabeth, was in effect the lady of the manor. The visits of the women of the parish to her afflicted daughter both reinforced her new position and helped to integrate her, as a newcomer, into the female network of the parish. And, as a neighbour, Alice Samuel would have expected to be welcomed. For 'neighbourliness' implied not only the day-to-day transactions of domestic proximity but a set of mutual social obligations which transcended differences in wealth and status.[9]

But a storm cloud was gathering over neighbourly relations with Alice Samuel. When Alice entered the Throckmortons' hall next to the fireplace, Jane was being nursed by the fireside by another woman. Jane's mother and her grandmother were also present. They were gathered around a wide and spacious ingle-nooked fireplace, sufficiently large to sit within. Alice, we are told, took a seat near the child in the chimney corner. Moments later, the child became still more agitated, pointed to Alice and shouted, 'Grandmother, look where the old witch sits... Did you ever see... one more like a witch than she is? Take off her black-knitted cap, for I cannot abide to look at her' (sig.A.3.r). One can only imagine the stunned silence that followed this outburst. While Jane's exclamation augured terrible events to come, it was also a serious breach of etiquette. Not only did it disrupt normative adult relationships but, in a world in which children should be seen and not heard, it ruptured relations between adults and children as well.

We have no indications of Alice Samuel's true likeness. The only 'contemporary' drawing of Alice was to appear over a century later in Richard Boulton's *A Compleat History of Magick, Sorcery, and Witchcraft* (see Plate 10). We cannot therefore expect this to convey any reliable information about Alice's appearance. It is quite possible that she presented, to Jane's mind, the stereotype of the witch with which the child would certainly have been familiar. It was her black-knitted cap that suggested a witch to Jane Throckmorton. It is unlikely that there was anything especially distinctive about Alice's cap to bring about witch associations. She was probably wearing a 'muffin cap' or 'bag hat' rather like a cook's hat, a large circle of cloth gathered into a band. Alice's was probably trimmed in black. It was the colour, not the hat itself, that evoked terror.

We know that children of the time were frightened of anything black. They were brought up to fear ghosts and goblins, black men, 'bogeymen' in general, the Devil and his minions – and, of course, witches.[10] Reginald Scot's collation of maids' tales deliberately exaggerated the horror. But it still bears witness to the kind of dark and threatening world which the children inhabited. 'But in our childhood,' he wrote,

> our mothers' maids have so terrified us with an ugly Devil, having horns on his head, fire in his mouth, and a tail in his breach, eyes like a bason, fangs like a dog, claws like a bear, a skin like a niger, and a voice roaring like a lion, whereby we start and are afraid when we hear one cry 'Boo!' And they have so frightened us with bull beggars, spirits, witches, urchins, elves, hags, fairies, satyrs, pans, fauns, silens, kit of the candlestick, tritons, centaurs, dwarfs, giants, imps, calcars, conjurers, nymphs, changelings, *Incubus*, Robin Good-fellow, the spoorn, the mare, the man in the oak, the hell-wain, the fire-drake, the puckle, Tom thumb, hob goblin, Tom tumbler, boneless, and such other bugs, that we are afraid of our own shadows.[11]

They inhabited, in Rudolf Otto's sense of the word, a genuinely numinous world, one that was mysterious, terrifying, yet at the same time fascinating and captivating.[12] A world where the supernatural was only a footfall away.

Apart from that fateful black-trimmed cap, we know little about Alice Samuel. She was probably born in Upwood, a village near Warboys some ten miles north of Cambridge. We know from the Upwood Parish Registers that an Alicia Ybbot married John Samuel on 5 May 1561. *The Witches of Warboys* informs us that, at the time of her trial in 1593, she was aged about eighty. So if this is true, she was born around 1513 and married at around the age of about forty-eight. However if – as the text suggests – she were eighty years of age, it is difficult to square that information with descriptions of her daughter Agnes as young and a 'maid'. It is unlikely that Alice was as old as the text claims, and it seems probable that her great antiquity is being emphasised to accentuate her physical conformity to a witch's stereotype: the old crone.

For reasons that we will see later, we do know that, at the time of her trial, Alice Samuel was considered to be well beyond child-bearing age. Unfortunately, we know little about the time of the menopause or 'the cessation of the flowers' in sixteenth-century England. Literary sources differed on the age when it was believed to occur, though fifty was a general estimate. In 1564, for example, the Dutch physician Levinas Lemnius thought a woman's cycle generally ceased between the ages of forty-five and fifty,[13] while, in 1615, Helkiah Crooke, physician to King James I and keeper of Bedlam Hospital, declared in his *Microcosmagraphia* that 'the courses' stopped after the fiftieth year.[14] We can assume, then, that Alice was well over fifty, if not the eighty the text makes her out to be.

The average age at which women got married during the period was twenty-five or twenty-six. So, if Alice were to have married in 1561 at twenty-five, then she would have been born around 1536. This would make her about fifty-seven years old at the time of her trial in 1593.

She was the right age, then, to be accused of being a witch. And she was the right gender too. Witches were most likely to be found among older women, menopausal and post-menopausal women in particular. As Lyndal Roper writes, 'Menopausal and post-menopausal women were disproportionately represented among the victims of the witch craze – and their overrepresentation is the more striking when we recall how rare women over fifty must have been in the population as a whole.'[15] Witchcraft accusations, she goes on to argue, were grounded in 'a powerful cultural current of hatred of elderly women in early modern Europe, an antagonism which was sometimes shared by women as well as men'.[16]

Even among those sceptical of witchcraft, prejudice against older women was not uncommon. Reginald Scot, for example, viewed witches' confessions as fantasies arising from post-menopausal melancholy: 'Now, if the fancy of a melancholic person may be occupied in causes which are both false and impossible, why should an old witch be thought free from such fantasies, who (as the learned philosophers and physicians say) upon the stopping of their monthly melancholic flux or issue of blood, in their age must need increase therein, as (through their weakness both of body and brain) the aptest persons to meet with such melancholic imaginations?'[17] Children, pregnant women, and babies were especially vulnerable to the activities of witches. Or, at least, they were thought to be. Printers of witchcraft pamphlets probably recognised a general cultural anxiety, and a market. Hence the title of a pamphlet translated from the Dutch in 1601: *A strange report of six most notorious witches who by their devilish practices murdered above the number of four hundred small children.*

From the above estimate of Alice's age, we can derive a likely age for Agnes. For if Alice was over fifty at the time of her trial, and if her daughter Agnes was born within a period of several years after her marriage, Agnes would have been around the age of twenty-five when her mother was first accused of being a witch.

At first, Elizabeth Throckmorton was furious with Jane for her accusation of Alice. And she rebuked her. This amounted to a serious denial by Jane of the respect due to a neighbour. After much trouble in quietening her down, the child was put to bed. Alice Samuel remained at her place by the fire, and said nothing. She looked rueful, as well she might. Jane may well not have known the seriousness of her denunciation. Alice would have. She was old. And she was female. She would have recognised only too well that to be 'cried against' as a witch was to run the risk of being created as one, regardless of anything she might or might not have done.

ii.

Worms and Urine

Bewitchment was seldom the first cause thought of. Nor was it in this case, no doubt to Alice's great relief. Although a sick child had pointed her out as a witch, no connection was made to Alice as the cause of the child's illness. Not yet, at any rate. So Elizabeth and Robert Throckmorton's first thought, like that of any modern parents, was to look for a natural 'medical' explanation.

After several days, Jane was no better. A sample of her urine was therefore sent by a messenger to a Doctor Barrow of Cambridge, a man, it is said, 'well known to be excellent in Physick' (sig.A.3.v). This is most likely to have been Philip Barrow or Barrough, author of a work published in 1583 called *The Methode of Physicke, conteyning the Causes, Signes, and Cures of Inward Diseases in Man's Body from the Head to the Foote*.

It was common practice for the gentry to send urine samples to physicians. Uroscopy, or the examination of urine, was central to the techniques of the medieval and early modern physician, and derived from the 'humoral' theory of the Greek physician Galen (second century CE). As Galen saw it, the human body contained four humours or bodily fluids – blood, phlegm, choler, and melancholy. Good health was the consequence of a balance within the body between these four humours, and sickness the consequence of their imbalance. Correct analysis of the colour, smell, and texture of the urine sample, together with any sediments in it, formed the key to diagnosing a patient's disorder:

> Now in every man's body are four qualities: heat and cold, moist and dry. Heat and cold, they be causes of colours. Dryness and moistness, they be causes of substance. Heat is the cause of red colour; dryness the cause of thin substance; moistness the cause of thick substance. As thus, if the urine of the patient is red and thick, it signifies that blood is hot and moist. If it is red and thin, it shows that choler has domination, for choler is hot and dry. If the urine appears white and thick, it betokens phlegm, for phlegm

19

is cold and moist. If the urine shows white and thin, it signifies melancholy, for melancholy is cold and dry.[18]

Barrow would certainly have given Jane's urine close attention, comparing it to the many possible combinations of substance (thick, average, thin), colour (white, pale, flaxen, yellow, red, black), texture, sediments, and taste in his texts. He would have consulted his colour charts. It is more than likely that he compared it to other samples in his possession, a complex activity rather like that of a contemporary wine taster. His patients would fully have expected such dedicated analysis.

But he would have also received information from the bearer of Jane's urine about her physical symptoms, the length of her illness, her diet, and so on. Indeed, Barrow's *Method of Physick*, while paying lip-service to Galen and humoral medicine, stands more in the tradition of the experimental and experiential medicine of the Renaissance Swiss physician Paracelsus. Richard Bostocke had popularised Paracelsus's work in England in 1585 in his own *The Difference betwene the Auncient Physicke and the Latter Physicke*. In contrast to those who emphasised the importance of book learning, Barrow recommended the efficacy of clinical experience: 'Since therefore the case so stands that art is weak without practice, and that (as Galen says) experience is gotten longo rerum usu: let the Physician (if he does not prefer lying fame and vile lucre before true and absolute knowledge) let him (I say) that his mind may be enriched, not leave the poorest house unfrequented.'[19]

Barrow diagnosed worms as the cause of Jane's illness. When we examine his chapter on worms in *The Methode of Physicke*, we can see why. There he distinguishes three kinds of worms – *teretes* (round and long), *lati* (broad), and *ascerides* (thin and short). All these kinds are caused by 'crude, raw, gross, and phlegmatic matter, and through convenient rottenness, such as is gathered specially in children, and in other great eaters'.[20] Those that have round worms, he tells us, feel an incredible gnawing in their bowels and belly, and issue thin and small coughs. In some, 'yesking', the sound in the nose from violent movement in the stomach, follows. In many, he later remarks, 'the belly throws out corrupt meats, and is puffed up like as it were a timpanie [like a drum, or a pregnant woman.]'[21]

These symptoms did sound like those of Jane.

The returning messenger was dispatched with medicine for the child. Barrow's intention was to kill the supposed worms with bitter herbs: wormwood, southernwood, calamine, horehound, pepper-wort, hyssop, rue, leaves of peachwort or dead arsesmart, seeds of coriander, hartshorn, lupin mint, pennyroyal, origan, centaury, fern, gentian, *Aristolochia rotunda*, seed of colewort, and root of elecampane, and aloes, mixed with milk, honey, or syrup of licorice to lure the worms to taste the bitter medicine. As he saw it, the dead worms had to be quickly driven out with suppositories and purgatives, and especially by 'pills of pestilence' and *hiera prica* – aloes and canella bark mixed with honey.

Barrow's medicine was ineffective. Within two days, another urine sample was sent to him, together with a more detailed description of Jane's symptoms. Her parents suspected epilepsy. But Barrow was certain she was no epileptic. Although her behaviour fitted some symptoms of the falling sickness, its decisive feature for Barrow – 'foaming at the mouth' – was presumably absent.[22] He sent further medicines to purge her, but to no avail. A further sample was sent. But the doctor's examination of this third urine deposit showed the child to be in good health.

Only then did he enquire of the parents of the possibility of the child having been bewitched. 'The answer was made, "No"' (sig.A.3.v). But Barrow was not so sure. He kept great faith in urine analysis. He was convinced that, were Jane to be suffering from a natural illness, there would *have* to be a sign in the child's urine. Bewitchment did not show up in urine. And therefore, because the child continued sick, and no sign of illness manifested in the child's urine, for Barrow a supernatural cause seemed to be the only diagnosis possible.

Could it be said that Barrow's suggestion of bewitchment was an excuse to cover up his own inability to diagnose and cure the child? Indeed it could. Thomas Ady, himself a doctor, put it clearly:

> Seldom goes any man or woman to a physician for cure of any disease, but one question they ask the physician is, 'Sir, do you not think this party is in ill handling, or under an ill tongue?' Or more plainly, 'Sir, do you not think the party is bewitched?' And to this many an ignorant physician will answer, 'Yes verily.' The reason is, *ignorantiae pallium maleficium & incantatio*, a cloak for a physician's ignorance. When he cannot find the nature of the disease, he says, 'The party is bewitched.'[23]

For Philip Barrow, the natural explanation was to be preferred. But when his medicine failed, he was not averse to seeking a supernatural explanation, even if it were only to fill in the gaps of his medical knowledge. Barrow was clearly not among those who, like Samuel Harsnett, chaplain to the Bishop of London, believed that the supernatural could be reduced to the natural. If any have an idle or sullen girl, wrote Harsnett,

> and she have a little help of the *Mother*, *Epilepsy*, or *Cramp* to teach her to roll her eyes, wry her mouth, gnash her teeth, startle with her body, hold her arms and hands stiff, make comic faces, girme, mow, and mop like an ape, tumble like a hedgehog, and can mutter out two or three words of gibberish, such as *obus*, *bobus*, and then with- all old Mother *Nobs* has called her by chance idle young housewife, or bid the Devil scratch her, then no doubt but Mother *Nobs* is the Witch, the young girl is owl-blasted and possessed.[24]

But, then, Samuel Harsnett was more concerned with refuting the claims of exorcists than he was with advancing the cause of natural explanations of illness.

The dichotomy between a natural and a supernatural explanation was much less clear to the early modern mind than it is to us. To put it another way, theological and medical discourses were never as distinct or separate then as they are today, and as we are apt to presume them to have been in retrospect.

Moreover, the symptoms of 'medical' and 'religious' diseases often overlapped. It was often hard, for example, to distinguish between hysteria (the suffocation of the Mother or womb) and demonic possession. In 1621, Edward Fairfax, 'neither a fantastic Puritan or superstitious Papist', as he put it, was eventually convinced that his daughter, Elizabeth, was the victim of witchcraft. But before this, he had attributed all she had said and done in her fits to 'the disease called "the mother"'.[25] Sir Kenelm Digby told of a woman who, though suffering the disease of the Mother, manifested the symptoms of possession.[26]

Bewitchment and epilepsy were also not easily distinguishable. The symptoms were similar: falling down suddenly to the ground, grinding the teeth, self-violence, deprivation of the senses, swelling of the body, and foaming at the mouth. So it is perhaps not altogether surprising that Barrow wondered whether, given her symptoms and with no sign of natural illness, witchcraft was present.

Worms, epilepsy, or bewitchment? The same alternatives were to appear in the case of the thirteen-year-old Thomas Darling six years later. On Saturday 27 February 1596 Thomas Darling accompanied his uncle to Winsell Wood, near Burton upon Trent. There he fell into an argument with an old woman named Alice Gooderidge. Shortly after returning home, Thomas fell ill. His fits and vomiting led his aunt to take a urine sample to a physician. Like Jane's physician, he diagnosed worms. His medicine was as completely ineffectual as Philip Barrow's, and Thomas's condition worsened. Convinced that it was a natural though strange disease, the possibility of bewitchment was rejected by his aunt. Many others thought the boy's affliction was epilepsy. It was only later that the diagnosis of bewitchment was made. To Alice Gooderidge's great misfortune, she was eventually arrested for herself bewitching Thomas. Tragically, she died in gaol while awaiting trial (see Plate 11).[27]

Many folk at the time considered natural and supernatural explanations to be compatible. So the diagnosis of a natural disease did not necessarily mean a corresponding denial of supernatural involvement. Some people saw natural diseases in general as being demonically caused. Others viewed those suffering from natural diseases as prime candidates for infiltration and infection by the Devil. Thomas Browne, author of a text called *Religio Medici*, testified in a 1664 witchcraft trial that the fits of some women and girls were 'natural and nothing else but what they call the mother'. But, he went on to say, they were 'heightened to a great excess by the subtlety of the Devil, co-operating with the malice of these which we term witches'.[28]

Possession by the Devil was also often linked with melancholy, itself an illness that was thought to embrace a vast array of symptoms. For Robert Burton, for example, writing in his famous *Anatomy of Melancholy*, religious melancholia was itself instigated by the Devil, while demonic possession was included in his category of diseases of the mind.[29]

There were occasions when those suffering from what Burton would diagnose as religious melancholy (and we would classify as severe clinical depression) were believed to be possessed by the Devil. Suicidal impulses were themselves seen as evidence of demonic activity. In August 1590, for example, Queen Elizabeth's astrologer John Dee diagnosed Ann Frank, a suicidal nurse in his household, as possessed by an evil spirit. His attempts at exorcising the spirit were unavailing. She died in late September of that year, having successfully cut her own throat.[30]

Philip Barrow was uncertain how to take matters forward. He therefore suggested that a second opinion be sought. Thus, the third sample of Jane's urine was sent on to a Master Butler. This is most probably William Butler, fellow of Clare College, Cambridge, licensed to practise medicine in 1572. He was described as 'the greatest physician of his time, and as much resorted to for his great knowledge in physic, as any person that lived before him'.[31]

Had it not been for Butler's eccentricity, we are informed, he would have been much more consulted. He was renowned for keeping patients, 'persons of quality' especially, waiting for hours. On one occasion, according to John Aubrey's *Brief Lives*, 'A serving man brought his master's water to Doctor Butler, he being then in his study (with turned bars [the doors barred]) but would not be spoken with. After much fruitless importunity, the man told the doctor he was resolved he should see his master's water; he would not be turned away – threw it on the doctor's head. This humour pleased the doctor, and he went to the gentleman and cured him.'[32]

In Jane Throckmorton's case, having examined the urine and had her symptoms described to him, Butler, like Barrow, thought the problem might be worms, although he could not detect this in the urine sample. And he went on to prescribe the same medicine as Barrow had done. Since the prognosis had had little if any effect before, this medicine was not in fact administered to Jane a second time, no doubt to the child's great relief. As we have seen, Barrow suspected witchcraft to be at the root of Jane's troubles, and he had accordingly advised Robert Throckmorton not to spend any more money on doctors. But at this point neither of the child's parents was yet convinced that this was the true cause of their daughter's ills.

The reluctance shown by Jane's parents to accept the diagnosis of witchcraft is an important element in their case against the Samuels. They preferred the 'old' medicine to the 'new' demonology. But eventually they were forced, even against their better judgements and, perhaps, their better natures, to accept as valid the identification of witchcraft and sorcery as being behind their daughter's increasingly troubling and perplexing symptoms.

iii.

Spectres and Spirits

A month later, they do become convinced. Two more daughters fall into the same 'extremities' as Jane. And both cry out against Alice Samuel: '"Take her away. Look where she stands here before us in a black thrumbed cap … It is she," they said, "that has bewitched us, and she will kill us if you do not take her away"' (sig.A.4.r).

What was it that finally moved Robert and Elizabeth Throckmorton to believe that their children were the innocent victims of witchcraft? That the same symptoms that afflicted Jane were hydra-like, now spreading to other children, must have worried them intensely. But they could just as easily have put this down to the contagious spread of a natural illness as to the malevolent acts of a sorceress. A month earlier, Jane had accused Alice of being a witch. She had not suggested that Alice was the cause of her sickness. But now, for the first time, the children not only accuse Alice of being a witch, they also claim that she has bewitched them. Moreover, they claim, she intends to kill them.

This too their parents might have ignored, however disturbing it might have been. Except for one thing.

Alice, we are told, 'was not then present' (sig.A.4.r). The children were seeing an apparition of Alice. And it was the sinister spectre of Alice, 'this thing', that 'did something move the Parents, and strike into their minds a suspicion of witchcraft' (sig.A.4.r).

Witches, spectres, and spirits went together. As Sir Thomas Browne put it in his *Religio Medici*, 'For my part, I have ever believed, and do now know that there are witches: they that doubt of these, do not only deny them, but spirits; and are obliquely, and upon consequence, a sort, not of infidels, but atheists.'[33] From denial of witches to denial of spirits, and from there to denial of God, for Browne and many others were but short steps.

For the Throckmortons, as for their contemporaries, the apparition of Alice strongly suggested witchcraft. Apparitions demonstrated the link between misfortune and its malevolent cause. The Throckmortons may well have been familiar with the story ten years earlier of Ellen Smith and the young daughter of Widow Webb of Maldon. Having been assaulted by Mistress Ellen, the child instantly sickened. Haunted by Ellen for two days, she cried continually 'Away with the witch, away with the witch,' and then died.[34]

Half a century later, and the materialisation of spectres is not only a part of witchcraft lore but also of witchcraft law. In Michael Dalton's guide to magistrates, *The Countrey Justice* of 1630, the author writes that '[t]heir apparition to the sicke party in his fits' is one of the keys to the discovery of witches.[35]

There is no suggestion in the Warboys text that the three children are hallucinating. On the contrary, underlying it is the assumption that the children are having a 'real', and not an 'imaginary', experience of Alice Samuel. Nor is there any suggestion that they are being deluded by the Devil into believing that Alice is present. That might have pointed to the Devil's trickiness – and Alice's innocence. Rather, the text reflects the popular belief that Alice herself has 'really' appeared in a 'spectral' form.

The 'real' appearances of ghosts and spectres could be theorised in terms of Aristotle's notion of a third substance between body and soul, 'pneuma' or spirit,[36] or in the Platonic notion of the 'aereal', as compared to the 'aethereal' and 'terrestrial' bodies of the soul.[37] However, in this case, that Alice has appeared in the absence of her 'physical' body would have been enough to condemn her for most readers. And Alice is 'visible' only to those bewitched by her.

Alice's appearance only to the bewitched children, but not to others, far from raising doubts about the 'reality' of the children's experience would, rather, have reinforced it. Her invisibility to those not bewitched was a complex sign and proof of her presence. The visual ambiguity served to authenticate rather than disconfirm this presence. The selective appearance of Alice to those bewitched served both to verify that witchcraft was really happening and, more importantly, to point to its source.

All this is not to suggest that the question of apparitions – like witches themselves – was uncontested during the sixteenth century. As Keith Thomas has reminded us, '[A]lthough men went on seeing ghosts after the Reformation, they were assiduously taught not to take them at face value.'[38] Both Protestants and Catholics were inclined to think that they were not as they seemed – the spectres of witches or the ghosts of the dead – but perhaps the fabrications of priests, the wiles of the Devil, illusions of nature, or the fantastic products of diseased bodies and troubled minds. In 1601, for example, in their *Dialogicall Discourses of Spirits and Divels*, the Anglicans John Deacon and John Walker would not have believed the spectre of Alice to have arisen from the activities of ghosts, witches, or the Devil but 'from disordered melancholy, from mania, from the epilepsy, from lunacy, from lycanthropy, from convulsions, from the mother, from the menstrual obstructions, and sundry other outrageous infirmities'.[39] But such sceptics were in the minority, and for those who believed in the reality of witches the appearance of their spectres was not unlikely, and in fact the very opposite of improbable.

But there was one thing that did hold Elizabeth and Robert Throckmorton back from believing that Alice Samuel had ensnared their children by casting spells. This was quite simply that, as far as they knew, she had no reason to: '[T]hey were but newly come to the town to inhabit... neither had they given any occasion (to their knowledge) either to her or any other, to practise any such malice against them' (sig.A.4.r). Elizabeth and Robert Throckmorton believe that, in the absence of conflict between their family and anyone else in the village, they should not be the victims of revenge through witchcraft. In other words, within this rural community is the cultural expectation that witchcraft will occur only as a payback by a witch as the consequence of a 'falling out'. And, in the absence of conflict with Alice Samuel, there is no reason at all to expect malign activity from her.

In witchcraft narratives before *The Witches of Warboys*, this assumption, that witchcraft is linked to vengeance, is already a commonplace. Thus, for example, the story of Mother Staughton of Wimbish in Essex, ten years before, in 1579:

> [S]he came one time to the house of Robert Cornell of Suersem, and asked for a bottle of milk from his wife. But being denied it, she departed for a little while, leaving her own bottle behind her, and took another with her that belonged to the aforesaid Cornell. After three days she came again, and asked for her own bottle, and returned the other, asking for milk as before. The wife of the house, always suspecting her to be a witch denied her request and barred the doors against her. Whereupon she sat down on her heels before the door, and made a circle upon the ground with a knife. After that she dug it full of holes within the compass, in the sight of the said

wife, her man, and her maid. They demanded to know why she did so. She answered that she made a shitting hole for herself after that sort, and so departed. The next day the wife coming out at the same door, was taken sick. And she began to swell from time to time, as if she had been with child, by which swelling she became so great in body that she feared she should burst. And to this day, she is not restored to health.[40]

Indeed, so stereotypical is the pattern – conflict, revenge, misfortune – that Reginald Scot in his *Discoverie of Witchcraft* could even parody it. Thus, in the voice of an accuser, he says of an imaginary witch, 'She was at my house of late: She would have had a pot of milk. She departed in a chafe because she did not have it. She railed, she cursed, she mumbled and whispered. And finally, she said that she would be even with me. And soon after, my child, my cow, my sow, or my pullet died, or was strangely taken.'[41] And it was certainly not uncommon, in the case of narratives about the possession of children, for their haunting to have occurred after conflict with an old woman.

The Puritan exorcist John Darrell, for instance, informs us that William Sommers' fits began after he encountered an old woman who extorted money from him and forced him to eat bread and butter.[42] Thomas Darling is convinced that he is bewitched after he remembers his meeting in a wood with an old woman on the same day on which he had become ill. 'As I passed by her in the coppice,' he reports, 'I chanced, against my will, to pass wind which she, taking in anger, said, "Gyp with a mischief and fart with a bell. I will go to Heaven and you will go to Hell."'[43] Mary Glover is reported to have been taken ill immediately after an argument with Elizabeth Jackson, Jane Ashton after threats from Edmond Hartley.[44] William Perry, the so-called Boy of Bilson, fell sick after he came across an old woman who accused him of ill manners 'saying that he was a foul thing, and that it had been better for him if he had saluted her'.[45]

As we will see, later there are others, wise after the event, who will 'remember' other encounters with Alice that led to similar misfortunes.

It is perhaps unwise to take at face value the text's claim that Elizabeth and Robert Throckmorton had had no conflict with Alice or, we may presume, with her husband John. It is clearly in the interests of the Throckmortons to present themselves, or to be presented, not merely as victims of witchcraft but as completely innocent victims. All the more easy to present Alice and her family as genuinely and unjustifiably vicious. And easy too to present their pursuit of her as not motivated by their own petty desires for revenge, and her pursuit of them as unprovoked and malicious.

Had the children returned to health, or the accusations ceased, all might have been well. But possession, like the plague, was horribly contagious. And others were soon to be infected. Alice herself stayed well away from the Throckmorton house, as well as the children. This was a wise thing to do. But it made no difference. Even if the physical Alice stayed away, the spectral Alice continued to make her present felt – and seen – at least to those who were bewitched.

We do not know whether the spectral evidence was introduced later into Alice's trial. There is no mention of it in *The Witches of Warboys*. And it was often recognised as fallible.[46] However that may be, we can now see 'behind' the text the reason for the Throckmortons' change of mind. For them the spectral evidence was decisive. Like other possessed children, as at Salem in a later century and land, the Throckmorton daughters took hostages. Their parents were on the verge of becoming so, metaphorically at least. Agnes, Alice's daughter, was also soon to join them – but, in her case, literally.

We know from the text that the two children who followed Jane into bewitchment are Jane's next two older sisters. The Titchmarsh Parish Registers inform us that the next oldest to Jane is Elizabeth. She was christened in St Mary the Virgin, Titchmarsh in Northamptonshire, her mother's home village, on 19 July 1579, and thus she was around ten and a half years old at the onset of her illness. Elizabeth's older sister Mary, christened in Warboys on 18 May 1578, joins Jane and Elizabeth in accusing Alice Samuel of being a witch.[47]

Less than a month after Mary and Elizabeth had cried out against Alice Samuel, around mid-January 1590, the youngest daughter, Grace, also fell ill. Christened on 10 March 1581, she was then eight years and ten months old. She too expostulated against Alice. A little later, and Joan, the oldest of the five sisters, succumbed in her turn. She was then around fifteen years and seven months of age.[48] She too denounced Alice Samuel, who, we are told, after she recognised that she was suspected of witchcraft, did not come to the house again. But still Alice was present to them in spirit if not in body: '[T]ake her away, Mistress,' screamed Joan, 'for God's sake take her away and burn her, for she will kill us all if you let her alone…' (sig.A.4.v).

Joan was, of all the children, the most tormented, at least initially. But their seizures were uniformly violent. They could hardly be held down: 'These kinds of fits would hold them, sometimes longer, sometimes shorter, either an hour or two, sometimes half the day, yea, the whole day. And many times, they had six or seven fits in an hour. Yet when it pleased God to deliver them from their fits, they neither knew what they had said, nor yet in what way they had been dealt withal' (sig.A.4.v).

During one of her seizures, Joan predicted that eventually there would be twelve who would be bewitched in the house, and she named them all: in addition to herself and her sisters, seven female servants. The seven maids were afflicted in exactly the same ways as the children. And all blamed Alice Samuel for their ills. Upon their departure from the Throckmortons' house, they recovered. But their replacements became similarly troubled. We hear no more of these servants, either of those who departed, or those who replaced them.

The Throckmorton children were the right age and gender to present with the symptoms of bewitchment and, as we will see, possession by spirits.[49] Of sixty-four English demoniacs whose ages I have been able to estimate from the sources, either directly or indirectly, only eight are over twenty years of age. Females, and particularly girls and young women, were also more prone to possession than males. In sixty-two cases of possession where the genders of the possessed can be determined, forty-four are females and eighteen males. Of the forty-four females, only three can be said to be of adult age. In sum, in early modern England (from 1550 to 1700), around two-thirds of those possessed with spirits are female children or adolescents, and around one-fifth are boys or adolescent males.

The possession of children by spirits is a peculiarly English phenomenon. In Catholic Europe, demonic possession by spirits seems to have occurred more often in convents among nuns. But in the England of Henry VIII, the monasteries and nunneries were disbanded. Monks and nuns had been sent forth into the world to fend for themselves. Possession was far more likely to occur among the children of pious Puritan households, just as it did in Warboys.

In England, like the overarching religion, possession was Protestantised, and then domesticated.

iv.

Arrives a Witch-hunter

Gilbert Pickering of Titchmarsh Grove, Northamptonshire, was the brother of Robert Throckmorton's wife Elizabeth. Pickering was to play a central role in the drama. He had heard of the children's illness. And he arrived in Warboys, around a month after Grace had fallen ill, on St Valentine's Eve, Friday 13 February 1590.

Gilbert Pickering, we can surmise, was drawn to Warboys not only by the news of the children's illness but also by the possibility they were indeed bewitched. If Elizabeth and Robert Throckmorton were not persuaded that their children were victims of witchery when he arrived, they were convinced soon afterwards. For Gilbert was something of an amateur witch-finder. In him, the bewitched children found an ally. And Alice found a dangerous foe.

Twenty years later, Gilbert, now Sir Gilbert, was still involved in the pursuit of witches. But by then, he had turned professional. In 1612, he was to 'swim' the suspected witch Arthur Bill and his father and mother. This practice followed from the belief that a witch would not sink since 'God has appointed (for a supernatural sign of the monstrous impiety of witches) that the element of water should refuse to receive them in her bosom, that have shaken from them the sacred water of Baptism, and wilfully refused the benefit thereof by making that breach and fall from God in participating thus vilely with the Spirits of Belial'.[50] Ropes were attached to the suspected witch to ensure that, were the suspicions ill-founded, the innocent did not drown (see Plate 12). What before was merely a suspicion was now, for Gilbert, confirmed. The unfortunate family floated on the water. And Arthur Bill was sent by Gilbert Pickering for trial. He was eventually hanged, declaring his innocence to the end.

By contrast, Gilbert Pickering did not attempt to swim Alice Samuel. His repertoire did not then extend to this unpleasant procedure. Swimming was not yet common practice. It was only popularised in England as a result of its inclusion in King James I's

Daemonologie in 1597. But this amateur sleuth did arrive with a whole armoury of experimental and 'scientific' strategies to test for the presence of witchcraft. And he was impatient to put them into action. He was, to be sure, disappointed to discover on arrival that the children were as well as any children could be, and untroubled by their episodic seizures and spasms.

Within half an hour of reaching Warboys, Pickering was informed that a Mistress Andley and a Master Whittle of St Ives had gone to the house of Alice Samuel to persuade her to visit the children. When the children had first accused her, Alice had promised to do anything to assist them, even venturing her life in water up to the chin, or losing the best part of her blood, to do them good. And, at that stage, she would have meant it. But Alice, living only next door, of course, had since heard reports of the ongoing accusations against her. She was, unsurprisingly, no longer willing to get involved in a situation that seemed to be spiralling out of control. Quite simply, she was mortally afraid. But her understandable refusal to co-operate was being read by the Throckmortons as a sign not of fear but of guilt.

It is now that we enter the world revealed to us by Gilbert Pickering's diary of events. He too, the Warboys text indicates, decided to go to Alice Samuel's house to add his persuasiveness to that of those persons already *in situ*. Pickering forcefully tells Alice that he has the authority to compel her to accompany him if she won't go willingly. Alice is constrained to return to the manor house 'together with her daughter Agnes Samuel, and one Cicely Burder' (sig.B.1.r). Both Agnes and Cicely, we learn for the first time, were themselves suspected of being witches, or at least as being in league with Alice Samuel.

The suggestion that Agnes and Cicely had to be forced to go with Alice and the others is intended to reinforce their complicity in the bewitching of the children. But it is unlikely that any suspicion had fallen upon either of them at this time. Following this episode, we hear of Cicely Burder twice more, and then just in passing. And we only hear of Agnes again, in late 1592, when the spirits within the children tell them to inform their father that, were he to go to John Samuel's house, he would find Agnes Samuel, who 'is not yet brought into question about any of these matters hiding herself' (sig.F.3.r). And, as we will see, it will be early 1593 before the children rail against Agnes for bewitching them. More likely, then, that Agnes and Cicely, the daughter and friend of Alice, accompany her willingly to the Throckmortons' to offer much-needed support and solidarity.

Gilbert Pickering's report of what happened on the way next door is also intended further to implicate Agnes. The tense procession to the Throckmortons' was led by Mistress Andley, Master Whittle, and others, followed by Alice, Agnes, and Cicely, with the hawk-like Gilbert Pickering cautiously bringing up the rear. He walked sufficiently close to them, so we are told, that Alice and her daughter and friend were unable to confer. When they arrived at the door of the Throckmortons' house, Mother Samuel curtsied to Pickering and bade him go ahead and enter in front of her. Pickering refused. Staying close to the Samuels, he overheard Alice say to her daughter 'I charge you, do not confess anything'. 'You naughty woman,' he said to Alice, 'do you charge your daughter not to confess anything?' 'No,' she said, 'I charged her to hurry herself home to get her Father his dinner' (sig.B.1.v). We can well imagine these words of warning being spoken. But not by Alice to her daughter; rather, by a wary Agnes to her beleaguered mother.

Three of the Throckmorton children were present when Alice Samuel entered the hall of the house. They were perfectly calm and untroubled before she did so. But their reaction upon seeing her was instantaneous. They all fell on the ground 'strangely tormented' and threw themselves desperately around the room like grounded fish taken freshly out of water. Their stomachs reached up into the air, their head and heels touching the ground like tumblers: 'And they would have drawn their heads and their heels together backwards, throwing out their arms with great groans, most strangely to be heard, to the great grief of the beholders' (sig.B.1.v).

Not long after this, Master Whittle took Jane aside into another room and laid her on a bed. He was as strong, we are told, as any man in England, and she but a child of nine. But he was unable to hold her flat on the bed. She would lift her belly up and down a hundred times in the space of an hour, her eyes closed as though she were blind, and her arms spread out so stiffly and strongly that no man had the strength to bring them back to her side.

These phenomena were clear signs of bewitchment, and they were damning for Alice. For they were also indications that evil spirits had taken up their abode in the bodies of the tormented. And those who witnessed the tortured children knew it. The criteria for possession evidenced in the New Testament would have been familiar to many at this time: crying, gnashing of teeth, wallowing, foaming, extraordinary and supernatural strength, supernatural knowledge, violence to self and others, inability to hear and speak, entering into coma-like states, and pining away.

I use the word 'possession' carefully here. The Throckmorton children appeared to have mischievous spirits operating within them that were the source of their troubles. Once the notion that the children were bewitched had taken root, it was only a short step from there to believe that spirits had taken up residence inside them. And an even shorter step to conclude that the spirits had been sent by a witch.

It is doubtful whether anyone present in the household would have made any very technical distinction between 'obsession' and 'possession'. According to the former, spirits were presumed to besiege the body from the outside. According to the latter, spirits set upon the person from within. It was then, and is now, a fine distinction. For then, if not now, spirits came and went, appeared to be both outside and in.

But we can get a clear sense of differentiation from the first recorded English pamphlet on the bewitchment of a child. The account is found in a publication entitled *The Examination and Confession of certaine Wytches* in 1566. This was not a case of possession but of the obsession of a twelve-year-old girl called Agnes Browne.

Agnes is haunted by a spirit in the form of a dog. This had been sent to torment her by Joan Waterhouse, after Agnes had refused to give her a piece of bread and cheese. Joan and her mother Agnes, along with Elizabeth Francis, are on trial for witchcraft at the Chelmsford assizes on 26 July 1566. Agnes Browne testifies against Joan Waterhouse as follows:

> And then she said that on such a day (naming the day certain) that [sic] she was churning of butter. And there came to her a thing like a black dog with a face like an ape, a short tail, a chain and a silver whistle (to her thinking) about his neck, and a pair of horns on his head.

> And he brought in his mouth the key of the milk house door. 'And then, my Lord,' she said,

> I was afraid. For he skipped and leaped to and fro, and sat on the top of a nettle. And then I asked him what he would have, and he said he would have some butter. And I said I had none for him. And then he said he would have some before he went.

And then he did run to put the key into the lock of the milk house door. And I said he should have none. And he said he would have some. And then he opened the door and went upon the shelf, and there upon a new cheese laid down the key. And after being awhile within, he came out again. And he locked the door, and said that he had made worthless butter for me. And so he departed.

And then, she said, she told her aunt of it. And then she sent for the priest. And when he came, he bade her to pray to God, and call on the name of Jesus.

And so the next day, my Lord, he came again to me with the key of our milk house door in his mouth, and then I said, 'In the name of Jesus, what do you have there?' And then he laid down the key and said that I spoke evil words in speaking of that name. And then he departed. And so my aunt took up the key, for he had kept it from us two days and a night, and then we went into the milk house, and there we did see the print of butter upon the cheese.[51]

The behaviour of the Throckmorton children pointed to something quite different. We can surmise that those who observed the children would have suspected that, if spirits were present, they were already 'within' the children. The Throckmorton children would have been included among those of their contemporaries who were classified as 'demoniacs'. Gilbert Pickering was certain of this from the outset. And he was soon to use the spirit within Jane to discern just who it was who was the cause of her possession.

Lists of the criteria for possession by spirits were common in contemporary texts. It is clear from these narratives that the early modern demoniac had elaborated and embroidered the biblical repertoire of the possessed. And, out of their creativity, a theological virtue was made. Thus, the author of a work on the possession of William Sommers in 1598 declared that 'seeing men in this matter are grown more incredulous than heretofore, it has pleased God, besides the signs of possession mentioned in Scripture, to give other signs also…to make his glorious works most apparent and certain'.[52]

From the depositions provided at the trial of the demoniac William Sommers, the author of *A breife Narration of the Possession, Dispossession, and, Repossession of William Sommers* in 1598 produced a list of twenty-three signs intended to prove the authenticity of his possession.[53] And, in order to assist jurymen in distinguishing natural disease from demoniacal behaviour, Richard Bernard listed ten true signs of possession.[54] Certainly, the

Throckmorton children, with their frightening physical strength, their rigidity, their clairvoyance, and their combination of coma-like states with intense hyperactivity, conformed all too well to these signals.

And, as demoniacs, they were soon to be very influential. The demoniac William Sommers read *The Witches of Warboys* soon after his own fits began in October 1597, as did the Puritan exorcist John Darrell. Anne Gunter's father had read the story of the Throckmorton children. And Anne – another supposed victim of sorcery – herself confessed to having been much influenced by the behaviour of the Throckmortons.[55] The disturbing show which they put on could hardly have been spontaneous.

But where did the children 'learn' their demoniacal repertoire? No doubt, like many other demoniacs, they were familiar with the New Testament stories of those possessed with evil spirits. These were stories that appealed to the 'ghoulish' in children, then as now. And, no doubt, as people began to wonder whether the Throckmorton girls were possessed, they rehearsed the arguments for and against. And the children listened and learned the art of demonic performance. Moreover, there were certainly stories of other demoniacs at the time with which they may well have been familiar.

Unfortunately, we do not know whether the Throckmortons or those others who saw the children in their fits were familiar with John Fisher's 1564 work, *The Copy of a Letter describing the wonderful Woorke of God in delivering a Mayden within the City of Chester, from an horrible kinde of torment and sicknes 16. of February 1564*. Nor do we know whether the Throckmorton children had ever heard the story of Anne Mylner recounted in this pamphlet. But the initial symptoms of the children were remarkably similar to those of Anne. In October 1563 Anne Mylner had fallen sick, became unable to eat or drink, and suffered fits and trances every hour. It was thought by some that she was possessed by a spirit.

She had been in that state for some seventeen weeks when she was visited, the text says, by a Master John Lane, Fellow of Christ's College, Cambridge, on 16 February 1564. In her trance-like state, we read, 'her belly began to move, swelling up and down, sometimes beneath her chest, sometimes up to the throat, in such vehemency, that a man would have thought she would have burst. Then suddenly, she lifts herself up in her bed, bending backwards in such a way that her head and her feet almost met, falling down sometimes on the one side, sometimes on the other, but rising again so suddenly, that the beholders could not imagine how it might be possible, so quickly could she without aid of hand, cast herself (her belly being upward) into the form of a hoop.'[56]

Like the Throckmorton children, Anne Mylner demonstrated two of the three defining criteria – extraordinary strength and physical rigidity – listed by King James VI of Scotland, soon to become James I of England, in his 1597 *Daemonologie*.[57] But, unlike the Throckmortons, Anne Mylner was cured by the prayers of John Lane and others there present after he blew vinegar from his mouth into her nostrils to revive her.

The following day, John Lane preached a sermon at St Mary's in Chester. The now recovered Anne was present, as was a John Throckmorton Esquire, Chief Justice of Chester. This John Throckmorton was related indirectly to the Throckmortons of Warboys. John Throckmorton's uncle was Robert Throckmorton's great grandfather.[58] Possession by spirits was common enough to be identifiable, but rare enough to excite public interest.

Were the Throckmorton children mimicking Anne Mylner? We do not know. We can only conjecture that the case of Anne Mylner was sufficiently exotic to have entered the oral tradition of the Throckmorton family. And the story of the girl who could turn herself into a hoop may well have been heard by the children of Robert Throckmorton.

They too could bend backwards into hoops, doubtless disorienting and horrifying all who witnessed them.

V.

The Scratching of
Alice Samuel

One of the reasons for Alice Samuel's reluctance to return to the Throckmorton household was that she 'feared the common practice of scratching would be used on her' (sig.B.1.r). She had good reason to be afraid. Scratching was not a test of witchcraft. It was an act intended to neutralise it. So to be scratched was not merely to be accused of witchcraft, but to be assumed to be guilty of it.

The act itself was a violent one. The witch was scratched, usually with the fingernails of the bewitched person, until blood was drawn. Supernatural violence was believed to have been perpetrated by the witch. Natural and very real violence was the response intended to countermand it. Thus were the spells broken, and threats removed. At its best, scratching destroyed the witch's power. At the very least, the effects of such power could be neutralised. Then, as now, questions about the possibility of violence done by witches were asked. No one could doubt that real violence was done to witches in response. Take the case of an old woman crossing the river at Newbury on a raft during the English Civil War.

In September 1643 a group of Parliamentary soldiers were foraging for food. They were terrified to see a tall, lean, slender woman who, as it appeared to them, was walking across the surface of the river. When she landed on the shore, the officers 'gave orders to lay hold on her and bring her straight to them. Some were fearful. But some, who were more venturesome than others, boldly went to her and seized her by the arms demanding what she was? But the woman did not reply to them at all. They brought her to the Commanders to whom, though she was strongly urged, she did reply as little.'[59] A decision was taken to execute her. But the Ironsides were unable to kill her by bullet or sword. Finally, they decided to kill her by 'blooding' her:

> [Y]et one amongst the rest had heard that piercing or drawing blood from veins that cross the temples of the head would prevail against

the strongest sorcery, and quell the force of witchcraft, which was allowed for trial. When the woman heard this, she knew then that the Devil had left her and her power was gone, wherefore she began to cry aloud and roar, tearing her hair, and moaning piteously, which was expressed in these words: 'And is it come to pass that I must indeed die?'[60]

Her pleas were in vain. She was eventually shot, we are informed, by a pistol beneath the ear. The woman's corpse was left for the worms (see Plate 13).

Whether intended completely to disempower the witch, or at least to counter her power, the ultimate aim of scratching was to cure the bewitched. A decade before the Throckmorton children fell ill, an ostler from Windsor gave evidence against the accused witch Elizabeth Stile. She had asked for alms, which he refused. Not long afterwards, he informed the court,

[H]e had such a great ache in his limbs that he was not able to take any rest, nor to do any labour. And having sought many means for remedy thereof, he could find none. At last, he went to a wise man, named Father Rosimunde, alias Osborne. He told him that he was bewitched, and that there were many ill women in Windsor. He asked him whom he mistrusted. And the said ostler answered, 'Mother Stile,' one of the aforesaid Witches. 'Well,' said the wise man, 'if you can meet her, and scratch her so that you draw blood of her, you shall presently mend.' And the said ostler declared on oath that he, watching her for a time, did so scratch her by the face that he made the blood come out. And presently his pain went away so that he has been grieved no more since.[61]

You did not have to be a cunning man or a learned one to know that scratching a witch was a cure for bewitchment. On the contrary, this seems to have been common knowledge. Richard Burt of Pinner in Middlesex, for example, knew exactly what would cure him. On Wednesday 8 March 1592, he was eating lunch in a barn when he was confronted by a monstrous black cat. Going to the door of the barn, with his apple pie in his hand, he was whisked into the air, carried off over Harrow, and into a place of 'Cymmerian darkness, plentiful in filthy odours and stinks, full of noise and clamours, insomuch that he seemed to hear infinite millions of discrepant noises, but saw nothing save only the fire...'.[62] Four days after his vision of hell, and unable to speak, he was returned to Pinner. The local parson pitied his plight. Having got his mouth open and with much ado unfolded his tongue, he was able to return to him his speech:

> [T]he first words he spoke were these: Woe to Mother Atkins, woe to Mother Atkins, for she has bewitched me. Whereupon he would not be quiet but ever requested that he might speak with her.
>
> Master Burbidge and Master Smith caused her to be sent for, who being present, he never ceased until he had scratched and drawn blood from her, persuading himself that was a remedy sufficient under God that would make him well. Neither was it or is it any capital error, experience testifies. For since that, he has mended reasonably, and now goes to the Church.[63]

Still, if Alice feared to go to the Throckmortons' because she would be scratched, her fears were groundless – at least at that time. For, we are told, both the children's parents and Gilbert Pickering had no intention of having her scratched. They had taken advice of theologians and been told it was unlawful. As an exercise in counter-magic it was theologically suspect. This was simply because, by reversing the roles of witch and victim, it blurred the distinction between them. The victim became the witch, and vice versa.

Suspected of bewitching Thomas Darling, the witch Alice Gooderidge was scratched on the face and the back of the hands by Thomas until he drew blood. The anonymous author of this account disapproved: '[T]ouching this practice of scratching the witch,' he wrote, 'though it is commonly received as an approved means to discover the witch and procure ease to the bewitched, yet, seeing that neither by any natural cause nor supernatural warrant of God's word it has any such virtue given to it, it is to be received amongst the witchcrafts, whereof there be great store used in our land to the great dishonour of God.'[64]

Put quite simply, it was a case of blood for blood. Richard Browne, victim of the Yorkshire witch Elizabeth Lambe, had the logic right. He argued that 'he was cruelly handled at the heart with one Elizabeth Lambe, and that she drew his heart's blood from him... he desired to scratch her, saying that she had drawn the blood of him, and if he could draw blood of her, he hoped he should amend'.[65]

Legally, it was assault – or worse. And the courts did not always turn a blind eye. 'Violence upon private motion,' Richard Bernard informed his jurymen, 'is a revenge, and we may not offer it to another to ease ourselves.' And, more pragmatically, it could incite the witch to even greater malice. As John Gaule reminded his readers, 'Banging and basting, scratching and clawing, to draw blood of the witch' was not only a superstitious practice but 'rather a provocation to the malice of the witch, than any fortification against it.'[66]

At worst, it was playing into Satan's hands. The Devil eased the body, the more easily to seize the soul, declared Thomas Cooper, 'resting it securely in these devilish charms'.[67]

Jane Throckmorton, we may recall, had been taken by Master Whittle by herself to another room. There they were joined by Gilbert Pickering. Jane stretched out her right arm to the side of the bed where Gilbert was standing and, scratching the bed covering, murmured repeatedly, 'Oh, that I had her. Oh, that I had her' (sig.B.2.r). While she was saying this, Gilbert put his own hand to Jane's. Jane did not know whose hand it was, for she was facing away from Gilbert, with her eyes closed, and pinned down by Whittle. But she would not scratch his hand. Rather, removing hers from his, she continued to scratch on the bed covering.

So the scratching of Alice was initiated neither by the Throckmortons nor by Gilbert Pickering, but by Jane. Or, rather, to remove any suggestion of her complicity in the assault on Alice, not even by her, but by the spirit. Since the opportunity was thus offered by 'the spirit in the child to disclose some secret whereby the witches might be made manifest and known by some means or token' (sig.B.2.r), Pickering went back into the hall and returned with Alice Samuel.

The Throckmortons were initially opposed to scratching Alice. But now they permitted it. Gilbert Pickering was probably persuasive. As happens to many modern parents, medicine had failed them. And, like many modern parents, the Throckmortons continued to hope fervently for a cure. So, at Jane's initiative, and perhaps with Gilbert's active encouragement, they turned to the supernatural alternative.

Resigned to do what others felt necessary, Alice went with Gilbert 'as willingly as a bear to the stake' (sig.B.2.r). The metaphor was an apt one. Alice was about to be 'tethered to a stake' and attacked, if not by dogs, then by the Throckmorton children.

But, if the Throckmortons acquiesced, why did Alice do so? Did she think resistance useless? Did she perhaps hope that if she were scratched the child would be cured, and that would be the end of the matter? We do not know. What we do know is that, while some resented and resisted, such passivity as we see in Alice was not uncommon among those about to be scratched.

George Gifford, for example, tells the story of a butcher whose son John broke out in incurable sores. A local sorcerer or cunning man identified the source of the boy's ills as an old woman who had previously lived close by but had moved out of the shire. On the cunning man's advice, the butcher forced the return of the witch by burning the boy's hair in a cloth in the open air. 'The woman,' we read, 'came home with all speed, came to his house, came to the boy, and said, "John, scratch me." He scratched her until the blood flowed, and whereas before nothing would draw his sores, they healed of themselves.'[68]

Alice Gooderidge too co-operated in her scratching. When the blood was flowing from her hand, she stroked Thomas Darling with the back of it, saying, 'Take blood enough child. God help you.' Thomas was, as usual, ungracious – and unmoved. 'Pray for yourself,' he said. 'Your prayer can do me no good.'[69]

So that Jane could not see Alice, Gilbert marched the alleged witch to the far side of the bed. Jane was still scratching the bed covering and moaning, 'Oh, that I had her.' Speaking softly so that the child could not hear, Gilbert instructed Alice to put her hand to that of the child. She refused. Without any malicious intent towards Alice, nor confidence in scratching, or so we are told, Gilbert then forced Alice's hand against that of Jane. As soon as she felt Alice's hand, Jane scratched it deeply. Indeed, she scratched with such force, we are told, that her own nails broke into splinters.

So Jane knew clairvoyantly when she was scratching Alice's hand and when someone else's had replaced hers. This was important. And Gilbert Pickering gave evidence of it at Alice's trial. Clairvoyance was one of the key signs of bewitchment. Indeed, as an indication of supernatural activity, it was a defining one. John Cotta, for example, in his 1616 text *The Triall of Witch-craft*, saw it as one of the key signs that 'detect and prove a supernatural author'.[70]

Like Jane, the demoniac William Perry, who became known as the Boy of Bilson, was able to discern when the woman who had bewitched him came into the room, even when she was secretly brought in.[71] Richard Dugdale, the so-called Surrey Demoniac, cultivated the useful skill of being able to predict the weather.[72] Clairvoyance was a skill in which the Throckmorton children were to become highly proficient, or so it would seem to those around them.

Gilbert Pickering continued his experiment. While Jane was scratching Alice's hand, Gilbert covered Alice's with his own. Jane ceased scratching. Sometimes, while Gilbert's hand superimposed Alice's, Jane would put one of her fingers between his and scratch Mother Samuel's with the one finger, all her other fingers lying dormant on Pickering's hand. Crucially, as Gilbert Pickering later said in court, Jane's eyes were closed all this time, and her head and neck were so thoroughly buried in the chest of Master Whittle that it was impossible for her to see those who stood on the other side of the bed.

The experiment was then repeated in the hall. For another of the three children had picked up the sinister refrain 'Oh, that I had her'. This time, Pickering conducted Cicely Burder to the child. And, as Jane had done with Alice, so this child did with Cicely. Robert Throckmorton and Francis Dorington, the vicar of the parish, would not allow any testing of the third child.

The scratching of Alice, and later of Agnes, is a central and recurring motif throughout the story of *The Witches of Warboys*. But this is because it fails to have its intended effect – the curing of the bewitched. Ironically, it continually reinforces the guilt of Alice and Agnes through its inability to function effectively as a cure of bewitchment. In fact, it is the failure of scratching to restore the bewitched Throckmorton children that later leads to doubts about the efficacy of the practice. In his *A Guide to Grand-jury Men* in 1627, Richard Bernard commented that not for all the scratching that went on in the case of the Throckmorton children 'did the children amend, but were again in their fits, and that often afterwards'.[73] And Richard Bernard, like William Perkins, found it a godless activity.[74]

Still, even within *The Witches of Warboys*, there is one example of its curative powers. In his evidence, the gaoler in Huntingdon told how, while Alice was imprisoned there, one of his sons fell sick with symptoms identical to those of the Throckmorton children. It was apparent that he was bewitched, and Mother Samuel responsible. The gaoler went into the prison and brought Alice to his son's bedside. There he held her tight until his son had scratched her. Presently, we are told, his son recovered from his sickness (sig.O.2.v). Scratching had not apparently diminished Alice Samuel's powers. Nor, it seemed, had the humiliation and trauma of being locked up in a cell.

vi.

Cunning Men and Cunning Women

I t must have seemed strange and incongruous to Robert Throckmorton that witchcraft had so suddenly afflicted his daughters. As we noted before, the Throckmortons had not long been in Warboys. And they had given no occasion to anyone to practise maleficence against them. Furthermore, we have no indication in the story of any falling out between Alice Samuel or any of the children.

The guilt or innocence of Alice Samuel was further complicated by two other issues. The first of these was the possibility of two modes of being possessed. In the one case, possession occurs as the direct consequence of the action of the Devil. In the other, it occurs as a result of the activities of witches. In either case, possession manifested itself in similar ways. But the two modes carried quite opposite moral weight.

When the Devil has directly entered the body of the possessed, it is as a consequence of the sin of the demoniac. The possessed are guilty, and are reaping just punishment for their sins. In the case of the Elizabethan Alexander Nyndge, his possessed body signals his wickedness. And the story of his possession reminded its readers of the need for vigorous self-examination to avoid the merited punishments of God.[75]

By contrast, when the Devil has entered the demoniac indirectly via the machinations of a witch, the demoniac is perceived as an innocent victim, the target of a witch's evil acts – maleficia. So it comes as little surprise that those who were possessed were eager to point the finger of blame away from themselves and onto others.

The second issue has to do with cunning men and women, local practitioners of magic. They were always susceptible to accusations of witchcraft, for reasons we shall see. But Alice Samuel was not one of these regional magicians. And, though the Throckmorton cause would have been assisted if Alice had been a cunning woman, the text makes no suggestion that she was.

The role of cunning folk was varied: to furnish folk medicine to those who were ill; to assist people to find stolen goods; to identify witches; indeed, to assist in a wide variety of personal problems. Their activities often conflicted with those of the clergy. And this opposition was acknowledged. As one Essex clergyman put it, '[A]s the Ministers of God do give resolution to the conscience, in matters doubtful and difficult; so the Ministers of Satan, under the name of wise-men, and wise-women, are at hand, by his appointment, to resolve, direct, and help ignorant and unsettled persons, in cases of distraction, loss, or other outward calamities.'[76]

As the early modern period's equivalent of practitioners of 'alternative medicine', these homeopathic magicians were in competition with the medical profession. In 1582 we read of the case of a sailor, Thomas Death, who, having been at sea and returning home to Ipswich, was told by a messenger from his wife that his daughter Mary was taken very strangely. Death took her urine to a physician and asked him if she were bewitched. The Doctor was unwilling to commit himself. Dissatisfied, Thomas Death took the urine sample to a cunning man, who told him that, had he not come so quickly, it would have been too late. The cunning man told him that within two nights 'the parties that had hurt his daughter should appear unto her, and remedy her'. Thomas sent the messenger home with medicine prescribed by the cunning man. When he eventually arrived home, he found his daughter restored, having taken the medicine and having seen the spectres of two women standing before her in the night.[77]

The demarcation between cunning folk and their activities and witches was often blurry, and for some indistinguishable. Black and white magic were all of a piece to their opponents. William Perkins saw cunning folk 'as the greatest enemy of God's name, worship and glory, that is in the world, next to Satan himself'.[78] Richard Bernard's jurymen must have been more confused than enlightened by his account. These good or white witches, he wrote 'are commonly called blessers, healers, cunning wise men or women (for there are of both sexes) but of this kind mostly men'.[79] Their profession, he went on to say, 'is to heal and cure such as be taken, blasted, strucken, forespoken … and bewitched'.[80] But he was convinced that, though their work was for the good, all their cures were done 'by their compact with the Devil'.[81] And there were some who had the double capacity 'both to bless, and to curse, to hurt, and to heal'.[82]

Take the case of Edmond Hartley. He did cross the line, both between white and black magic, and sexual propriety and impropriety.

When, in December 1596, seven members of the household of Nicholas Starkie, a gentleman of Cleworth in Lancashire, began to show signs of being possessed, he called in Edmond Hartley, who was a local cunning man. Initially, the possessed responded well to his treatment of 'certain popish charms and herbs' for eighteen months. But Edmond Hartley was not just cunning but lecherous as well. His habit had been to kiss all the possessed maids. This was his undoing. The sexual and demonic became entangled: 'His manner was that, when he meant them a mischief, then he would kiss them if he could, and therewith breathe the Devil into their bodies.'[83]

The practice of laying his lips on theirs may well have been intended by Hartley to help rather than harm. The spirits were often thought to have entered by the mouth. And they could be sucked out through the same opening. But, to the onlookers, breathing the Devil in or sucking him out would have looked much the same. And Hartley paid the penalty.

He was tried at the Lancaster assizes in March 1597, and convicted of having bewitched the children. Although he denied any wrongdoing, the rope broke at his execution, at which time he 'penitently confessed'.[84] He was hanged a second time – on this occasion successfully.

So, unlike Edmond Hartley, Alice Samuel was not by trade a cunning woman. And she was unlikely to be confused for a witch. At least at that time. But, in the context of her trial, matters change. Half-forgotten misfortunes are remembered, half-remembered conversations recalled. Her neighbours and friends must then have thought that she *was* a witch, after all.

vii.

A Demoniac in Titchmarsh

The next day, St Valentine's Day 1590, Gilbert Pickering returned to his home at Titchmarsh Grove. He took the second child, Elizabeth Throckmorton, with him. As we have seen, he was willing to test the validity of scratching. During her stay with him, from 15 February to 8 September in this year, Elizabeth became for him part of an ongoing experiment.

For the duration of Elizabeth's visit, Pickering took detailed diary notes. We have daily entries over the month from 16 February to 16 March, occasional reports over the month from 29 July to 30 August, and a general description of the period from 31 August to 8 September, which was the day of the child's return to Warboys. We can follow her activities, and his, quite closely over this period.

We cannot determine the degree, if any, to which Elizabeth attuned herself to the expectations of those around her to act in the way demoniacs were supposed to and behaved accordingly, or whether, away from her sisters and without other influences, she refined her demoniacal crafts alone. Gilbert Pickering's witch-sleuthing expectations were high, and she may well have tried to come up to them. Certainly, he was the first to see 'Satan' as being intimately involved, and the spirit within Elizabeth acting at his direction: '[I]t would take too long,' he wrote, 'to show all the tricks and collusions of Satan in wrestling and over-ruling all the parts and members of this child' (sig.B.4.r). Elizabeth's demon was evil. But he was also playful, a prankster, 'a ring-leader of new fashions' (sig.B.4.r).

However that may be, what we can say with some certainty is that, towards the end of her time at Titchmarsh Grove, Elizabeth's 'inventiveness' appeared to be waning, her health was becoming jeopardised, and, in all probability, Gilbert Pickering was glad to return her to her parents.

Elizabeth was 'in her fit' when she left Warboys on the journey to her uncle's home. She quickly recovered when she rode out of

Warboys on the twenty-mile journey west to Titchmarsh Grove. But her fits returned the instant that she reached Gilbert's house at Titchmarsh. Suddenly, she was rendered speechless, deaf, and blind. She pitched herself backwards, and thrust out her stomach so forcefully that none could bend her back again. Her legs and arms shook.

Elizabeth's repertoire is typical of other demoniacs of the period. Like other child demoniacs, she preferred to play rather than pray. She would delight especially in playing cards. She would pick out one person with whom to play, not seeing, hearing, nor speaking to any other. Coming out of her trance, she would not remember anything she had done. There were variations on these basic themes. Sometimes she could speak but not hear or see. Sometimes she could only hear, and then only those whom she liked. And at other times, perversely, she could only see, and not speak or hear.

Prayer was likely to bring about seizures. Pious Puritan households were especially prone to prayer. And the more pious the household the more demonic possession took place under its roof. Or so it seems. Prayer in particular was likely to stir up the devils within. The Throckmorton residence was no exception.

The night before Elizabeth left Warboys, the evening of 13 February 1590, the children were all well. Doctor Dorington, the vicar of the parish church of St Mary Magdalene, had wished to have those there pray together. No sooner had he begun to pray than all the children fell into their fits 'wonderfully tormented, as though they would have been torn into pieces' (sig.B.3.r). Dorington stopped mid-prayer. 'Should we go on?' he asked. At the same time, the children had ceased shrieking. It was a pattern that continued. He prayed, they shrieked. His prayer ended, they were quiet. When Dorington stopped praying, the children ceased to shriek. When he began to pray again, 'the children, or rather the wicked spirit in the children, forced them as before' (sig.B.3.r).

The Pickering household in Titchmarsh was a pious one as well. Titchmarsh was a Puritan centre. Gilbert Pickering had married into the staunchly Puritan Browne family. It was his wife Dorothy's family from Tolthorpe in Rutland that had produced the Puritan separatist Robert Browne. The Pickerings themselves were patronised by William Cecil, Lord Burghley, who had strong Protestant leanings.[85]

It was an atmosphere in which Elizabeth throve. On her first night at Titchmarsh Grove, at the time of prayers, the same occurred.

She was tormented during grace, and then again during prayers after the meal. The whole company was terrified. But, prayers having ended, she went quiet, though she still seemed in a trance.

Prayer was one thing, reading the Bible was another. Protestant demoniacs generally reacted badly to that most sacred of Protestant objects, the Bible. It played the role among the possessed in Protestantism that the consecrated host played among the Catholic possessed. The demon's response to the spoken word of the Good Book corresponded to the visual sign of the sacrament. The violent reaction of the demons to the Bible reinforced and confirmed its authority.

The cunning man Jesse Bee, for example, saw the Devil's reaction to his reading of the scriptures in the presence of the possessed Thomas Darling as a way of inspiring 'due and godly regard' for the Bible among the spectators.[86] Bee would call Satan to battle by reading the first chapter of the Gospel of St John.

The first chapter of John's Gospel was particularly provocative. In its opening verses, it emphasised the Protestant primacy of the Word rather than the Catholic primacy of the Sacrament of the Mass. 'In the beginning was the Word, and the Word was God.'

Gilbert Pickering well knew the power of the opening chapter of the Gospel of John. At Titchmarsh, with Elizabeth, he repeated an experiment he had tried successfully beforehand. One of those present would read the first verse of the first chapter of the gospel, at which Elizabeth would go into a tormented state, wailing and shouting out. When the reading ceased, she stopped also. It was proven many times. Elizabeth even raged at the mention of the word 'God' or any words that tended in the direction of 'godliness'. The next day, since it was recognised that public prayer would cause her only to be tormented, she was encouraged to pray inwardly and secretly. This was sufficient to cause that which it was intended to forestall. Such was the noise and disturbance which she created that prayers had regularly to be interrupted.

Gilbert Pickering also re-enacted another experiment which had been tried at Warboys. There, when the children were in their fits, they were carried into the churchyard that adjoined the house. Once removed in this manner, they became well. But, on being carried indoors again, they relapsed. So too Elizabeth, for the next three days: '[I]f she were carried abroad in her fit, it would leave her, and not take her again until she was brought into the house' (sig.B.4.v).

Those around Elizabeth rejoiced at the result. They could now control the spirit – and her seizures.

Why the spirit within her should be so malleable was much debated. The demon, they decided, had no commission to molest Elizabeth outside. He was under instructions from Alice only to torment her indoors. No sooner had this been determined than 'the said experiment presently failed' (sig.B.4.r). For now, as soon as she was carried outside, she was tormented.

The spirit in Elizabeth was both malevolent and cunning.

viii.

Familiars and Fairies

At Titchmarsh, Elizabeth continued to see visions or materialisations of Alice Samuel. But Alice was no longer alone. On 26 February Elizabeth saw her accompanied by various animals. Alice would put these – a mouse, a frog, a cat, sometimes a toad – in Elizabeth's mouth. Elizabeth ran from the room, crying, 'Away with your mouse, Mother Samuel. I will have none of your mouse' (sig.C.1.r). But after that Elizabeth was convinced that she had a mouse in her stomach.

On 31 August 1590 she cried out grievously about a vision of Mother Samuel with a black child sitting upon her shoulder.

To the contemporary reader, this was more than merely unpleasant. This was truly sinister and macabre. For it was further evidence of Alice's malevolence. These were her familiar spirits. They were a central feature of the Warboys story, increasingly elaborated on by the children – and eventually, as we will see, by Alice herself.

Witches and their familiars were never a central feature of witchcraft on the Continent. But, during the Elizabethan period, they did become a familiar feature of English witchcraft. In the Elizabethan statute of 1563 familiars were not mentioned. But for the remainder of the century witches were seldom without their familiars (see Plate 14). By 1604 the familiar had become sufficiently integral to people's perception of witchcraft to be mentioned explicitly in the Witchcraft Act of that year. This decreed the death penalty for any person who, 'after the said Feast of Saint Michael the Archangel next coming, shall use, practise or exercise any invocation or conjuration of any evil spirit, or shall consult, covenant with, entertain, employ, feed or reward any evil and wicked spirit to or for any intent or purpose'.

First published in 1618, and reprinted thirteen times that century, Michael Dalton's *The Countrey Justice* viewed the having of familiars as one of the two decisive proofs of witchcraft. Ordinarily, he wrote, witches have a familiar or spirit, 'which appears to them, sometimes in one shape, sometimes in another; as in the shape of a man, woman, boy, dog, cat, foal, fowl, hare, rat, toad, &c. And to these their spirits they give names.'[87] They had a quasi-bodily nature. They entered individuals through the openings in the body – nostrils, ears, wounds, the anus, most commonly the mouth, and so on. And they exited in similar ways.

So animal familiars were common – dogs, cats, and toads especially. All three were present in the earliest pamphlet on a witch trial in England.

In this defining trial of witches in Chelmsford in Essex on 26 July 1566, Elizabeth Francis told how, at the age of twelve, she was given a familiar in the form of a white spotted cat named 'Satan' by her grandmother. Every time the cat did something for her, it required a drop of her blood. She gave it blood by pricking herself in various places, the marks of which remained to be seen. She gave the cat to a Mother Waterhouse, who, like Elizabeth Francis, offered the cat a drop of her blood 'when he did anything for her, by pricking her hand or face & putting the blood to his mouth which he sucked...the spots of all the which pricks are yet to be seen in her skin'.[88] She went on to confess that she had turned the cat into a toad. Later on, it appeared to her daughter in the form of a dog with horns on its head.

The interrogation of children produced interesting information about familiars. In the 1589 trial of three witches, also in Chelmsford,[89] the son of Ellen Smith confessed that his mother kept three spirits (see Plate 15). One was called 'great Dick', another who lived in a wicker bottle was called 'little Dick', and the third – 'Willet' – was kept in a woolpack.[90] Seven years earlier witchcraft had broken out in St Osyth's, north-east of Chelmsford. Ursula Kemp's eight-year-old son, Thomas Rabbet, claimed that she had four spirits:

> The one called *Tyffin*, the other *Tittey*, the third *Pygine*, and the fourth *Jacke*: and being asked of what colours they were, saith, that *Tittey* is like a little grey cat, *Tyffin* is like a white lamb, *Pygine* is black like a toad, and *Jacke* is black like a cat. And he says, he has seen his Mother at times give them beer to drink and a white loaf or cake to eat. And he says that in the night time the said spirits will come to his Mother, and suck blood of her upon her arms, and other places of her body.[91]

These were variously sent to punish or to kill those who had crossed her. The spirit Jack sucked upon her left thigh, which, when she rubbed it, she said, 'will at all times bleed'.[92]

So witches paid a price for their familiars. They had to be fed – bread, milk, animals, the blood of the witch. We hear of it as early as 1510. A schoolmaster of Knaresborough, John Stewart, was then reputed to have kept three spirits in the shape of bumblebees, to each of whom he gave a drop of blood from his finger.[93]

Similarly, a spirit, in the shape of a ferret called Bidd, was said to have been nourished by blood taken from the finger of Joan Prentice between 1 November and 1 December 1584. Having drunk that which she willingly offered to him, he disappeared. A month later, the ferret reappeared to make her an offer. It was one she could no longer refuse, even if she were inclined to. 'Joan', he said,

> 'Will you go to bed?' To him, she answered, 'Yes, that I will by God's grace.' Then presently the ferret leapt up upon her lap, and from thence up to her bosom. And laying his former feet upon her left shoulder, sucked blood out of her left cheek. And then he said unto her, 'Joan if you will have me do anything for you, I am and will be always ready at your commandment.'[94]

The witch, then, was a bad mother, the dark side of the maternal. She was one who fed and nurtured spirits. She suckled them with blood, not with milk (which was blood purified). She had an alternative family of familiars, usually animals, occasionally child-like creatures. She attacked good mothers. And she brought sickness and death into the house of other mothers, not only directly but through their babies and children.

Alice Samuel had her animal familiars. But she was also seen by Elizabeth with a child sitting upon her shoulders – a demonic *black* child. As we shall see, Alice was later to be accused of being a bad mother to her daughter Agnes – and that her familiars sucked blood from her chin.

We do not know how this peculiarly distinctive feature of English witchcraft trials arose. But we get a clue from the second earliest English pamphlet on witchcraft. On 20 August 1566, scarcely a month after the trial of the three witches in Chelmsford, the Catholic John Walsh is undergoing an ecclesiastical examination for witchcraft and sorcery. John Walsh saw himself quite clearly as a wise or cunning man, a healer, a conjurer, and a finder of lost property. So, being asked whether he had a familiar or not, he denies it utterly. At this point, at least, he seems to believe that to confess to having a familiar is to confess to malevolent witchcraft. But he does not deny that he is helped by fairies in determining if someone is bewitched. 'How do you know when anyone is bewitched?' he is asked. 'He says that he knew it partly by the fairies. And he says that there are three kinds of fairies, white, green, and black. When he is disposed to use them, he speaks with them on hills where, as there are great heaps of earth, as namely in Dorsetshire. And between the hours of twelve and one at noon, or at midnight, he uses them. Whereof (he says), the black fairies be the worst.'[95]

His distinction between familiars and fairies is not one he was able to sustain. Or perhaps it was not accepted by his examiners. For he also said, we are told, that 'he had a book of his said master, which had great circles in it, wherein he would set two wax candles across a cross of virgin wax, to raise the familiar spirit. Of the spirit he would then ask for any thing stolen, who did it, and where the thing stolen was left, and thereby did know. And by the fairies, he knows who is bewitched.'[96]

Walsh's familiar appeared to him in various forms, sometimes like a grey, blackish pigeon, sometimes like a brindled dog, and sometimes like a man, although with cloven feet. Like Satan the cat, he needed to be fed. And, again like Satan, his preferred form of sustenance was blood. When John wished to make use of his familiar, he had to give him some living thing – a chicken, cat, or dog. And when he first had the spirit, 'his said master did cause him to deliver him one drop of his blood, which blood the spirit did take upon his paw'.[97]

Fairies, familiars? It is difficult to tell the difference. In Scottish witchcraft, witches often had personal fairies. Like English familiars, they offered their services at a price, though, as Diane Purkiss points out, 'Scottish fairies behave like lovers, and often want children, while English familiars behave like children and often want love.'[98]

Morally too, they were a mixed bunch. Familiars could do good and fairies harm. Familiars offered to do as they were commanded. Satan the cat, the familiar of two of the Essex witches, was generally malignant. But his offer to Agnes Waterhouse was 'to do for her what she would have him to do'.[99] He found Elizabeth Francis a herd of sheep, and slaughtered a hog for Agnes.[100] So it was recognised that witches turned to their devilish imps 'for the health of themselves or others, and for things lost'.[101]

Fairies were also morally ambivalent. They were capable of doing good. But they were just as likely to do harm. They offered to help, but they could also demand your soul in return. They were, in fact, just like familiars, as the Lancashire witch Elizabeth Sowtherns discovered. This was her confession:

> About twenty years past, as she was coming homeward from begging, there met this examinate near a Stonepit in *Gouldshey*, in the said forest of *Pendle*, a spirit or devil in the shape of a boy, the one half of his coat black, and the other brown. He bade this examinate stay, saying to her that if she would give him her soul, she should have any thing that she would request. Whereupon this examinate demanded his name. And the spirit answered that his name was Tibb. And so this examinate, in hope of such gain as was promised by the said devil or Tibb, was contented to give her soul to the said Spirit.[102]

We cannot tell from *The Witches of Warboys* whether the Throckmorton children and those around them knew the stories of the witches of Essex, and St Osyths, and of their familiars. Nor can we tell the extent to which the published stories influenced popular beliefs about familiars, or popular beliefs the stories. But the children did inhabit a world thoroughly populated – at least in the contemporary imagination – by familiars, fairies, and witches. Elizabeth's vision was of Alice alongside her familiars. And another fateful link to her witchcraft was forged.

By late 1592 the Throckmorton children were well aware of the notion that familiars were fed by their witches. They began to accuse Alice, when she was not with them, of absenting herself in order to feed her spirits. Around this same time, a Master John Lawrence reported to Robert Throckmorton and Francis Dorington that Alice Samuel's chin was bleeding. Examining the handkerchief with which Alice had wiped her chin, they judged it 'to be bloody to the quantity of eight or ten drops' (sig.F.2.v). Upon her chin they observed only a few little red spots, 'as if they had been flea-bitings' (sig.F.2.v). Robert Throckmorton asked her whether her chin had always bled so. 'Very often,' she replied, 'but only when I was alone. I never told anyone about it.'

After she was condemned she was to confess that, even as she spoke to Throckmorton and Dorington, the spirits were then sucking at her chin. She had six spirits, she later said, that tormented the children. They sucked her blood before she sent them away, and when they returned they were rewarded 'by sucking of her blood oftentimes when they were outside her body' (sig.H.2.r).

ix.

A Girl Possessed

Meanwhile, at Titchmarsh Grove, Elizabeth's vicissitudes continued. We can hear Gilbert Pickering behind the text making his diary entries. From 16 February to 26 February 1590 Elizabeth had six or seven seizures a day, though sometimes as many as ten. There was much sneezing and drowsiness. She bent her limbs forwards and backwards. There were many fits of weeping, and paroxysms of laughing. She bled from the mouth and nostrils. She lost her sight, hearing, and understanding. She hopped for days on end.

The spirits became more active. On 27 February, like others possessed by spirits, Elizabeth's mouth gaped open widely, and she gasped for air. The spirit forced it open, she claimed. She was persuaded to try and close her mouth. She was able to do so, but only after much effort. It was said, in her hearing, to be 'a spirit of the air', one which entered when she inhaled and departed when she exhaled.

At least one spirit had taken up residence in her stomach. The belly was thought to be the body's 'hell'. And Devils spoke from the stomach. Elizabeth would often ask if others could hear the spirit in her belly lapping the milk she had drunk.

On 1 March her sneezing was so severe that she bled at least a pint of blood from her nose and mouth. She wept inconsolably all night. 'The witches will kill my Father,' she cried. 'And they will destroy me and my sisters.'

Her range of activity was wide and varied. It was not all blood, sweat, and tears. The second day of March was punctuated by laughing fits and 'merry jests of her own devising' (sig.C.1.r). She preferred to play cards with a person of her own choosing, rather than read books:

> She did choose one of her uncles to go to cards with her ... soon after there was a book brought and laid before her, at which presently she flung her self backwards, which being taken away, she presently recovered and played again. This was often proved and found true.

And thus playing at cards, her eyes were almost clean shut. But even if the sight of her eyes was clean covered, she saw the cards and nothing else. She knew her uncle and no man else, she heard and answered him, and none other. She perceived him when he played foul, or did steal from her, her counters or cards. But any other might take them out of her hands, she not seeing or feeling.

Left in the company of other children, playing bowls or other games, there were no fits to be seen. 'The more foolish the sport,' remarked the Puritan Gilbert, 'the more the spirit spares her.'

Elizabeth too had a Puritan streak. On 10 March she decided that playing cards was impious. She burned all the cards she could come by, and took up reading instead. The spirit was not impressed and took its revenge at this display of 'goodness':

> Sometimes it quite closed up her eyes, sometimes it tied her tongue, sometimes it set her teeth, sometime it would fling away the book, especially at any good word. If she could catch the book, and be able to hold it still by striving, she would clap it fast to her face, until she could see. For sometimes in her reading, it would fling her backward, and swell her belly in such sort and strange wise, that two strong men were not able to hold her down. (sig.C.2.r)

If the spirit didn't like words in general, it liked the Word of God even less.

> On 11 March she was asked (or rather the spirit within her was asked) whether she loved the Word of God. She was tormented. 'But do you love Witchcraft?' It was content. Opportunities to support Protestantism were taken. 'Love you the Bible?' It shook her. And to attack Catholicism! 'Love you Papistry?' It was quiet. 'Love you prayer?' It raged. 'Love you the Mass?' It was still. 'Love you the Gospel? It heaved up her belly. 'Whatever good thing you named it misliked, but whatsoever concerning the Pope's rubbish, it seemed pleased and pacified'. (sig.C.2.r)

The spirit reacted violently to mention of Satan. While reading, and when she came to the word 'Satan' or 'the Devil', she would have difficulty keeping the book in her hands. The spirit within would violently shake her arms and her body, so that she would often say, 'Will you not allow me to say my prayers? Will you not allow me to read? I will say them, I will read.' She would not forsake her reading: 'It cast it forth from her hands (as many times it did). Yet she would receive it again, being brought to her, and many times fetch it herself.

And in the end, after much contention and much striving, she would read quietly' (sig.C.3.v). At the mention of Satan or the Devil, Elizabeth would twitch all over. At the name of Alice Samuel, she would be shaken so hard by the shoulders and arms that it was as if she would be vibrated to pieces.

On the last day of August her jaws were set so tight that she was unable to eat or drink. Elizabeth was joining a long line of religious women who appeared to be unable to eat. Such an illness was the terminal point of something that was more central to medieval women's religiosity than to men's. As Caroline Bynum has eloquently put it, 'Since late medieval spirituality valued both renunciation and service, each gender renounced and distributed what it most effectively controlled: men gave up money, property, and progeny; women gave up food.'[103]

So those around Elizabeth Throckmorton would not have been surprised at the sight of a young woman suffering from such an infirmity. They would, I believe, have been quite familiar with the stories of medieval women who, if they did not rejoice in their inability to eat, nonetheless made a theological virtue out of necessity.

And, just as 'holy anorexia' was not unheard of among saints, so too 'unholy anorexia' was not uncommon among those possessed with spirits. It empowered their 'spiritual' selves, with no loss to their 'physical' selves.

The early sixteenth-century demoniac Mary Glover, for example, at the end of eighteen days of fasting, was said to 'be impaired neither in flesh nor strength'.[104] The pious demoniac Margaret Muschamp would let nothing come within her jaws, though her lips were moistened with milk and water. Her sixteen weeks of fasting caused her no harm. Margaret, ever the model of the pious child, 'would smile and show her arms and breast, and say that God fed her with angel's food'.[105]

Elizabeth's suffering was visible to all: '[I]t could not but grieve even a merciless tyrant's heart (but that the Devil has no mercy) to see how the child wept and lamented, many times putting her hand to her mouth, and lifting up her head, as if giving thirsting signs of a hungry desire for meat and drink' (sig.C.4.r).

In the staunchly Protestant household of Gilbert Pickering, it was impossible for Elizabeth to mimic those 'holy anorexics' of medieval Catholicism who survived on the Eucharistic wafer. Such relics of popery were not available to her. But the closing of Elizabeth's mouth was nonetheless seen as a sign of her deep piety, of God's regard for her, and of her deep resistance to Satan. Those around her were convinced that 'God's merciful Providence and care towards the child' would see her through (sig.C.4.v).

It is unhelpful to apply modern understandings of anorexia nervosa or sixteenth-century variants to Elizabeth Throckmorton or other sixteenth-century demoniacs who were unable to eat. Our information about Elizabeth is too limited.[106] And, even if it weren't, her cultural context is sufficiently different to lead us to question whether such a modern diagnosis would be helpful or illuminating.

But it is legitimate to ask if she were able to eat though refusing to do so or whether she were genuinely unable to bring herself to swallow food. With some conviction we can say that Elizabeth chooses her inedia or inability to eat as the battleground on which she engages with Satan. She invests it with religious meaning. Paradoxically, at her most powerless – her inability to eat and drink to sustain her own life – she powerfully exerts her will against what she takes as the cause – the Devil.

On the evening of 31 August, when it was time for her to go to bed, Elizabeth's carers realised that she could be fed milk by a quill inserted through the gap left by a lost tooth. Elizabeth greatly rejoiced, we are told. Being unable to speak, she expressed her joy at having deceived the malice of the Devil by outward signs, clapping her hands on her chest and stomach. Like the other children whenever they could speak, she defied Satan's machinations: 'Do what you can, you can do me no hurt. You see that God is stronger than you… I am glad in my heart that you cannot overcome me' (sig.C.4.v). In these utterances of joyous defiance, verbal and non-verbal, the piety of the children was reinforced. Elizabeth was taken to bed still in her fit. Determined to say her prayers, she was severely tormented throughout. In spite of this, she continued until they were finished, a sign of 'the spirit and grace of God in the child' (sig.C.4.v).

The next evening, Satan sought revenge for her defiance. Whereas, beforehand, Elizabeth's teeth had been set against each other, now they overlapped. This new devilry made it impossible to use the quill. In spite of this setback, Gilbert Pickering was certain that the outcome would not prove fatal: '[W]e were truly convinced,' he wrote, 'that the malice of the Devil, and of his wicked instruments whosoever, was limited, and his mischievous purposes towards the child so far forth restrained, that although he might endanger her health (which many times he did), yet he should never actually permanently damage it, much less her life' (sig.C.4.v).

Her torments were undoubtedly severe, but Elizabeth endured them all patiently. And, in her capacity to endure, she exemplified for those around her the very ideal of the womanly response to illness: 'If a strong man in his perfect health had struggled in such a storm, and suffered such a violent attack but for one hour, as she did for half a day or longer, it would have not been a wonder had he been sick for a month afterwards, no, not if death itself had soon followed after it' (sig.C.4.v).

But, like others possessed by spirits, Elizabeth had no memory of what had happened to her during her seizures. After her fits, we are told, she was as happy as anyone else. Her sufferings were to her as if in a sleep or dream. There were a number of evidences for this. Her claim that she couldn't remember anything was one. Her cheerful countenance after her fits was another. Her immodest laughter in some of her fits was such that the 'child's modesty would have blushed at' it (sig.D.2.v), had she been aware. Her insensitivity to pain during her fits, and her courage in entering into them, all pointed to her obliviousness afterwards of what occurred in them.

Often Elizabeth had said that she would not be well until she returned to Warboys, or had travelled a mile or so along the way to her village. Thus, on 1 September 1590, accompanied by Gilbert's wife among others, she set out on horseback for her home. Before they had gone a mile, she began to cheer up. Her jaw unlocked and she was able to speak again. She predicted that by the time she had traversed a mile, she would be well. Having gone the mile, she rubbed her eyes, came to herself, and wondered how she had got there and what she was doing there. Alighting from the horse, she found her leg, no use to her for the previous three weeks, marvellously restored. She was able to eat and drink again. And she was able to read her prayer book, at least until she came to the word 'Satan'.

But as soon as mention was made of returning to Titchmarsh Grove, she fell once again into a fit. Her eyes closed. She was no longer able to stand. Her jaw clenched shut again, and her stomach began to heave and swell. A further experiment was tried repeatedly:

> Now as long as she is walking forwards from the Grove as if to Warboys, so that you don't speak of going back again ... she is very well and merry without any sign of dislike as long as you are going on or standing still. But as soon as ever you turn her about to go homewards, she presently sinks down in your arms as one fallen into a sudden swoon, struggling between life and death. And she

continues so, striving for a little time, until she is clean overcome, if you don't in the meantime turn her face again. But if you do, as one awaking from a dream, she is returned to her former state. (sig.D.1.v)

They returned to Titchmarsh Grove. Elizabeth's inability to eat returned that night. She was able to take milk through the quill. But, when something more solid was brought to her, she pointed in the direction of Warboys. Elizabeth has regressed to infancy – 'a suckling and sucking child' (sig.D.1.v).

The next afternoon, Wednesday 2 September, she was taken on the same route to Warboys. She recovered at the identical spot as the previous day and was able to eat. Before finishing and giving thanks, however, Satan appeared to her, and made it impossible for her to pray coherently.

Before she was turned round towards Titchmarsh Grove to return there, a twig was placed between her teeth to keep her mouth open. Elizabeth strove with her hands to remove the twig. But it was held so strongly between her jaws that it could not be removed, 'which appeared by the great marks of her teeth made in the stick' (sig.D.2.r). After great difficulty, it was finally removed. But this way of keeping her mouth open was not tried again. When she was informed that she was being fed with a quill, she was amazed and would not believe it.

The contrast between Elizabeth as she is in her fits, and before and after them, is extreme. It is the afternoon of 2 September 1590. Gilbert is sitting in the fields near his home. Elizabeth is close by. He is watching her. 'And now here in this place which is the open fields, she is willing and eager in every movement to turn herself around, and to set her face homewards' (sigs. D.2.v–D.3.r). Not for one moment does he think that she is a fraud. Nor does he ever seem to have thought so. For him, she is assuredly possessed by spirits, and he is aghast at what they can do to her. As he watches the child prepare to be tormented while she turns towards the Grove, he continues,

And surely it may be thought, there are very few ... if they had but once seen the child in that pitiful and woeful case in which she has been a hundred times, that would voluntarily cast themselves into so great an extremity and hazard of life ... And yet has this little child (such is the pre-eminence of God's spirit over all Spirits of wickedness) seen many of her sisters and some others, divers times in the like state, or worse (if it were possible) handled and tormented. (sig.D.3.r)

There, in the fields, he reflects in his diary on the psychology of possession, on what he calls 'the great question'. 'Does she consciously feel and partake either in anguish of mind, or grief of body,' he asks, 'those pangs and torments which to outward judgement she appears to?' A happy oblivion both during and afterwards is his conclusion. Granting his acceptance of her possession, anything else, we can surmise, would be unthinkable. These are the reasons 'that draw us to believe it':

First, the testimony of the child her self (when she is recovered) might be sufficient to persuade the matter, if there were nothing else. For why should not she rather by showing her grief cause us to moan and pity her (as all do that see her) if she felt any cause why? The smiling and cheerful countenance which she has always used to those that ask her how she does presently upon her fit ended, may something also strengthen this point. The earnest desire she has always had in time of her greatest extremities, to finish her prayers, or any such good exercise, although her torments (as they appeared to be) were the more increased thereby, as usually they were. Her exceeding hearty and immodest laughter in some of her fits, and such indeed as the child's modesty would have blushed at, and could not have permitted, if she had been well. To these may be added, that the not feeling of her blow and hurt, nor knowing any thing of it, until she was recovered, which she received in her forehead by the latch of a door … with many such like arguments which might be alleged. And not to leave out that which is most force of all: her open contempt at all times, and in all places, both in speech and gesture, immediately before her fit took her; her boldness and good courage at all times to adventure upon it, though she knew assuredly it would assault her; as namely, in the beginning of her visitation, at the naming only of God, or Jesus, or any good word, which if you had seen, you could not have sufficiently admired; also at the giving of thanks after or before meat received, at the entering upon any good exercise, as reading or praying, she never once used to give any sign of fear or discouragement, in any respect. And at the naming of the Devil, Mother Samuel, or any such black word, that keeps the colour, as Sathan, or Cicely, (which is another woman's name, that is suspected to be confederate in this wicked practice) she never feared nor would stick at them, but always showed herself ready (though she very well knew that she should have her fit for it) to cast herself upon the present danger. (sig.D.2.v)

There is the strong suggestion that, during this period, still eating little, Elizabeth became what we would think of as depressed. She was sad most of the time, and unable to eat. She wept often, and suffered from headaches and muscle pains. And she was lonely. Such was the anguish caused to the other children in the house by seeing her in her fits that they were kept away from her.

Gilbert attributed her misery to her having perhaps heard how she acted during her fits, and being deprived of the company of other children for much of the time. She was more 'like the image and shadow of a child', he wrote. Still, the regime of daily trips to the fields to ensure that Elizabeth received some sustenance continued from 3 until 8 September. On that day, having come to the usual place where she made her recovery, she happily continued on to Warboys.

Her only unhappiness was that she was departing from Titchmarsh Grove. Gilbert Pickering gives us no hint of his own feelings at Elizabeth's departure. But, given the stresses and difficulties of the last several months, he may well have been not quite as unhappy to see her going home as she was.

X.

A Lady, Bewitched to Death

The story now returns to the village of Warboys, but some six months earlier. It was mid-March 1590, and a month or so after Gilbert had left for Titchmarsh with Elizabeth. The Throckmortons were visited by Lady Susan Cromwell, second wife of Sir Henry Cromwell, together with her daughter-in-law, the wife of Oliver, Henry's son and Susan's stepson.[107] Her visit came almost exactly nine years before the birth of the step-grandson who would change England's history for ever – Oliver Cromwell, future Lord Protector of the Commonwealth. But, as we shall see, Lady Susan would not live to see him born.

The Cromwells of Huntingdonshire were new aristocracy, and represented new money. Sir Henry joined the upper echelons of society in 1563. In that year, he was knighted by Queen Elizabeth. He was civic-minded. He was the Member of Parliament for his county. Four times he served as High Sheriff of Cambridgeshire and Huntingdonshire. He was appointed a commissioner for the drainage of the fens. He had even made some progress on local fen drainage, since it seems that in 1586 and 1587 he was leasing 'fenn closes' and 'closes of pasture' to his tenants around Ramsey and nearby Higney.[108]

But, assessed in terms of the four degrees of people in England as described by William Harrison in 1587, he was not quite top drawer. Knights stood towards the bottom of the first rank, and beneath princes, dukes, marquises, earls, viscounts, and barons.[109] But then, as now, their money made up for it.

Sir Henry's wealth came from his father, Richard Williams. Richard had been raised from obscurity by Henry VIII's Chancellor, Thomas Cromwell. The reasons for his having done so remain opaque. He may have kept a public house in Putney. Henry's mother may have been Thomas Cromwell's sister, for he was referred to as 'cousin' and 'nephew' by Thomas. Whatever his origins, he throve in the environment of Henry's court. He was knighted in 1540 and changed his name to Cromwell. Following the abolition of the monasteries, he was granted the estates of the nunnery of Hinchinbrook and the abbey of Ramsey. He not only survived the fall of Thomas Cromwell in mid-1540, he gained from it.

Henry Cromwell continued to live in the style of his father. His generosity was such that he was known as 'the Golden Knight'. He wintered at the rebuilt Hinchinbrook House in Huntingdon, where he was visited by the Queen in 1564. He summered at Ramsey Abbey, some four and a half miles from Warboys. And it was from there that Lady Cromwell and her daughter-in-law journeyed to the village. She had learned of the troubles that afflicted the family whom she knew well. And she went to Warboys to visit the children and to comfort their parents.

Lady Cromwell had not long been in the house when the children who were still there all fell into their fits. They were so grievously tormented that Lady Cromwell was moved to tears. Having been informed that Alice Samuel was under suspicion, she sent for Alice. Alice was obliged to respond to Lady Cromwell's demand. John Samuel was a tenant of Sir Henry. Reluctantly, Alice came. After her arrival, the children's torments grew even worse. This was sufficient to convince Susan Cromwell.

Lady Cromwell, we are told, took Mother Samuel aside and accused her of having bewitched the children. It was a charge that Alice vehemently denied, claiming that the Throckmortons did her great wrong in so accusing her. To this, Lady Cromwell responded that it was not the parents who accused her, but the children, or at least 'the spirit by them' (sig.D.4.r). Alice's declaration of innocence was overheard by Joan, the oldest of the girls. She was, at the time, in a state of possession. 'It was she that caused all this,' declared Joan, 'and there is something that now tells me this' (sig.D.4.r). And she went on to say that it was squealing very loudly in her ears. She expressed her surprise that no one else could hear it. Alice Samuel persisted in her denials. And seeing the danger she was in, she wanted to go home.

Lady Cromwell had power over Alice. She knew it, and she used it. She may well have been told that the scratching had failed. So she adopted another form of counter-magic, or, in this instance, sympathetic magic. The witch's power ran through a sorceress's body. It even 'rubbed off' on her clothing. Hair and therefore head-cloths were especially powerful witching devices. And fire and heat were particularly efficacious ways of countering the power of a witch.

No doubt ignoring her protests, Lady Cromwell clipped off a lock of Alice's hair and, together with Alice's headband, gave these items to the children's mother to burn. It was a sure indication of Susan Cromwell's conviction that Alice was indeed a witch, intended both to identify her and neutralise the witchcraft. Alice was aghast. 'Why do you use me thus? I never did you any harm as yet' (sig.D.4.r). Except for these last two words, we can see Alice's comment as arising from her genuine puzzlement that she should be so treated. She, like most others, was aware of the origin of witchcraft accusations in a social disagreement between witch and victim. And she was disclaiming any knowledge of any conflict between them. But we can see the hand of the author of the text in adding 'as yet' to Alice's words. For, though not realised at the time, they point to what was soon to happen, and Alice's presumed part in it.

It seems incontrovertible that Alice was not only nonplussed but also angered and dismayed by her treatment at the hands of Lady Cromwell. Much later on, when she was to confess to having bewitched Susan Cromwell to death, it was this incident that she cited as the cause of her anger at the visiting aristocrat.

Lady Cromwell returned to Ramsey that same day. That night, she dreamed of Mother Samuel. And she was grievously tormented in her sleep by a cat which, as she imagined, Alice Samuel had sent to haunt her. The cat threatened to pluck all the flesh from her body. So greatly did she thrash around that she awoke her daughter-in-law, with whom she was sharing a bed in the absence of the latter's husband, Oliver. It is to her daughter-in-law that we probably owe this account. She, in her turn, roused Lady Cromwell from her tossing and turning and was informed of her dreams. The disturbing spectre of Alice and her familiar, whether as dream or vision, certainly portended no good to anybody.

Lady Cromwell slept no more that night. The horror of what she had experienced lay heavily upon her.

She was soon to fall strangely ill. Her symptoms were comparable to those of the children. She continued in this state until, the text informs us, she died a year and a quarter after her visit to Warboys. If we consider that she had her encounter with Alice Samuel in mid-March 1590, then, according to *The Witches of Warboys*, she met her fate in June 1591. The death of Lady Cromwell can be verified in the All Saints, Huntingdon, Parish Registers in the Huntingdon Records Office. There we find a reference to 'My Ladye Susan Cromwells funeral' in an entry from 12 July 1592.[110] So *The Witches of Warboys* places the death of Lady Cromwell a year earlier than that in which it occurred. We cannot tell whether this is a simple (albeit important) error on the editor's part or a deliberate attempt to heighten the dramatic impact of the encounter between Lady Cromwell and Alice by shortening the period between it and her subsequent demise.

In either case, the strategic intention of *The Witches of Warboys* is clear. This is the point at which Alice Samuel did the harm to Lady Cromwell that she had implicitly threatened earlier in the day. 'I never did you any harm as yet' has moved from veiled menace to terrifying consequence. The contretemps between Alice Samuel and Susan Cromwell has led to Susan's bewitchment and ultimately, her extinction.

We do not know the cause of Lady Cromwell's death, though we may reasonably assume that it was a long and lingering one. But, granting that she had such a dream, it is not unfeasible to suppose that in her terror she frightened herself to death. The ominous words of Mother Samuel, 'I never hurt you as yet', we read were 'never out of her mind' (sig.D.4.v). We can be certain that she genuinely believed that witchcraft was all too present in the house of the Throckmortons. Consciously or unconsciously, Lady Cromwell brought back from Warboys deep fears of Alice Samuel and the efficacy of her powers. They were fears that surfaced in the dark watches of the night.

In the everyday world, Susan Cromwell was a figure of some consequence and authority. But, on the plane of the supernatural, she had been confronted by a power that she could not match. Her dreams of Alice accompanied by an animal familiar confirmed that supposition. And such dreams were not to be dismissed lightly. They resonated theologically. In the words of Philip Goodwin, 'Good dreams are God's good working in mens' sleepings. And bad dreams be the evil workings of the Devil in sleeping men.'[111] Nightmares did cause mental illness. The seventeenth-century physician Richard Napier noted a number of cases of people who had become mentally ill as a result of their terrifying dreams.[112] And early modern dreams were often taken seriously as signs of what the future held: '[D]reams seen by grave and sober persons do signify matters to come,' wrote Thomas Hill in 1576.[113]

Lady Cromwell did not need to be familiar with the English translation in 1518 of Artemidorus's *The Interpretation of Dreams* to know that 'domestic beasts which show themselves fierce and savage signify ill'.[114] Her dream image of the stripping away of her flesh by a spirit being, in effect the reduction of Lady Cromwell to her skeletal state, was more than enough to convince her. Her dream signified the coming transition of Lady Cromwell from life to death.

xi.

A Visiting Demonologist

Between the departure of Lady Cromwell from Warboys in mid-March and around Christmas of that same year, 1590, Robert Throckmorton made no further notes, although, we are assured, 'there befell a hundred wonders' (sig.D.4.v) during that time. The narrative moves then to December 1590, and to the encounter of Henry Pickering with Alice Samuel. Henry Pickering was the brother of Elizabeth Throckmorton and Gilbert Pickering, and hence the children's uncle. *The Witches of Warboys* designates him as a 'scholar of Cambridge' (sig.D.4.v). He graduated with an MA from Cambridge in 1590, the year of his visit to Warboys recorded in our text. The seventh son of John Pickering of Titchmarsh, he was baptised there on 10 December 1564. Perhaps he was visiting Titchmarsh and Warboys to celebrate his twenty-sixth birthday with his family.[115] He was later to become rector of the church of All Saints in Aldwinckle, Northamptonshire, near Titchmarsh. It was in this church that, on 14 August 1631, he was to baptise the dramatist-to-be John Dryden, his grandson, and the son of his daughter Mary and her husband Erasmus Dryden.

Henry gave evidence against Alice at her trial (see sig.O.1.r). So the account we have has been written back into the narrative from the trial evidence. If his brother Gilbert was the careful experimentalist, Henry Pickering, the ink still fresh on his degree, is the brash, young theologian.

It was inevitable that, having heard the story of the children, and having seen them in their fits, he would wish to speak to Mother Samuel. Several days after his arrival, therefore, and unbeknownst to any others in the Throckmorton household, or so we are led to believe, he went in search of Alice. He took with him two other scholars of his acquaintance, then staying in Warboys.

Coincidentally, as the men were heading towards her cottage, Alice Samuel emerged and crossed the street in front of them. They followed her for a long time, for her journey was to take her all the way to the village pond, about a mile distant from her home next to the Throckmortons' (see Plate 16). Alice was carrying a little wooden tankard and a little barley in her apron, hoping to exchange the grain for some ointment of balm. The balm, we are told, was not to be had. And, as she prepared to return home, Henry and his colleagues waylaid her, and began to question her. Scholars they were. But gentlemen they may not have been. Alice was clearly not impressed.

The Alice of Henry's report is different from the Alice we have encountered thus far. This was a noisy, truculent, and belligerent woman, unwilling to be questioned, loud and impatient in her responses, unwilling to allow any to speak but herself. One of the scholars asked her to follow the womanly virtue of being more silent. She reacted angrily with words to the effect that they could expect no better from one born of humble beginnings. The greatest part of her speech, though, was railing against Robert Throckmorton and his children.

It is clear that, by this time, her patience is exhausted. She now believes that Throckmorton is culpable for allowing his children to continue their accusations against her, and that their fits are faked: 'He misuses me,' she said, 'in allowing his children to play the wantons in such a way, accusing me and bringing my name into question. The children's fits are nothing but wantonness in them,' she said repeatedly, 'and if they were my children, I would not allow them to escape so without punishing them, one after the other' (see sig. E.1.r). She was accusing Robert Throckmorton of being an irresponsible father. And she was accusing them of being wicked children. The Throckmorton children heard of this accusation of it being nothing but wantonness in them. They were later to take their revenge, and accuse her of being a bad mother.

Her attempt to be righteously indignant and to take the moral high ground cut no ice with the Cambridge scholars. Henry Pickering had studied theology, so he knew a thing or two about looking down on others from the moral mountain top. It was Alice's faith, or lack of it, that interested him, not her judgement on Robert's childcare. And so they questioned her about her service of God and profession of her faith. She stubbornly and persistently replied only to the effect that 'my God will deliver me, my God will defend me and revenge me of my enemy'. But, in her use of the personal pronoun 'my', they saw a chink in her armour. And the weakness which they believed they detected was her apparent though inadvertent statement of faith in a religion other than Christianity.

We do not know the extent to which Henry Pickering and his friends were familiar with Continental demonology and its construction of witchcraft as an anti-religion focused on the worship of an alternative deity, the Devil. But they could not have been unaware that, for the past decade or so, the great European witch-hunts had been under way, as much in Protestant as in Catholic lands. And they too probably believed that they were engaged in a life and death struggle against Satan and all his works.

These men were part of a generation that viewed the history of the world apocalyptically, determined by the opposing agencies of light and darkness, good and evil. On the negative side stood Satan, the Beast, the Antichrist, and Catholics. On the positive were to be found God, the company of saints and angels, and Protestants. Witches, as the demonologists saw them, had made a formal contract with the Devil. And, through them, diabolical powers were running the world. Or, if they were not yet quite running it, they were running riot in it.

It was in 1597 that Continental demonology was formally to make its entrance into England. And it did so, via Scotland, in the person of King James I and his book *Daemonologie*. In this important work, James introduced to English theologians and demonologists those two features of witchcraft that dominated the European witch-hunts: the notion of the compact between the witch and Satan, and the notion of the Sabbath, the gathering of witches together to worship the Devil. Coincidentally, if not ironically, perhaps, James was acquiring his knowledge of witchcraft in the winter of 1589 on a visit to Denmark, just as the demons were becoming active in faraway Warboys.

Still, Continental demonology may have impacted on Henry Pickering and his friends more indirectly. For Jean Bodin's *De la Demonomanie des Sorciers*, first published in Paris in 1580, was known in England soon after its publication. And it was quoted by the author of the preface to the 1582 account of the Essex witches, *A true and just Recorde of the Information, Examination and Confession of all the Witches, taken at St Oses in the Countie of Essex.* He goes on to accuse them of idolatry and apostasy 'for they worship Satan, unto whom they have sworn allegiance'.[116] And, in the light of the heinous nature of the crime, he endorses the Continental practice of burning witches.

So it was probably with a burgeoning sense of excitement that Henry Pickering and his friends began to question the woman who, as they saw it, had rejected God and sworn allegiance to the Devil and all his foul works.

One of them asked her, 'Do you have a God alone? Do you not serve the same God that others do?' No doubt she saw the trap they were laying for her: a confession that she worshipped a different God – the Devil.

'Yes,' she said, 'I do worship the same God.'

But they had much trouble getting her from the phrase 'my God' to 'the God of Heaven *and Earth*'. To them, this reluctance on her part would have been tantamount to a refusal to confess her faith in the Christian God, a denial of the credal statement 'I believe in God the Father Almighty, the Creator of Heaven and Earth'. Her reluctance is hard to explain, unless we assume that she believed they were trying to entrap her. Perhaps she recalled that Satan had been cast down from Heaven and now 'prowls around like a roaring lion seeking whom he may devour'. She heard 'the God of Heaven and Earth' as a synonym for the Devil.

Not surprisingly, Alice was anxious to escape from the bullying scholars, saying that her husband would beat her for her long absence. Henry Pickering, more hostile than his friends, was not to be deterred either by her anger or her pleading. If she had brought this wickedness upon the children, he self-righteously declared, the vengeance of God would wait upon her at the time of her death.

'However much you may deceive yourself,' he told her, 'there is no way to prevent the judgements of God but by your repentance and confession. If you do not confess in time,' he went on, 'I hope to see you burnt at a stake. And I myself will bring fire and wood, and the children will blow on the coals.' It was the Continental punishment for witchcraft with which he threatened her.

Alice was not to be browbeaten. 'I would rather see you knocked head over heels into this pond,' she said, and went on her way.

xii.

A Case of Clairvoyance

I n the context of Alice's trial, the story that was told of the conflict between Alice and the scholars of Cambridge may have reinforced the suspicion that Alice had been recruited to a heretical anti-religion. But in the narrative of *The Witches of Warboys*, it had a different purpose. The episode served as much to demonstrate the possessed nature of the children as it did the defiance of Alice to the threat of divine judgement. For, while Alice was arguing with the scholars, Joan, the oldest of the Throckmorton daughters, fell into a trance at home while in the parlour with her father and grandmother. Clairvoyantly, Joan told those present of the confrontation between Alice and Henry Pickering as it unfolded. She is said to have reported verbatim every word that passed between Mother Samuel and the scholars.

For the author of the text, it was important that the credibility of Joan should be established. This ensured the veracity of her clairvoyance and therefore the truth of the possession. Thus, after Joan reported that Alice and the scholars had parted, Robert Throckmorton asked about the whereabouts of Henry Pickering. He was informed that Henry had not yet returned from the church since evening prayer. Thus he went in search of him.

Robert met Henry and his friends coming back from the direction of the pond, and enquired where they had been. They recounted their meeting with Alice. 'I could have told you as much myself,' he said. And he repeated to them the whole episode of Joan's rendition of their encounter. When they all returned to the parlour, another of the sisters was in her fits. This sister could hear Henry Pickering and no one else, while Joan could now hear no one but her sister. So her uncle's questions were relayed to Joan via her sister, and she told Henry Pickering all that had occurred.

This clairvoyant capacity became an ongoing part of the girls' demonic repertoire. The spirit, the text tells us, would appear many times to them after this, while they were in their fits. The spirit, or 'the thing', as the children called it, manifested itself in many shapes. But most often they saw it as a 'brown chicken'. It would talk familiarly to them, indicating that it emanated from Mother Samuel and was sent by her to the children expressly to torment them. But this was a spirit (or spirits) which seemed to be working more on behalf of the children than for Alice. For it 'informed' on her activities. So the children were able to tell at any time what Mother Samuel was doing, in what part of her house she was, or where else she may have been. The children's precognition was verified by messengers despatched explicitly to test their insight into what Alice was up to.

How are we to explain the children's knowledge of events apparently beyond their ken? One possible explanation is that this reportage is merely a fictional device on the part of the author. But foresight is such a central feature of the girls' possession, and clearly well attested to by many witnesses, that it is better to assume that the account is bearing witness to events that did occur (at least in some sense of the word 'occur'). Another explanation, that provided by *The Witches of Warboys* itself, is that the girls' clairvoyance is the consequence of the spirits within them informing the children what is happening elsewhere. But that is not an explanation I would wish to accept. Another more satisfactory explanation might be that, in the especially unusual heightened states of consciousness which these children attained, they really did perceive in some sense 'clairvoyantly' that which, in a normal state of consciousness, they could not have known.

The real explanation is probably at the same time both more banal and more interesting than any of these: more banal, because supernatural knowledge cannot be involved and we must seek a more straightforward and naturalistic explanation of the children's activities; more interesting, because of the desire of those around them to credit them with such attributes, and because of the girls' ability to sustain credible performances in the face of persistent questioning, testing, and experimentation by their parents and relatives. The will to believe and the capacity to persuade came potently together to reaffirm a supernatural atmosphere. Had either the will to believe among the adults or the capacity to persuade among the children faltered even for a while, the supernatural fog through which everything was being viewed would quickly have evaporated. In this important sense the context created its own reality.

Over a hundred years later, sceptics such as Francis Hutchinson would see all the children's activities as the consequence only of their imaginative creativity. 'The Children could manage their own Fits,' he wrote, 'and also took great Pleasure in making Strangers wonder.'[117] But, in early modern England, childhood and clairvoyance went well together. Children, because of their innocence and purity, were popularly considered to be conduits of the preternatural, both the divine and the demonic. The line between the sacred and the profane was often a fine one, and was frequently determined only by the eye of the beholder. But, in the case of the Throckmorton children, the division was evident. The children plausibly claimed their clairvoyance was caused by their demons within. And those around them, perhaps credulously, but fully in line with the sensibilities of the day, took them at their word.

Later on, many commentators saw the Throckmorton children as exemplars of the connection between preternatural knowledge, bewitchment, and possession. For example, John Cotta in *The Infallible True and Assured Witch* (1625) declared that '[s]ome sick men also have revealed and declared words, gestures, actions done in far distant places, even in the very time and moment of their acting, doing, and uttering, as I have known myself in some, and is testified likewise to have been heard, known, and seen by divers witnesses worthy credit in our country, in divers bewitched sick people'. And in the margin he refers to 'a Treatise of the Witches of Warbozyes' (sic).[118]

The spirits' accusations of Mother Samuel now moved progressively to the story's centre. Whenever the children were having seizures, and were carried to Alice's house, or she was forced to come to them, they would instantly become well. It was problematic to induce Alice to come to the Throckmortons'. Her resistance was growing. But, whenever the children appeared on her doorstep, having been carried there in their fits, they would wipe their eyes and say, 'I am well. Why do you carry me? Set me down.' While they stayed at Alice's, they were well. But as soon as they left her front door, they clattered down to the ground again, and were taken home in the same highly disturbed state in which they had arrived.

On those occasions when Alice Samuel came to the Throckmorton house, in whatever kind of fit the children then were, they would 'be as well as any in the house, and so continue while she was present' (sig.E.2.r). But, as soon as she prepared to depart, they would all sink down like stones to the ground. If she turned around and came back towards them they would all recover. Such histrionic performances were repeated 'twenty times in one hour' (sig.E.2.r). As soon as she did leave the house, their fits returned.

No doubt the strain was telling on Robert and Elizabeth Throckmorton. This is a reasonable inference to make from the conclusion to the first part of the story. For we read that Robert thought it good to disperse his children, sending some of them to one friend's house, some to another, to see whether things would eventually settle down. Although separated from each other, the girls continued to demonstrate their knowledge of each other's activities.

For the next eighteen months, their seizures continued regularly. But, relative to what went before, and what was yet to come, it was a time of quiet. Alice Samuel, for one, must have hoped the worst was over.

It was a forlorn hope. For the storm that was coming was more violent and destructive than perhaps she, or any of the protagonists, could have foreseen – with or without the gift of second sight.

Part Two

An Infestation of Devils:

Michaelmas Day 1592 to
31 December the Same Year

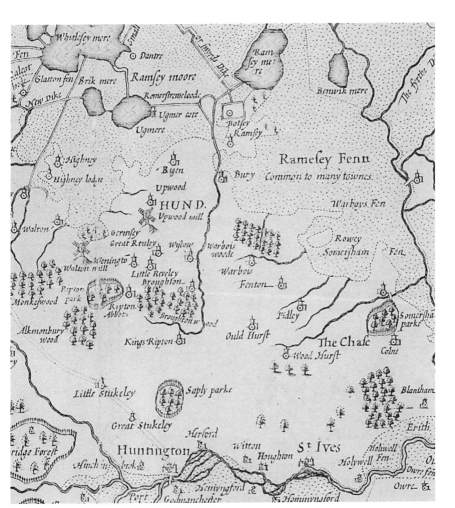

Detail of Huntingdonshire, with Warboys in the centre, from John Speed, *The Theatre of the Empire of Great Britaine* (London, 1611).

The moſt ſtrange and

admirable diſcouerie of the three Witches of *Warboys*, *arraigned*, *conuicted*,
and executed at the laſt Aſſiſes at Huntington, ſor the bewitching of the fiue daughters ot
Robert Throckmorton Eſquire, and diuers other
perſons, with ſundrie Diuelliſh and grie-
uous torments :

And alſo for the bewitching to death of
the Lady Crumwell, the like hath
not been heard of in this
age.

LONDON
Printed by the Widdowe Orwin, for Thomas Man, and Iohn Winnington, and are to be ſolde in Pater noſter Rowe, at the
ſigne of the Talbot. 1593.

The title page of *The Witches of Warboys*.

Christeninges

Jane Throckmorton filia Robarti baptized the xxjth of August

Henry Lavender sonn of his baptized the ixth of September

Margret Elmer D of Robert baptized the vth of October

Maria Poulter baptized the same daye

Christiana Wilson bapt the xxviijth of October

Edwardus Freeman baptized the xxixth of October

Richard Elmer sonn of Richard bapt the xth of November

Margaret Meade baptized the xxjth day of February

Johanna Samuell baptized the vith of March

Richard Bulmer baptized the xxiijth of March

Anno Elizab: xxiijth

Anno dm̄ Richarde Catlin was bapt the xxvth of June

1581 John Robyns baptized the seaventh of July

Bartholomewe Frisby sonn of John bapt the xxjth of August

Katheryne Willsher baptized the vith of September

Grace Storke baptized the viijth of October

Joane Longe D baptiz: the xxvijth of November

Ffrancis Abbott baptized eodem die

Ffrancis Smyth so of Mr Gilbert Smyth of Henton baptise
at Warboys the xxjth of December

Richard Willsone son of Robert bapt the xxvth of December

Robert Hinde sonn of John baptized the xxixth of January

Elizabeth Loraine bapt the xxviijth of January

Richard Ellington bapt the first of February

Agnes Rowell bapt eodem die

Willm̄ Cromwell baptized the   of March

Grace Throckmorton D of Robert bapt the vth of March

Anno Elizab: xxiiijth

Anno dm̄ Richarde Deconanson was baptis the xvijth of April

1582 Thomas Lavender baptiz: the xth day of April

Henry Kendall John Conor, Margaret Daviss bap the xxth yi April

Ffrancis Dorington the so of Mr John Damgie of London bapt xxjth June

Gilbert Royden was baptized the xxth of July

Allyn Morris was baptized the viijth of August

Willm̄ Hankin was bapt the first of   November

Joane Dorington D of Ffrancis bapt the viijth of November

Robert Freeman was baptized the xxvth of November

Ffrancis Dorington   Wytnesse

        of malte   diverse   of malte   O Ffrances Charyewald
        of ....   of Robt

Page from the Warboys Parish Registers showing Jane Throckmorton
as the first entry. She was baptized on 21 August 1580.

A true and particular obseruation of a no-
table piece of Witchcraft, practiſed by *John Sa-*
muel the Father, *Alice Samuel* the Mother, and *Agnes Samuel*
their Daughter, of Warboiſe in the Countie of Huntington,
vpon fiue Daughters of *Robert Throckmorton* of the
ſame towne and Countie Eſquire, and certaine o-
ther Maid-ſeruants to the number of twelue
in the whole, all of them being in one
houſe: Nouember, 1589.

Bout the tenth of Nouember which was in the yéere
1589. Miſtris Iane one of the daughters of the ſayd
Maſter Throckmorton being néere the age of tenne
yéeres, fell vpon ý ſodaine into a ſtrange kind of ſick-
nes and diſtemperature of body, the manner whereof
was as followeth. Sometimes ſhe would néeſe very lowde and
thicke for the ſpace of halfe an houre together, and preſently as one
in a great trance and ſwoune lay quietly as long: ſœne after ſhe
would begin to ſwell and heaue vp her belly ſo as none was able
to bend her, or kéepe her downe: ſometime ſhe would ſhake one
legge and no other part of her, as if the paulſie had bén in it: ſome-
times the other: preſently ſhe would ſhake one of her armes, and
then the other, and ſœne after her head, as if ſhe had bén infected
with the running paulſie: Continuing in this caſe two or thrée
daies, amongſt other neighbours in the towne there came into the
houſe of Maſter Throckmorton, the foreſayd Alice Samuel to viſite
this ſicke child, who dwelled in the next houſe on the Northſide of
the ſayd Maſter Throckmorton. The childe when the old woman
came into the parlour was held in another womans armes by the
fire ſide, ſo ſhe went into the chimney corner and ſate downe hard
by the child, the Grandmother of the child, & the mother being alſo
preſent, ſhe had not bén there long, but the child grew ſomething
worſe then ſhe was at her comming, and on the ſodaine cryed (ſay-
ing) Grandmother looke where the old witch ſitteth (poynting to
the ſayd mother Samuel) did you euer ſée (ſayd the child) one more
like a witch then ſhe is: take off her blacke thrumbd cap, for I can
not abide to looke on her. The mother of the child little then ſuſpec-
ting any ſuch matter, (as afterwards fell out) was very angrie

A 3   witch

The opening page of *The Witches of Warboys*.

The interior of St Mary Magdalene. The thirteenth-century font is in the foreground.

The southern view of St Mary Magdalene, Warboys. The manor house can be seen in the left background.

St Mary Magdalene, Warboys, from the North East and rectory side.

View of the manor house in Warboys from the eastern side.

View from the northern side of the Elizabethan front
of the manor house in Warboys. The ingle-nooked
fireplace can be seen to the right of the front door.

Detail from frontispiece to Richard Boulton, *A Compleat History of Magick, Sorcery, and Witchcraft*, vol. 1 (London, 1715). The only contemporary illustration of Alice Samuel. There is no moment in the text matching this imaginative construction.

The title page of *The most wonderfull and true Storie, of a certaine Witch named Alse Gooderidge* (London, 1597).

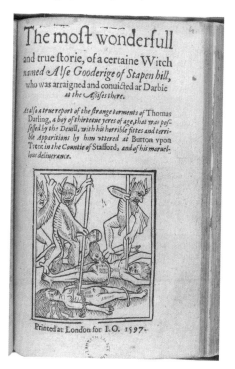

The most wonderfull and true storie, of a certaine Witch named Alse Gooderige of Stapen hill, who was arraigned and convicted at Darbie at the Assises there.

As also a true report of the strange torments of Thomas Darling, a boy of thirteene yeres of age, that was possessed by the Deuill, with his horrible fittes and terrible Apparitions by him vttered at Burton vpon Trent in the Countie of Stafford, and of his maruellous deliuerance.

Printed at London for I. O. 1597.

Swimming the witch. Detail from title-page of *Witches apprehended, examined and executed* (London, 1613).

The title page of *A most certain, strange and true Discovery of a Witch* (n.p., 1643).

A MOST
Certain, Strange, and true Difcovery of a

VVITCH.

Being taken by fome of the Parliament Forces, as fhe was ftanding on a fmall planck-board and fayling on it over the River of *Newbury*:

Together with the ftrange and true manner of her death, with the propheticall words and fpeeches fhe vfed at the fame time.

Printed by John Hammond, 1643.

THE
Discovery of Witches:

IN

Answer to severall QUERIES,

LATELY

Delivered to the Judges of Assize for the
County of NORFOLK.

And now published

By MATTHEVV HOPKINS, Witch-finder.

FOR

The Benefit of the whole KINGDOME.

EXOD. 22. 18.

Thou shalt not suffer a witch to live.

may. 18

LONDON,
Printed for R. *Royston*, at the Angell in Ivie Lane.
M. DC. XLVII.

Frontispiece to Matthew Hopkins' *The Discovery of Witches*
(London, 1647).

¶ The Apprehension and confession
of three notorious Witches.

Arreigned and by Iustice condemned and
executed at *Chelmes-forde*, in the Countye of
Essex, the 5. day of Iulye, last past.
1 5 8 9.

¶ With the manner of their diuelish practices and keeping of their
spirits, whose fourmes are heerein truelye
proportioned.

IOAN PRENTIS
& hir Bid

JACKE

GILL

The title page of *The Apprehension and Confession of three notorious Witches*
(London, 1589).

The pond in Warboys.

Orchard Lane, Huntingdon. On the right, one of the windows to the Huntingdon Gaol cellars in which Alice, Agnes and John Samuel were held awaiting trial.

The Huntingdon Gaol Cellar in which Agnes and Alice Samuel were imprisoned.

The field outside Huntingdon which held the gallows.

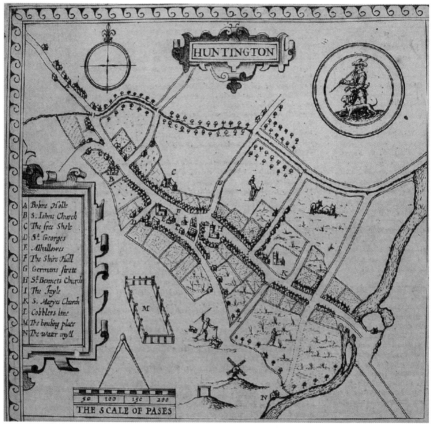

Detail of Huntingdon from John Speed's *The Theatre of the Empire of Great Britaine* (London, 1611). The gallows can be seen in the centre foreground.

i.

Conversations with Spirits

Michaelmas, 29 September 1592. The children have returned, and – with the exception of the eldest – the family is once again together. Only Joan is away from home, residing for a while in Titchmarsh Grove at the home of her uncle, Gilbert Pickering.

If Robert Throckmorton hoped that the dispersal of his daughters would bring their possession to an end, he was soon to be disabused of such hope. For in a while the children all fell back into their earlier deranged patterns of behaviour, although – as their father despairingly realised – they were to seem more strangely vexed and more seriously tormented than at almost any time since the beginning of their affliction. Whether their hyperactivity resulted from an increase in the maliciousness of the spirits or of those who controlled them, or both, Robert Throckmorton was uncertain. That his patience and that of his wife was now stretched to breaking point is admitted.

Again it is Jane, the second youngest of the daughters, and the first to be possessed at the start, who begins this next series of possessions. Just over nine years old when she first accused Alice Samuel of bewitching her, she has recently turned twelve. For three weeks she has daily paroxysms, sometimes more, sometimes fewer. In the course of these, while perfectly sedate between intervals, she would lose the use of her senses, would sob and groan, and her belly would swell uncomfortably.

The recurrence of her fits coincided with the presence in the house of a newborn infant. The text informs us that the baby was the child of an aunt then living in the house. We can establish from the Warboys Parish Registers that this child was Gilbert Pickering, christened in Warboys on Sunday 17 September 1592. His father was John Pickering, cousin to Elizabeth Throckmorton and Gilbert Pickering, and his mother was Elizabeth Cervington. John and Elizabeth had been married on 15 November 1591. The

Throckmortons' house was filled with relatives and friends of the parents. Perhaps in an attempt to restore some kind of equilibrium to neighbourly relations, Mother Samuel too paid a visit. It was a selfless act which she would not live long to regret.

On her arrival, Alice Samuel was conducted upstairs to the room which Elizabeth and the child were occupying. If the advent of a new child in the house had diverted attention away from Jane, the latter was about to retrieve it. Jane had been in a fit in which she could neither hear, see, nor speak. But, as soon as Alice entered the room, Jane seemed to regain normal consciousness. She bade Alice welcome, saying that she had been too long a stranger to the house. Jane served her with food and drink. Soon afterwards, Mother Samuel gathered the baby in her arms.

'Who does that baby belong to, and what is its name?' asked Jane of Alice.

'It is your Aunt Elizabeth's,' said Alice. 'His name is Gilbert.'

'Has my aunt had her baby?' asked Jane. 'I am very glad of it.'

She asked which other relatives were in the house, some of whom were in the room with her. And Mother Samuel told her who was present.

'I can see nobody but you and the child in your arms,' said Jane.

When Mother Samuel departed, Jane reverted to her trance-like state. Three weeks later, she recovered. But she claimed to have no memory of what had happened since Alice Samuel had entered the house.

While Jane's sister, Elizabeth, was at Titchmarsh, Gilbert Pickering pondered on her forgetting of her torments. However, amnesia was not restricted to Elizabeth but was common too among the rest of the children. The Throckmorton girls never seem to have remembered what had happened to them in their seizures. We cannot determine whether this was a matter of fact or a matter of convenience for the children. Certainly, to those watching, it made them appear less culpable for their activities. But their unwillingness to admit to what they had said or done, as well as their total lack of recall, were without doubt a source of great comfort to their parents and those who had witnessed their vicissitudes: '[W]hen these children were in their greatest torment and miseries as might be devised, in such a way as made the heart of the beholders many times to melt in their bodies, being without all hope ever in this world to see them alive again, yet whenever it pleased God to deliver them out of their fits, they would wipe their eyes and be presently well as if it had never been they, not knowing anything that had befallen them' (sigs.E.4.r–v).

In the latter part of October 1592, Grace, Elizabeth, Mary, and Jane became re-infected. It was now Halloween, a time when spirits and witches were believed to be especially and energetically active. The Warboys spirits were no exception. Towards the end of their fits, when the worst was over, the children would have long conversations with their unwelcome visitors. And, as was usual among demoniacs, their voices changed timbre as they spoke on behalf of the spirits within them.

For the most part, the conversations revolved around what kind of fits they would have. But Mother Samuel was again a central part of the girls' lives. The spirits spoke much of her as the cause of it all, and how 'they would bring her to shame for it in the end' (sig.E.3.v). The spirits were invariably accurate in what they said, Robert Throckmorton tells us. And he put it all in writing precisely as it happened, to guarantee the veracity of his account.

If the children were to ask their spirits, when they would come out of the trance they were having, or when they would have another, their spirits would inform them. If the children were to ask how many fits they would have the next day, or the following day, or any day of the week, or how many fits they would have on any particular day, what manner of fits they would have, and how extreme, or how long every fit would continue, in what part of the day they would begin, and when they would end – once again, the spirits would tell them. And thus it went on. Robert's written record enabled him to verify the spirits' predictions. Perhaps the children were enabled too, through Robert's diary notes, to keep track of the predictions that the spirits made, and ensure their conformity to subsequent happenings.

Nevertheless, it is undeniable that there was a pattern to these outbursts. The girls screamed when they were supposed to get out of bed, or were out of bed or dressed, or when they asked their father's, mother's, or grandmother's blessing. They exclaimed and ex-postulated when they went to breakfast, or dinner, or supper when the food was placed on the table, as soon as they started eating or finished eating.

Their mania was often concurrent with religious activity – as soon as they began to pray or finished praying, times of grace before and after meals, or on any Sabbath day or other day on which the church bells were rung.

The reaction of the Throckmorton demons to religious observance was not peculiar to the Warboys manor house. Demons were particularly active in pious households. The Devil seems to have been especially agitated and annoyed by Puritanism. And vice versa. As William Hunt puts it, 'Puritans saw the hand of Satan (not to speak of his horns and tail) in virtually everything of which they disapproved, from the Spanish Inquisition to the dirty joke. They envisioned all their opponents enlisted under a single banner. It was a motley crew: drunkards, morris dancers, great-bellied wenches, good-humoured curates, murderers, sodomites, ribald minstrels, lenient magistrates, epicurean bishops, Jesuit martyrs, Spanish dons. Satan's legions on the march must have been quite a sight, even in the mind's eye.'[1]

ii.

Gods, Witches and Devils

By early November 1592, around a month after the children began once more to be possessed, there is a shift in the spirits' activities. For now they begin to say that before long they will bring Mother Samuel to confession or confusion. The text is uncertain on this question: whether the spirits were weary of their Dame Mother Samuel, as they often told the children, or whether through the power of God's goodness and his protection of the children, they were unable to kill the Throckmorton girls as they wished.

God's role in the shenanigans of witches, devils, and spirits in early modern England is a puzzling one – certainly to us, probably to them. Was God actually an accomplice in every evil act perpetrated by the Devil and his earthly servants? Or was the Devil an autonomous and co-terminous force acting independently of, or even in opposition to, the divine will? The answer is – and was – both 'yes' and 'no'. God was, in the final reckoning, omnipotent, able not only to act as he wished within the laws of nature, but to transcend them in miraculous acts. But the Devil, by contrast, was not all-powerful. He could act only within the laws of nature, even though at times he was capable of deceiving human beings into believing he could in fact act outside them. Consequently, God had the ultimate control over Satan's sorties. It followed that there was no demonic act, therefore, which was not carried out without God's (at least) tacit approval. Notwithstanding this higher divine guidance, granting that every misfortune could be laid at the feet of the Devil or his witches, it must often have seemed that – in a cosmic battle of co-equals in a world of misfortunes – the Devil held the upper hand.

There was thus a paradox at the heart of demonology. The Devil was both dependent on and independent of God. As Alexandra Walsham puts it, the Protestant reformers

> faced the problem of having to reconcile a renewed emphasis on Satan's power to corrupt humanity with the claim he could only

83

work within well-defined limits. Their conviction that the Devil was launching a fresh assault on the forces of good in the world, in league with an army of witches whom he had bound to his service by means of a pact, coexisted a little uneasily with the full logical consequences of their belief in divine omnipotence.[2]

This conundrum comprised an early modern version of that of theodicy in general. If God is both good and all-powerful, why does evil exist in the world? For either there is evil which God cannot control although he would like to, in which case he cannot be all-powerful, although he is good; or there is evil which God can control but chooses not to, in which case he cannot be good, although he is all-powerful.

One solution proffered in early modern England was, in effect, to maintain the goodness of God, give up God's omnipotence, and view the Devil as an equal and opposing force of evil. Demonological discourse reinforced this Manichaean view in practice if not in principle. The more orthodox solution was one pioneered by St Augustine. It reinforced God's omnipotence, though it could never quite overcome difficulties in connection with his absolute goodness. And it was to the effect that Satan and his minions were only carrying out God's will.

This is the position adopted in *The Witches of Warboys*. From this point on in the story, the reader cannot but see that the spirits, far from being the servants of Alice, the witch, and the Devil, are now the servants of the possessed. Are the children now the agents of Lucifer? No, for God has actively intervened and has taken matters into his own hands. God has determined that the matter should be brought to an end and has decided to use the spirits not against the children but against Alice Samuel. It was a solution which certainly demonstrated his ultimate power over the Devil. Whether it demonstrated his benevolence was another matter altogether.

God's providential intervention into the lives of the Throckmorton children constituted clear evidence of Alice's guilt. Only through his action could the sufferings of the children be ended. But it represented more than this. For, unfathomable as God's actions had been in allowing the children to suffer thus far, it was clear that, in having their sufferings brought to an end, they were especially favoured.

iii.

A Witch in Residence

The children now begin to claim that they will never again be well unless they go to live with Alice Samuel, or she comes to live with them at the Throckmortons'. Moreover, unless one or other of these eventualities occurs, they declare, their condition will deteriorate further.

The general assumption in the early modern period about the veracity of demons was that those within the possessed spoke the truth. They were, after all, ultimately divine employees. The alacrity with which their accusation, via the children, of Alice Samuel was accepted by everybody attests to the acceptance of the view that spirits had access to truth.

But still Robert Throckmorton did not trust the possessors. He would have known that biblical authority also pointed in another direction. In the Gospel according to John, Christ had called the Devil a liar, and the Father of Lies.[3] So Robert Throckmorton did not rush seriously to disrupt his life even further by moving his children to live at the Samuels or Alice to move in with them. Still 'thinking that the spirits might lie' (sig.E.4.v), he waited for three weeks. To no avail; far from the children improving, their torments increased – just as the spirits had predicted.

Robert Throckmorton made John Samuel an offer. If Alice were to come to the Throckmortons' on a permanent basis, he would pay £10 a year board and wages for the best servant in Huntingdon to provide a substitute for Alice's domestic duties. Along with this went his promise and bond that Alice would be well treated by him while she was resident with the Throckmortons. John Samuel was having none of it. From his superior position in the social hierarchy, Throckmorton, with the determination born out of desperation, forced John Samuel's hand. If John Samuel would not allow Alice to come to them, he would take the children to her. He did just that. And, as soon as the children entered the Samuels' cottage, they recovered.

This was enough for Robert Throckmorton. He now knew what had to be done. He told John Samuel that his children would be staying there, that they were not to leave the house, and that he would provide their necessities. Samuel acquiesced, though not without saying that he would starve them and, extinguishing the fire, (literally) freeze them out. No one would ever accuse John Samuel of being a gracious man. He used 'very many evil words' (sig.E.4.v), we read.

The reality of John Samuel was that he was a violent, abusive, and quarrelsome man, not only to his wife but also to others in the village of Warboys. The Warboys court rolls dating from the 1580s reveal an antisocial and anti-authoritarian figure, regularly fined for misdemeanours – having cattle in the common, failing to repair ditches, breaking the confidentiality of the jury while a member, infringing local ordinances regarding hedges, chickens, and pigs.[4] And his reputation in the district was well known. When Henry Pickering and his friends from Cambridge went to see Alice Samuel, they followed her some distance from her house before talking with her. They were trying to avoid a confrontation with John. And, in attempting for her part to avoid talking with them, Alice had pleaded her fear of being beaten by her husband.

Agnes Samuel, the daughter of Alice and John, was present too. Agnes was no shrinking violet. But we should take the claim that she too used 'evil words' with a large pinch of salt. 'Like father, like daughter' was by no means an inexorable truth.

For the remainder of that day the children were well and happy, eating, drinking, and reading their books. By the time evening had come, John Samuel realised that, all things considered, he would be better off with £10 per annum in his pocket for a servant to replace Alice than tolerating the imposition of four children in his house on a permanent basis. He promised Robert Throckmorton that, next morning, he would send Alice to the manor house to stay. Trustingly, Robert took his children home. As soon as they left the Samuels' house, their fits restarted. They continued all that night.

We can surmise that it was early in the morning that Robert Throckmorton set out for the Samuels' to bring Alice back to his house. No doubt he was mortified to be told by John that Alice had left the house, and no one knew where she had gone. John had called his bluff. He called John's. The children were once again delivered to the Samuels' cottage for the day. As soon as they entered, again they became well.

Towards evening, Alice Samuel came to the manor house to explain that she had been two or three miles out of the town all day. She confided to Robert Throckmorton and others present that her husband had known of her going, since he did not wish her to go to the Throckmortons'. Later, he was confronted by Robert in the presence of witnesses, with Alice there, with her claim that amounted to his having clearly tried to renege on the arrangement with Robert. This he vehemently denied. But he must have known that Alice had exposed his ruse. And he suddenly and shockingly attacked her with a cudgel and severely beat her before those present could come to her aid.

When Samuel desisted, Robert again pressed his claim that Alice should come and reside at the manor house. This time he demanded that she should come immediately. John Samuel, realising that Throckmorton was this time determined that she should accompany him, was content to let his wife go to the manor.

For the first nine or ten days, while she was present in the Throckmorton household, the children were all in a better state than they had been for the whole of the previous three years. Alice was treated by the Throckmortons as a welcome guest.

At the end of this period, with all well in the house, Alice made a request of Elizabeth Throckmorton.

'I need to return home to fetch something,' she said.

We may suppose that she invented an excuse to break the pattern of her stay at the Throckmortons' in the hope that her return to her own house might become something more permanent. Elizabeth Throckmorton was loath to agree to her request. The risk involved for the children's mother must have seemed too high.

'Rather than your going,' said Elizabeth, 'I will go and fetch what you want.'

'No one else will be able to find what I want,' she replied. 'But I promise I'll come back straightaway.'

Reluctantly, Elizabeth allowed her to go.

The children reacted quickly to this new development. As soon as she was gone, their seizures returned as before. The reason why only Alice could go, and no other, was revealed instantly to them. The spirit, then talking with the children, informed them that Mother Samuel had gone to feed her spirits and make 'a new league and composition with them' (sig.F.1.v). Mother Samuel, the spirit said, had made a new contract with them so that the children would now be none the better for her being in the same house but, rather, the worse for her presence.

Alice had finally escaped the manor house. And she had absolutely no intention of going back. The Throckmortons weren't going to put up with that. They demanded her immediate return. So it was four or five hours later that, having been sternly summoned, she came back with much reluctance. It was as the spirits had foretold. Those children who were still in their convulsions on her return continued in them, while those that were not fell immediately into fresh moaning and juddering.

'Mother Samuel has entered into a new agreement with the spirits,' the innocents cried. 'We will now be no better for her presence but rather the worse.'

The children were insinuating that Mother Samuel had wanted to return home to force the spirits into ensuring torments that were worse for them during her presence than her absence. Her objective, they were suggesting, was to bring pressure on the Throckmortons to allow her to return home permanently for their own good. This was a result with which Mother Samuel might well have been happy. It must have seemed to her that, for once, the spirits were on her side. For, since the children's condition had now deteriorated in her presence, a return home for *their* sakes appeared to be a real possibility. But this was a double-edged sword. For it demonstrated too that the spirits would proactively work to her demands and her advantage.

Be that as it may, matters might still have worked out well for Alice when Robert Throckmorton came home that evening. For he did find his children in a far worse state than when he had left them that morning. And we can presume that he was quickly informed that the spirits had foretold that the children would fare better for Alice's absence than her presence. So we might have expected Robert Throckmorton to be sanguine about repealing his injunction, and to send her home. She would no doubt happily have departed. But the children now, convulsed as they were, were not able to hear, see, or speak to anyone but her, and some of them could take nothing but that which she gave to them or had touched with her hands.

So, in order for any communication at all to be possible with the children, Mother Samuel had to remain in the manor. Beforehand, the children had explained her returning home as her having to go there to feed her spirits. Now, whenever Alice happened to be somewhere alone in the manor house, the children would claim that she was even then feeding her spirits on their own turf. The manor was not large. It would not have been difficult for the children to make very good guesses as to where Mother Samuel might be. Apart from the entry hall downstairs, there was one other room on that level, and two bedrooms upstairs, in one of which the parents slept, in the other of which the girls themselves. If the children were downstairs in one room, there were only three other rooms in which Alice could possibly be. So it is perhaps not surprising that, when people went and looked to see if Alice was where the children had (clairvoyantly) said she would be, there they would find her. The feeding of her spirits was not an activity that could be seen publicly. Whether she was 'doing any such thing or not, God and her conscience are the best witnesses' (sig.F.1.v).

Or, rather, we should say that the feeding of her spirits was not an activity that others besides Alice and the children could view. For the children could see the spirits, and, so they claimed, could Alice. Many times, the text informs us, as she sat talking with the children by the fireside, they would say to her, 'Look here, Mother Samuel, don't you see this thing that sits here by us?'

And she would answer, 'No!'

'Why,' they would say again, 'I marvel that you don't see it. Look how it leaps, skips, and plays up and down.' And they would point at it with their fingers, here, and here, and there, as it leapt capriciously about.

And sometimes they would exclaim, 'Listen, Mother Samuel, don't you hear it? Listen how loud it is. I marvel you don't hear it. No! You cannot but hear it.'

And she would deny all and say, 'Ask your father if he hears it,' or suggest that they ask their mother, or anyone else who was there, whether they heard it or not.

'But there's no one else here to ask,' the children would say.

In the world of demonology, evil is both one and many. There is both 'spirit' and 'spirits'. And it is impersonal and personal: both 'the Thing' and Pluck, Catch, Blue, and so on. Moreover, many demonic personalities were thought to co-exist in the bodies of the possessed at any one time. There was, of course, clear biblical precedent for the phenomenon of multiple possessions. Jesus asked the Gadarene demoniac for the name of the spirit within him. And he answered, 'My name is Legion, for we are many' (Mark 5.9). And the Throckmorton children were not alone among their contemporaries in being thought to have many devils inside them. The French demoniac Nicole Obry, for example, was at one time possessed by around thirty, of whom the chief was the biblical

Beelzebub.[5] Beelzebub was active not only in France but also across the Channel in England, where the demons Brother Glassap and Brother Radulphus, who had taken up residence in Thomas Darling, reported to him.[6] Rachel Pinder was reputed to have 5,000 legions of demons within her.[7] And, as we will see, Joan Throckmorton was possessed by Blue, Pluck, Catch, and Smack – four of the nine spirits that Alice Samuel is said by Smack himself to have at her disposal.

A sceptic and rationalist such as Samuel Harsnett would come up with good reasons for the presence of many demons, not least that the expulsion of a large number prolonged the exorcism and was guaranteed to heighten the reputation of the exorcist.[8] At the very least, the presence of so many demons all fighting to be heard increased the awe, terror, and wonder with which those present heard these supernatural beings speaking from the stomach of the possessed while the demoniac's mouth remained firmly shut. The capacity of demoniacs to speak without moving their mouth, lips, or tongue, and generally from the stomach (literally, ventriloquy) reinforced the belief that the Devil was present here. So both the eyes and the ears of witnesses were assailed by the terrifying presence of the demonic, for demoniacs spoke in tones and timbres other than their usual voices.

For their later, genuinely theatrical descendants, the ventriloquist's dummies, the ventriloquist's purpose was to persuade onlookers that the dummies' moving lips expressed the latter's own self, not that of another. But, unlike their wooden counterparts, these demoniacal 'dummies' did not move their lips. The voices came from another (or others) within them, and not outside them. Therefore, to the onlooker, the voice that spoke from within expressed the thoughts of another self within the demoniac.

The children would not tolerate Alice's refusal to co-operate. 'The thing tells us,' they said, 'that you do see it and hear it, and that you sent it.'

Robert Throckmorton, like Gilbert Pickering, had become something of an experimentalist in occult matters. He too desired to test Mother Samuel's control of the spirits. Was he genuinely interested in testing the spirits, or was he deliberately setting out to trap her? We cannot tell. The text rather disingenuously claims that his request to Mother Samuel was one that he might have made to anyone there present, as if it were merely a matter of convenience that she was asked. One night, we read, he asked her to say how many seizures the three children then present, and already convulsing, would have on the following day, what kind of fits they would have, when they would begin, and how long they would continue.

If Robert, in the presence of his children, really expected to derive an objective outcome from this test, he was at best naïve. More likely, we should read his effort as another attempt further to entrap her, or at least to persuade her that she should admit the truth of his girls' accusations. With all this taking place within earshot of the children, Mother Samuel detected a trap being laid for her, and she was not inclined to co-operate. Yet, at Robert Throckmorton's insistence, she finally relented. Each one of the children, she said, would have three fits, in such a way and at such a time that another would have two of a similar kind, at such and such a time, and the third none. And, as she had forecast, so it happened the next day.

That Robert Throckmorton was deliberately trying to bring her to a confession becomes apparent soon afterwards. With Alice's presence now apparently making the children only worse, he continued to pile on the pressure. Even within a text written to show Alice's guilt, we can clearly see Robert attempting to manipulate her.

It has been shown that the children claimed to be able to see Alice feeding her spirits. The text refers to Robert's brother-in-law, Henry Pickering, being at the manor house again. I suspect that we are once more relying upon his account. Pickering's demonological expertise comes to the fore again. And it is probably he who prompts Robert Throckmorton to press Alice on the issue of her giving succour to her familiars.

'Tell me, Mother Samuel,' Robert disingenuously said, 'I've heard that those who are acquainted with these spirits, as the children say you are, and have retained them for their service to do what they command, feed them and reward them with something from themselves. I have heard that it is usually with their blood, and every day. Now therefore,' he said, 'confess and shame the Devil by telling the truth, whether you do any such thing or not.'

Alice Samuel reacted angrily to this. She vehemently denied it. 'May God show a sign from Heaven this instant,' she exclaimed, 'if I am the kind of woman you suspect me to be, or if I use any such thing, or reward them in any such way, or have any spirits. I don't even know what they are.'

To invoke God's active intervention was not something to be done lightly in sixteenth-century rural England. Nor was such an oath lightly received by Robert Throckmorton and Henry Pickering. Convinced as they were of her guilt, and being half terrified that her words would call the judgements of God down upon all their heads, they quickly exited the house.

They had gone scarcely ten paces from the manor when they were overtaken by John Lawrence, a cousin of the children, who had been present with them in the house.[9] Alice had called for a sign from God if she were indeed culpable of what she had been accused. Apparently, and unfortunately, it seemed that God had taken her at her word. For John told Robert and Henry, 'Since you left, Mother Samuel has begun to bleed from her chin.'

By the time the three men returned to the manor, Alice's chin had stopped bleeding. But they saw the handkerchief with which she had wiped away around eight to ten drops of blood. There was now no blood to be seen on her face, merely a few spots like flea bites.

'Does your chin bleed like this often or not?' Robert Throckmorton asked her.

'It does,' she replied, 'very often.'

'Has anyone seen it bleed but you?' he asked.

'Nobody,' she replied. 'It always bleeds when I am alone, and I have never told anybody about it.'

This is the first important physical piece of evidence thus far. And, for Henry Pickering, the most significant, though its true significance became apparent only after Alice was condemned.

She is said to have confessed the true meaning of her bleeding to Henry Pickering after she was convicted on 5 April 1593. Pickering was no supporter of hers, so why she would have chosen to open her heart to him is a mystery. However that may be, it was to him that she is then reported to have said, 'When I said that God should show a sign from Heaven if I had familiar spirits, the spirits were even then sucking on my chin.'

'When I brushed them off,' she continued, 'my chin bled. It had sometimes done this after their sucking, but not often, and never so much as then. No, hardly a drop at any time before.'

iv.

Agnes, Apprehensive
and Apprehended

It is now sometime in late November or early December 1592. Nothing has been heard of Agnes Samuel since February 1590, almost three years before. Then she was painted as being uncooperative, if not actually complicit in her mother's activities. But she has not yet been singled out. As the text reminds us, Agnes 'is not yet brought into question about any of these matters' (sig.F.3.r). But it is all but certain that she has lived for a long time with the prospect and fear of being dragged into them. That fear was about to be realised. For now, for the first time, the children drew Agnes too into the epicentre of their drama.

Mother Samuel was present, as was Robert Throckmorton. The children were in convulsions. The spirits informed Robert Throckmorton that, if he were to go to John Samuel's house, Samuel's daughter would hide herself, not wishing to be seen by him. Robert Throckmorton agreed to go 'to make trial thereof' (sig.F.3.r). The episode is intended to point towards Agnes's guilt: if she were innocent of witchcraft, why would she hide? We can read it as evidence of her terror at being implicated.

The Samuels' house was not untypical of the period. It was a timber-framed thatched cottage, with one or more rooms downstairs accommodating the whole family, and an upstairs attic reached by ladder stairs. While Robert Throckmorton knocked at the door of the Samuels' house, Agnes ascended the stairs, moved through the trapdoor in the ceiling, and climbed into the one-roomed attic. Clearly fearing the worst, she placed sacks of corn and tubs on the closed trapdoor. Throckmorton, hearing movement in the house, suspected her of concealing herself. This, after all, was precisely what the spirits had predicted she would do. He persisted in his knocking. Eventually, John Samuel responded. 'Who are you, and what do you want?' he asked.

Throckmorton identified himself.

'Go away,' shouted Samuel.

Robert Throckmorton went around to the back of the house and, finding the back door open, let himself in. When he came into the parlour, John Samuel was in his bed. It was about eight o'clock at night.

'I would like to see Agnes,' announced Throckmorton. 'Where is she?'

'As God is the judge of my soul,' said Samuel, 'I don't know where she is.'

'When did you last see her?'

'She has been here since night fell,' he replied, 'but where she is now, I don't know.'

'Isn't she in the room above?' asked Robert.

'I don't know,' retorted Samuel.

The roof was low, and John could not but have heard her, were she there. The stairs up into the attic room were at the foot of his bed. Robert Throckmorton, not surprisingly, was unconvinced. He called up to her three or four times.

'Agnes, are you up there? Answer me if you are. I only want to know where you are.'

She was silent. He took the candle and began to climb the stairs. The trapdoor, weighed down with its load, was so heavy that he could not shift it.

'I will break down this door or break through the ceiling. I will come up there before I go home. Fetch me a bar of iron or something like it,' he said to another person who had come with him, 'for I'll do it.'

Realising he was set on this, Agnes answered, 'I am here.'

'Come down,' he commanded.

Removing the sacks and tubs from the trapdoor, she did as she was ordered. Accusing John Samuel of being a liar, a charge he continued angrily to deny, Robert Throckmorton went home. Agnes was left alone. At this stage she was not implicated by the children in her mother's witchcraft. That she hid herself from Robert Throckmorton was no doubt suggestive of her complicity. The spirits had predicted that she would do so. They were right. Yet again they were vindicated.

V.

Alice 'Pines' Away

Alice Samuel was growing more and more weary of the Throckmorton household. There was no activity that she could do in the manor which was not revealed by the children. The psychological strain on her can only be guessed at. They seemed also to pick up on their father's determination to extract a confession. Perhaps too they realised that her confession would enable them finally to return to normality. For now they began to tell Alice in their fits that she would confess to bewitching them before the Tuesday after Twelfth Day – that is, before Tuesday 9 January 1593.

'The spirits,' they pronounced to Alice, 'will force you to confess and you know that whatever the spirits foretell proves most true.'

Although it was not then yet known, this Tuesday was, the text tells us, the assizes Sessions day in Huntingdon. The children now made this their common refrain in their seizures. They often wished that it would come soon for the spirits had told them that, after that day, they would have no more fits. Were she to confess sooner, then they would be the sooner well. Now in their convulsions, they continually exhorted Mother Samuel to confess to witchcraft. Mother Samuel resisted. 'I will not confess that about which I know nothing, nor have ever consented to,' she declared.

To this the children retorted, 'We don't want you to accuse yourself of anything. We're merely telling you what the spirits have told us.'

But they exhorted her nonetheless to confess. In so doing, they showed a piety that was characteristic of demoniacs. They were vessels not only of the demonic but of the divine. They manifested within themselves angry rebellion against societal norms. This was excused them and laid at the Devil's door. But they also demonstrated passionate adherence to these same norms. And, in so doing, they lost themselves as integrated personalities. Their bodies and minds were tortured sites of conflict between good and evil.

In a cosmic sense, they played both sides off against the middle. They were possessed by demons, but they were also exemplars of Puritan piety: 'Such were the heavenly and divine speeches of these children in their fits, to this old woman, some at one time, some at another, concerning her confession of this fact, that if a man had heard it, he would not have thought himself better edified at ten sermons' (sig.F.4.r).

We may assume that Alice herself, at least in the eyes of the Throckmortons, was not a paragon of Puritan virtues. And they attacked her for it. They primly lectured her on the joys of Heaven that she would lose, and the torments of Hell that she would endure were she not to confess if she were guilty. They emphasised the joys of Heaven that would be hers were she to do so. They were their parents' Puritan children. They also had a clear notion of the proper behaviour of parents and children (at least, when not possessed by demons). They rehearsed to her 'her naughty manner of living, her usual swearing and cursing at all that displeased her, and especially of their parents, and of them, which she could not deny, her negligent going to Church and slackness in God's service' (sig.F.4.r). All this she accepted and, we are told, would begin to amend.

Alice's parenting skills were also criticised – 'her lewd bringing up of her daughter in allowing her to be her dame, both in controlling of her and beating of her' (sig.F.4.r) to which she had previously confessed. As we have seen, the witch was a bad mother – indeed, an anti-mother. So, in accusing her of being a bad mother, they were not merely demonstrating their own piety as Puritan children, but also reinforcing the accusation of witchcraft.

It was in the interests of the author of *The Witches of Warboys* to present Alice in this way. But it is not mere invention. The Alice whom we see behind the story has a good heart. She visits sick children, she is present at the birth of others. She does the best she can. But she is not a forceful or determined person. She has a violent and abusive husband, and, if the text is to be believed, an assertive, even headstrong, daughter. She seems more passive than aggressive. She is more likely to be a victim than a persecutor, easily imposed upon by others. On occasion, though, she is emotionally volatile, and likely to lose her temper. More than probably, she was the subject of village gossip – gossip to which the Throckmorton children had been privy.

It would be surprising if everyone in the village of Warboys had accepted at face value that the children were possessed. Some, like their parents did at first, would no doubt have thought the children were sick. But there must have been others who thought they were faking it. Alice was clearly one of these. And around the village she had been putting the word out that the children were indeed dissembling. This had reached the manor house, and the ears of the children. And this was something they couldn't allow. So they reminded Alice that, being out of their fits, they had heard people say that she thought their seizures 'were but wantonness in them' (sig.F.4.r).

'Are you still of that mind?' they asked her.

Whether she was or not, we do not know. But prudence dictated her answer. To call the children fakes was too dangerous. 'No!' she unambiguously replied.

They concluded with a hearty prayer to God, saying, 'We will forgive you from the bottom of our hearts if you will confess so that we might be well. And we will ask our parents and friends to forgive and forget all that was past.'

All this was accompanied with much weeping, both by the children and those who heard them. We are told that only Mother Samuel 'was little or nothing moved' (sig.F.4.v). Slowly but certainly, she was being psychologically clubbed into submission.

Alice's health was now beginning to suffer. She began to have nose bleeds almost every day. It is not unreasonable to conjecture that this was the result of high blood pressure precipitated by stress. She looked sufficiently pale for Robert Throckmorton and his wife to be seriously anxious that some genuine harm would come to her. Whether their concern for her was real, or whether they were concerned for their own reputation should she come to grief in their home, we cannot tell. They claimed to have looked after her as well as they could, ensuring that she ate properly and was not overworked. Worried for one reason or another, or both, they may have been. But Robert Throckmorton kept up the pressure on Alice.

It was common among the children to have their mouths 'locked up' so that they were unable to drink, eat, or speak. One of the girls in particular, Elizabeth, was especially prone to this incapacity. We recall her inability to eat during her stay with Gilbert Pickering at Titchmarsh Grove. She was now almost thirteen and a half years old.

At supper, one night, she was not able to tell her parents the cause of her weeping, nor was she able to eat or drink. Again, Alice was suspected to be the cause.

'I think, Mother Samuel,' said Robert Throckmorton, 'that you are disposed to pine that wench.'

This amounted to a direct accusation of witchcraft. For it was a declaration that Alice was using image magic against Elizabeth. This was the practice of making wax or clay images of those against whom harm was intended, and doing to the image that which you wished done to the person it represented. Images pricked or burned sympathetically created analogous sensation in the intended victim. Other methods led to a slow and lingering death. One of the clearest accounts of image magic is given in the confession of Elizabeth Sowtherns, one of the Lancashire witches, in 1612:

> The speediest way to take away a man's life by witchcraft, is to make a picture of clay, like unto the shape of the person whom they mean to kill, and dry it thoroughly. And when they would have them to be ill in any one place more than another, then take a thorn or pin, and prick it in that part of the picture you would so have to be ill. And when they would have any part of the body to consume away, then take that part of the picture, and burn it. And when they would have the whole body to consume away, then take the remnant of the said picture, and burn it. And so thereupon by that means, the body shall die.[10]

A person's slowly pining away suggested an image buried in the ground and slowly decaying. When asked in 1566 what end images in wax or clay served, John Walsh put it simply: 'Pictures made in wax will cause the party (for whom it is made) to continue sick two whole years, because it will be two whole years before the wax will be consumed.'[11] So it is not a matter for surprise that Alice denied any suggestion that she was the cause. Indeed, she said, 'I am sorry to see it.'

'Well,' he replied, 'what is sure is that you won't eat or drink again until she can do both. Therefore, while she fasts, so will you. And when she can eat, so can you. But not before, whether you're the cause or not.'

Supper continued with all eating but Elizabeth and Alice, 'the one fasting of necessity because she could not eat, and the other for Master Throckmorton's pleasure, because she might not' (sig.G.1.r). At the end of supper, as the table was being cleared, Elizabeth, who had been weeping throughout the meal, sighed.

'If I had some food now, I could eat it,' she said.

Food was given to both Elizabeth and Alice. Elizabeth's hunger was, for Robert Throckmorton, a clear indication of Alice's guilt in 'pining' Elizabeth. Alice had lifted the curse. Both Elizabeth and Alice ate heartily, we read. And, although before this it had been very common for one or another of the sisters to go to bed having been unable to eat their evening meal, from this time on, we are told, 'neither that child, nor any of her sisters, had their mouths shut up at any time when they should eat their meat, or if they were they did not long continue so' (sig.G.1.r). Alice's greediness for food, we are supposed to infer, had got the better of her desire to 'pine' the children.

vi.

Sex with the Devil

As Christmas approached, Alice Samuel's health grew progressively worse. She complained on a daily basis of some new ailment or other, sometimes of painful sensations in her back, sometimes of pains in her head, heart, or stomach. At other times, pain in her legs would force her to go limping about the house. There is no suggestion in the text that this was pretence. On the contrary: 'And to speak the truth about her, it would seem that there was something that troubled her, whatever it was, for she would so groan and moan in the night time, one time complaining of this part of her body, another time of that, that indeed she rested but little in the night time herself, and greatly disquieted those also that lay in the chamber by her' (sig.G.1.v).

One night in particular stood out. Sleeping in Robert and Elizabeth's room, she cried out so piteously about her stomach that she woke them both up.

'In God's name, Mother Samuel,' said Robert, 'what's wrong? Why are you groaning?'

'I have an enormous pain in my belly all of a sudden,' Alice replied, 'and I don't know what's caused it. There is something in it which is moving,' she went on. 'It is about the size of a penny loaf and is causing me awful pain.'

Elizabeth got out of bed and went and felt Alice's stomach. Her stomach was swollen, as she had said, though Elizabeth could not feel the lump moving. The weather was so cold, we read, that Elizabeth returned quickly to her bed.

Had she stayed longer, she indeed might have felt sensation in Alice's belly. For now comes the hint that there may well have been active movement within her. More importantly, the text insinuates that, at precisely this moment on this cold December evening, she might have unnaturally conceived a child by the Devil: 'It may be that she bred then that child with which she said she was, when she was asked what she could say to my Lord the

Judge, why sentence of death should not be given against her' (sig.G.1.v).

The text here looks forward to her trial, when Alice was asked by the judge whether there was any reason to stay her execution. There was sadness and pathos in her answer: 'I am with child,' she said. The crowd gathered in the court roared with cruel laughter. They knew, as we do, that she was beyond the age at which conception was thought to be possible.

Alice laughed too, believing that the audience was laughing with relief at the prospect of her escaping the noose, at least for a while. Judge Fenner, like the rest of those present, was not convinced by her claim to be pregnant. And he tried to persuade her to withdraw it. She was not to be gainsaid. The judge had little choice but to initiate the formalities so that her assertion might be tested. A jury of women was sworn in to examine her.

'Pleading the belly' was not uncommon in criminal cases of the time. The execution of a female defendant found to be pregnant was postponed until such time as the child was delivered. And it was not uncommon for women to be pardoned after the child was born. As in the case of Alice Samuel, when the defendant 'pleaded the belly' a 'jury of women' was formed. It was their role to determine the truth of the claim to be pregnant, or, more specifically, whether any foetus in the womb had 'quickened', or shown signs of life. This was generally expected to have occurred during the third to fourth month of pregnancy. Were there no evidence of the child in the womb having quickened, the mother could be put to death, since, it was believed, even if she were pregnant, prior to quickening there was no 'living being' within the womb.[12] It is likely that, in this case, the jury were drawn from married women present in the courtroom. They soon determined that Alice was not with child 'unless (as some said) it was with the Devil' (sig.O.2.v).

In late sixteenth- and early seventeenth-century England, the notion of a witch having sex with the Devil was virtually unheard of. It was only later, in the 1640s, and under the aegis of the witch-finder general Matthew Hopkins, that accusations of demonic copulation became prominent.

But, in the suggestion of the jury of women that Alice might have been impregnated by the Devil, they had no doubt been influenced by Henry Pickering. For he would have known, from his readings of Continental demonology, that sexual relations with the Devil were a central feature of the demonic pact and of the witches' Sabbath.

Alice had not done anything to help her cause. For, only a short time before the jury of women examined her, Henry Pickering had persuaded her to confess that it was a William Langley 'who gave unto her the spirits, and had carnal knowledge of her body when she received them'. Some villagers were of the opinion, we are told, 'that it was the Devil in mans likeness'. Indeed! Who else could it be? The Devil often appeared in the guise of a human being. And generally he behaved like the worst of them.

We do not know if Henry Pickering had read the demonological manual of the Dominican inquisitors Heinrich Kramer and James Sprenger, the *Malleus Malificarum*, first published in 1486. But it is more than likely that he had. Certainly, if he was familiar with Reginald Scot's sceptical *Discoverie of Witchcraft*, he would have known of it. For Scot had referred to the text as early as 1584 as a book which contained nothing but 'stinking lies and popery'.[13]

As we have noted, Pickering may well also have been familiar with the *De la Demonomanie des Sorciers* of Jean Bodin, published in 1580. And he may have read the Burgundian witch-hunter Henry Boguet's 1590 work, *Discours des Sorciers*. Both texts were to become favourites among English demonologists. Such works would have provided Henry Pickering with all that he needed to know about the bodies of devils, the means whereby they had sex, and their capacity to procreate.

From his demonological readings he would have known, for example, that the pain which Alice experienced on the night when it was suggested she conceived of the Devil was entirely consistent with demonic intercourse. Some witches confessed that sex with Lucifer was extremely pleasurable. But often it was said to be quite the opposite. As Henry Boguet reported:

> Thievenne Paget said…that when Satan copulated with her she had as much pain as a woman in labour. Francoise Secretain said that, while she was in the act, she felt something burning in her stomach; and nearly all the witches say this intercourse is by no means pleasurable to them, both because of the Devil's ugliness and deformity, and because of the physical pain which it causes then.[14]

One problem that all demonologists had to get around was that of how beings such as angels and demons could have sexual relations at all. For intercourse requires bodies. And spiritual beings such as angels and demons were not considered to have them. The solution offered by the *Malleus Maleficarum* was that the Devil 'assumes an aerial body'.[15] It was a solution that the authors of the *Malleus*, like many others, had taken from Thomas Aquinas. For him, angelic and demonic bodies were what we would think of as being 'virtually' real. 'The angels, then,' declared Aquinas, 'assume bodies made of air, but condensed by divine power in an appropriate manner.'[16] And they did so, not for their benefit but for ours. And inversely, so did demons – but to our loss rather than our gain. That demons could interact 'physically' with us was the key proof of their reality.

Still, with only 'virtual' bodies made of condensed air and not 'real' physical bodies, how could the Devil create children? The *Malleus Maleficarum* again looked to Aquinas.[17] And his solution involved gender switching, semen stealing, and artificial insemination:

> But let us suppose that occasionally an offspring *is* born from copulation with a devil. In such a case, the semen would not come from the Devil himself, properly speaking, nor from the body he had assumed; it would be taken from a man for that purpose; and the same devil would receive semen from a man and impart it to a woman ... And the child so begotten would not have the Devil for its father, but the man whose semen had been used.[18]

Thus, the Devil takes on the bodily form of a woman (as a succubus) and has sex with a man, whose semen he steals. He then swaps to the form of a man (as an incubus) and injects the stolen semen into the body of the woman with whom he is having sex.

Would the fact that the air was cold in the room within which Alice was tormented suggest the presence of the Devil? It may well have done. For Satan's body was often said to be cold. The Cambridge Platonist Henry More put forward a pretty reasonable 'scientific' explanation for this:

> And indeed it stands to very good reason that the bodies of *Devils* being nothing but *coagulated Air* should be *cold*, as well as *coagulated Water*, which is *Snow* or *Ice*, and that it should have a more keen or piercing *cold*, it consisting of more subtile particles, than those of *Water*, and therefore more fit to insinuate, and more accurately and stingingly to affect and touch the nerves.[19]

So, Alice would seem to have become an early English victim of Continental demonology: of the belief that sexual intercourse with the Devil was possible, that it was painful, and that impregnation by Satan could result from sex with him. While some may have conjectured that this was the time when Alice was impregnated by the prince of demons, Alice's own interpretation of her pains was less theologically resonant. Sex with the Devil had not at this time crossed her mind. But she did believe that, like the children, she had become possessed and that a spirit had now taken up residence in her stomach.

'I truly believe,' she said, 'that one of them has got into my belly. This is an evil house,' she went on, 'and haunted with spirits. And I wish I had never come into it.'

Her strategy is clear. As someone who was now herself possessed by a spirit, she is claiming that she too has become one of the victims. Consequently, her suggestion was that she therefore could not be the perpetrator. But Robert Throckmorton was to have none of this.

'If there are any evil spirits haunting this house,' he declared, 'then you are the one that sent them.'

Alice's claim that an evil spirit had invaded her stomach failed to foster the role of victim that she had no doubt hoped to garner for herself. It served, on the contrary, further to entrench the beliefs of the Throckmortons that she was intimate, in all senses, with the realm of the demonic.

vii.

Alice Confesses to Sorcery

On Saturday 23 December 1592 a crisis was, once again, precipitated by Jane. As we have seen, it was Jane who had first become ill, and it was just over three years beforehand that she had done so. She fell into a fit more terrible than either she or any of her sisters had suffered for more than a year. Mother Samuel was genuinely mortified by it, and terrified that the child was about to die. She prayed earnestly for Jane's deliverance. But the more assiduously she prayed, and the more often she said the words 'God' or 'Jesus', the worse the child's seizure became. After two hours of these torments, the spirit within the child spoke to her (or more mundanely, the child spoke to herself).

'There is a worse fit than this to come,' it declared, 'in which you will be even worse troubled than this.'

'I care neither for you nor your Dame,' Jane said. 'Do the worst you can to me, for I hope God will deliver me.'

Soon afterwards she recovered. Mother Samuel didn't. The sight of Jane's afflictions was so terrible to her that she continued praying that she might never see the like in any one of the girls again. She was clearly near breaking point. The children didn't let up. They all continued to call upon her to confess.

'You must do it before long. If you do it now so that we are well by Christmas, we'll owe you. Christmas is almost here. If you confess now, we'll soon be well. And then we can have a happy Christmas.'

'I'll do all the good I can for you,' Mother Samuel replied, 'but I will not confess this matter, for I didn't agree to it. And I know nothing about it.'

Hearing the children and Alice conversing, Robert Throckmorton stepped in and also did his best to persuade her once again to confess.

'You know that, in their fits, they don't lie,' he said. 'Now therefore, in the name of God, if you have anything to confess, do it now. It is never too late to repent and ask for mercy.'

But, as she had with the children, she denied knowing anything about the cause of their illness.

'But what do you have to say about that grievous fit which the spirit recently threatened that Jane would have?' he responded. 'I'd like to know when that will be.'

'I trust in God that I will never see her in such a state again, nor any of them,' said Alice.

'I truly think that she will have it, and soon. For the spirit never fails them in anything he promises,' he declared. Mother Samuel, we are now led to infer, rises to the challenge of who it is that controls the spirits.

'Oh,' she said, speaking very confidently, 'I trust in God that she will never have it.'

'Well then,' retorted Robert Throckmorton, 'charge the spirit in the name of God that Jane may escape this fit that's threatened.'

And Alice complied. It was a fatal move. Did Alice naïvely hope that the spirit would not obey her, and her absence of control over all the spirits would prove her innocence? Had she come to believe that she 'really' was in control of them and could genuinely help the children? We don't know. What we do know is that, on this occasion, the spirits did as they were told by her.

'I charge you Spirit, in the name of God,' she said, 'that Jane never have this fit.'

And Jane, sitting by, heard the spirit agree. 'The Thing speaks truly,' she said. 'I thank God that I will never have this fit that he has foretold of me.'

Throckmorton pushed Alice further. 'Well, that's good, thanks be to God,' he said. 'Go on, Mother Samuel, and charge the spirit in the name of God – and speak from your heart – that neither Jane nor any of them all have any more fits.'

So she did his bidding and said what Throckmorton wanted. Again Jane heard the spirit agree to Mother Samuel's charge.

'The Thing speaks truly,' Jane then said. 'I thank God that I will never have any more fits after the Tuesday after the Twelfth Day.'

'That's good, thanks be to God,' said Robert Throckmorton again. 'Charge the spirit again, in the name of God,' he went on, 'and speak from your heart – don't be afraid – that he depart from them all now, and that he never return to them again.'

Very loudly, and very boldly, we read, Alice repeated these words. As soon as she had finished, the three children, who were even then in their convulsions, and had been for the last three weeks, wiped their eyes as if they had just come to themselves. And they pushed back the stools on which they had been sitting, and stood up. And they were 'as well as ever they were in their lives' (sig.G.2.v).

When the children were recovering and he was attending to them, Robert had his back turned to Mother Samuel. Unbeknownst to him, Alice had fallen down on her knees behind him.

'Good God, forgive me,' she said.

Turning around in surprise, he saw her on her knees, and said, 'Why, Mother Samuel, what is the matter?'

'Oh, sir,' she said, 'I have been the cause of all this trouble to your children.'

'Have you, Mother Samuel? And why? What cause did I ever give you to use me and my children in the way you have?'

'None at all,' she answered.

'Then you have done me the more wrong.'

'Good master,' said Alice, 'forgive me.'

'I do, and may God forgive you. But tell me, how did you come to be such a kind of woman?'

'Master,' she replied, 'I have forsaken my Maker, and have given my soul to the Devil.'

No doubt or ambiguity is to be left in the readers' minds. 'These were her very words' (sig.G.3.r), the text informs us.

It is tempting to view Mother Samuel's confession of having given her soul to the Devil as a later invention intended to reinforce her guilt, and to view the claim 'These were her very words' as a malicious underlining of her culpability.

But at this point in the story, having herself been confronted with the obedience of the spirits to her commands, Alice may well have believed that she *must* have had truck with Satan. Stories of individuals selling their souls to the Devil for gain were a popular feature of medieval and early modern literature. Perhaps the only surprise is not that people were willing to sell their souls, but how low the price was that they were after. The title of Lawrence Southerne's 1642 book would have strongly resonated with the public: *Fearful news from Coventry, or a true relation and lamentable story of one Thomas Holt… who through covetousness and immoderate love of money, sold himself to the Devil.* Fearful and lamentable it may have been. But it wouldn't have been out of the ordinary.

And witches also, perhaps especially, were thought to have sold their souls to Satan. In 1608 it was said of some local women in

Bury, Lancashire, that 'they are all witches, they have given their selves to the Devil'.[20]

Moreover, as we have seen, the agreement between the witch and her familiars was a commonplace of English witchcraft. And, between the familiar and the Devil, no great gulf was fixed. To be on intimate terms with the one was to be closely acquainted with the other. In 1566, and again in 1582, we find familiars named 'Satan'. In 1589 Joan Cunny confessed to having acquired her familiars after she had prayed 'unto Sathan the chief of the Devils'.[21] And in the village of Warboys, at least, witches, familiars, and Devils all seemed to play for the same team.

That the essence of witchcraft lay in the league made between the Devil and a witch was central to elite demonological theory. But in Mother Samuel's expression of the link between bewitchment and the Devil, we seem to be witnessing the expression of a genuine folk belief in the relationship between witchcraft and the prince of darkness. In her realisation that she may well have been the cause of the children's sufferings, there is the recognition that she must, whether consciously or not, have given her soul to Satan. And Robert Throckmorton duly noted it.

Hearing raised voices, Robert Throckmorton's mother, Emma, and Elizabeth, his wife, came into the entrance hall. When Mother Samuel saw Elizabeth, she likewise begged her forgiveness. Though not knowing what had happened, Elizabeth, we are told, forgave her with all her heart. Mother Samuel then pleaded forgiveness from the three children who were present, and later from the rest, kissing all of them. At this point the children, who, we may recall, were said to know nothing about what they said or did in their fits (although aware when out of them of what their sisters did), readily forgave her too.

Alice Samuel was in a condition to do nothing but weep and lament what she had done. Robert and Elizabeth were moved to comfort her as much as they could. But Robert's sympathy had an edge to it. There is a hint of proffered clemency, but any leniency necessitated the reiteration of guilt.

'We freely forgive you from our hearts,' said Robert, 'if the children are never again to be troubled.'

'I trust in God,' she declared, 'that they will never have their fits again.'

Robert Throckmorton then sent for his brother-in-law, Francis Dorington, and recounted to him all that had happened. He asked for Francis's help in comforting Alice. Even with Throckmorton's promise of forgiveness, and Dorington's pastoral care, she could not cease weeping. She wept all night.

Why did she confess? Had she really been involved in maleficia against the Throckmorton family? There was no reason for her to have been so. She had no reputation as a cunning person or as a witch. The text would have made much of this, had it been so. To recapitulate, the Throckmortons had newly come to town in 1589 when the children were first possessed. Even Robert Throckmorton did not claim that Alice had any reason to persecute his family, though he therefore thought her activities more heinous, rather than less, in consequence. She had done nothing but try to be neighbourly, visiting sick children, paying her respects at the birth of a child in the family, eventually even being willing to live under the Throckmorton roof to help the afflicted daughters. So we should not take her confession at face value as an admission from her that she genuinely was involved in evil doings against the children.

So the alternative is that she has made a false confession to acts of which she is innocent. In order to understand why, we need to look more closely at the psychology of confession. As one suspected of having bewitched the children, she has been living in fear of the outcome of this for the best part of three years. Although she has not yet been specifically accused by any of the children of bewitching Lady Cromwell to death, it is less than six months since Susan Cromwell died. Doubtless, her name was being mentioned as the cause. She, no doubt, would have heard the gossip from wagging tongues in the village.

Since early October 1592 she has seen the suspicions and accusations resurface. She has been the unhappy witness to increasing activity by the spirits in the children. Since coming to live with the Throckmortons, she has also been the victim of progressively more frequent finger-pointing. There is nothing she can do which is not reported on by the children. And we have seen her becoming increasingly desperate as the psychological pressure on her has been ratcheted up. Her health has got commensurately worse. She is cowed by both the children and the adults in the Throckmorton household. From her husband, she has received no help, only abuse and even physical violence. Her daughter Agnes, understandably fearful for herself, has deserted her. There is no indication in the text of there being other friends and neighbours present to support her, no hint that there is anyone there to defend her. Psychologically and emotionally, she has become completely isolated.

The children threaten punishments and hold out the promise of leniency – eternal torments if she does not confess her sins and guilt, eternal happiness in the future and forgiveness in the present if she does. They predict she will confess to her crimes soon after Christmas, but they also appeal to her 'better nature' in hoping she will let them be well by Christmas. 'It is never too late to repent and ask for mercy,' Robert Throckmorton had recently reminded her.[22] Back in December 1590, Alice believed that the children were just malicious. 'The children's fits are nothing but wantonness in them,' she had then said. That may have been a defence back then. And she may have believed it in 1590. Two years later, the children reminded her that, being out of their fits, they had heard people say that she thought their seizures 'were but wantonness in them' (sig.F.4.r). 'Are you still of that mind?' they had asked her. 'No,' she had replied. And now she has seen and heard it for herself: when she speaks, the spirits do seem to obey her. Of the authenticity of the bewitching of the children, Alice no longer has any doubts. Overjoyed at seeing the girls restored to health, overcome by the relentlessness of it all, and buffeted by a storm of conflicting emotions, it is little wonder that she confessed.

Her confession was a false one, one forced out of her by the unremitting pressure placed upon her in the Throckmorton household. Specialist literature in the psychology of confession distinguishes between false confessions which are compliant and those which are internalised.[23] The former are confessions made by those who, in full knowledge of their innocence, confess in order to make strategic gains. In short, the consequences of confession – an end to questioning, and a more lenient outcome – are deemed preferable to the consequences of resistance: ongoing interrogation, continued denial, and a harsher punishment. In the case of Mother Samuel, we can surmise that she hoped for an end to it all by Christmas. The prospect of forgiveness had been held out to her. She must have weighed this against the evidence that was stacked up against her, the prospect of ongoing incarceration at the Throckmortons', and the strong likelihood of criminal action. It was better to confess than to continue to deny her involvement. At best, she would be allowed to return home with the nightmare over; at the worst, she faced a year in prison. Unpleasant, yes; but not a terminal eventuality.

But was Alice's false confession an internalised one? Had she come to believe, along with others, that she was indeed guilty of the bewitching of the children? Her behaviour subsequent to her confession is, as we shall see, consistent with this. Alice's apparently genuine acceptance of her ability to command the spirits, her contrite behaviour over the next twenty-four hours, and her extensive elaborations of her guilt in later confessions – all point to her having come genuinely to believe in her own guilt. She had lost the capacity to distinguish the true and the false, the real and the unreal.

These two categories of false confession are not mutually exclusive. Internalised false guilt is not something which is necessarily maintained consistently. Nor are coerced confessions of either sort necessarily adhered to permanently. Alice's confessions and denials are context-dependent. She does seem to be more genuinely convinced of her guilt when surrounded by others who genuinely and manifestly believed in it, and less convinced when outside the immediate interrogatory context.

At this stage, it would appear that the Throckmortons were also willing to make an end of it. Or almost. Because on the morning of the next day, Sunday 24 December 1592, Alice went to church to make her confession and her repentance visible and public.

A superficial reading of the text would lead to the conclusion that her appearance in church was a matter of voluntary willingness on her part. But there can be little doubt that this act of contrition was imposed upon her by both Robert Throckmorton and Francis Dorington. For even the brief description we have of Alice Samuel as she was in church that morning allows us to conclude that this was a formal public penance, of the sort ordered by the Church courts. In this case, no formal proceedings against Alice in the courts had been instituted. Throckmorton and Dorington had in effect taken the law into their own hands.

It was a public punishment – a humiliation in front of the whole community. And it was intended to shame Alice.[24] As a penitent she would have appeared in a white sheet. She probably came barefooted, perhaps with her hair worn loose. She would have stood in the centre aisle of the church, in full view of everybody present. Before the Reformation, she would have been expected to carry a candle. In post-Reformation England, a white wand would have been carried instead.[25]

She would also have been compelled to listen to a sermon intended to emphasise the impropriety of her conduct. According to *The Witches of Warboys*, the purpose of this address was to comfort her. Francis Dorington chose to preach on a text from the Psalms.

According to the earlier of the two versions of our story, the text in question was Psalm 32, verse 5: 'I acknowledged my sin unto thee, and mine iniquity have I not hid. I said I will confess my transgressions unto the Lord; and thou forgavest the iniquity of my sin.' Dorington declared to all there present the substance of Alice's confession. Far from comforting her, the sermon increased her distress. Throughout its delivery, Alice did nothing but weep and lament, and 'many times was so very loud with sundry emotions so that she caused all the congregation to look upon her' (sig.G.3.r).

She had avoided prison. She had now been very publicly shamed and humiliated. But she had as yet confessed to nothing in front of her community.

viii.

A Matter of Honour

Did she over-egg her performance? The answer depends on whether we believe that she was sincere in repenting for the sin which she now genuinely believed she had committed – the actual bewitching of the Throckmorton children – or was putting on an act for the sake of the villagers gathered in the church.

It was usual, in a context of public penitence, for the penitent to make a confession of his or her sin, and then to ask for forgiveness. In this case, neither Robert Throckmorton nor Francis Dorington had forced Alice into a formal declaration of guilt. But, while Throckmorton may have been convinced of Alice's contrition while he was in church, he soon had second thoughts. For the service had hardly ended before he recalled that only he, Francis Dorington, and his own household were privy to the substance of her confession the previous night. And all of them might be thought partial in this matter.

According to the text, Throckmorton was fearful too that she might renege on her confession, because of 'the old woman's inconstancy before' (sig.G.3.v). His actions suggest a man who was worried about the validity of her confession in the light of the pressure brought to bear upon her, or at least concerned that others might question her admission as a consequence of such pressure. He therefore brought her back into the church. There and then, in front of their neighbours, he demanded that Alice agree that the confession which she had given the night before was by no means coerced out of her, and that it was given freely of her own volition. Mother Samuel admitted that what she had said constituted a voluntary act on her part.

'I desire you all to pray for me, and to forgive me,' she stated.

At last Throckmorton was satisfied. Alice had confessed in front of the village, and had asked forgiveness of her neighbours as well, we can assume, of God.

That evening, the night before Christmas, news came to Francis Dorington that Alice continued still to weep. He prevailed on Robert

Throckmorton to allow her to go home to her husband. John Samuel was consulted and retorted bluntly that, if Alice wished to return home, she could do so. Francis volunteered to accompany her and offered to mediate between Alice and her disagreeable husband.

So it was that Alice returned home on Christmas Eve. She did so in the fervent hope that the children were cured, and in the expectation that Robert Throckmorton would take the dreadful matter no further. She might have also been looking forward to a warm welcome from her own family. But, if that were the case, she was soon to be disabused of any optimism on that score.

Alice had been shamed before the whole village. But, more particularly, she had brought recrimination on her immediate family. All their reputations had been compromised. And, as a middling yeoman family, their social standing was now severely diminished. John and Agnes could not permit such a catastrophe to continue.

Alice was set upon, we read, by both her husband and her daughter, who convinced her to change her position. By Monday morning, Christmas Day, she had denied all that she had previously admitted. If Alice's confession was actually a studied and strategic one, was she now persuaded by her husband and daughter that self-abasement would not be in her best interests, and that the prior admission of guilt should be retracted? If she had indeed come to believe in her own culpability, were John and Agnes able to 'turn' her again? We do not know for certain.

What is clear is that when Robert Throckmorton heard that 'his new convert had revolted again' (sig.G.3.v), having already been reassured that this was unlikely by virtue of her public confession in church, he simply could not believe it. That evening, he and Francis Dorington stormed around to the Samuels' cottage to find out. As they came to the door, and within earshot, they heard the Samuels talking animatedly inside. They remained on the outside to listen. It seems reasonable to suppose that the Samuels were arguing whether Alice's confession would result in her being forgiven by the Throckmortons or being charged with witchcraft. Alice perhaps felt confident that all would be well. But Agnes was clearly unconvinced by the outward expressions of good faith by the Throckmortons. Robert and Francis overheard Agnes saying earnestly to Alice, 'Don't believe them, don't believe them, for all their fair speeches.'

At this, Robert and Francis made entry to the house and demanded of Agnes if that was indeed what she had said. She denied it, as did her father and mother. Throckmorton then challenged Alice with the rumour that he has heard.

'I have heard that you have denied the truth of your confession,' he said.

'I will deny that I am a witch, or the cause of the troubling of your children.'

'But didn't you confess as much to me?'

'I did,' she rejoined, 'but it meant nothing.'

'Well then,' said Throckmorton, 'I cannot show you the favour which I promised. I will surely have you before the Justices. But tell me,' he continued, 'why did you confess it to be true, if it isn't so?'

'For joy,' she said.

'For joy, and why for joy?' he asked, smiling out of genuine puzzlement at what she could possibly mean.

'Because,' she replied, 'I saw your children so well, after your good prayers and mine.'

'I pray that God will so continue them,' said Robert.

So Alice admitted to having confessed to bewitching the children because she had herself become convinced that, granting she was the cause of their cure, she must also have been the cause of their illness. Yet, as soon as she had come under pressure from Agnes and John, she had had second thoughts. Robert Throckmorton, we may well imagine, was furious at this turn of events.

'However that may be,' he said, 'I will not let this matter pass. For seeing it is made public, either you or I will bear the shame of it in the end.'

And, with that parting shot, Robert and Francis departed, leaving the Samuels to reflect on his threat. The next morning, Robert went to the rectory to underline to Francis that he would not let 'this matter thus to die in his hand, lest the worser sort of the people should imagine that this was but some device of theirs, to bring the old woman into further danger' (sig.G.3.v).

This was no longer a matter of Alice's guilt or innocence but of public shame and disgrace. Robert instantly perceived the threat to his honour and esteem in the eyes of the village and elsewhere, were he to allow Alice to escape with a denial of her confession's veracity. This would be tantamount to his admitting that all along he had been mistaken in his assurance of her responsibility. Granting his certainty in the matter, his peers, his family, the villagers of Warboys, and others besides would not have expected him to allow Alice to get away with any denial of her culpability.[26] It was way too late for Alice's admission to be hushed up, even if he were so inclined to allow this. And, what's more, her confession of guilt lay on the public record. In a hierarchical rural society in which status and public honour were significant, any acquiescence in her denial would mean Throckmorton's own public humiliation.

No doubt he had thought long and hard during the night. He simply could not back down. If he did so, most of his neighbours would believe that he lacked the courage to force the issue. And, as he told Francis the next morning, some of 'the worser sort' might even come to believe that any evasiveness on his part might be construed not so much as lack of courage as part of a more malicious plan to bring Alice into even greater danger, perhaps as the victim of rough village justice orchestrated by him. This action too would hardly sit well with what he would wish others to think of him.

Only two possibilities remained open. Either he now had to proceed with the legal action against Mother Samuel, or she once again had to be made to confess. Robert and Francis decided to give her another chance. They sent for her to come to the church.

Alice's resolve too had strengthened overnight. She was now further from confessing anything that she had said or done than at any time beforehand. She left Robert with no choice: 'You and your daughter will go with me to my Lord the Bishop of Lincoln.' Sending for the parish constables, Throckmorton charged them with delivering Alice and Agnes to Bishop William Wickham in Buckden, a village near Huntingdon.

At the final moment before departure, under enormous pressure and with the constables ready to take their leave, Alice went to Robert Throckmorton with another change of heart.

'Master,' she said, 'if you will go with me into the parlour, I will confess all to you.' And, in the parlour, she confessed to him all over again.

'Tell me then why you have denied it all this time,' he said.

'Oh,' she replied, 'I would never have denied it but for my husband and daughter, who said that I was a fool for confessing. They said that it would have been better to have died as I was, than to have confessed myself a witch. For, they said, now everybody will call me "old witch" for as long as I live.'

The text leads us to believe that Robert Throckmorton would not have willingly pursued the matter as far or as determinedly as he eventually did. For, once again, he offered Alice a reprieve.

'If you will keep on confessing the truth,' he said, 'I will show you all the favour I can.'

For reasons which we will soon see, it is difficult to believe that he was being completely honest or open with her. In the meantime, Francis Dorington arrived on the scene. With Dorington present too, Alice was again reluctant to confess. Perhaps in the hope that, in his own absence, she would be more forthcoming, Robert Throckmorton left them alone together. Dorington called for pen, paper, and ink, and wrote down the confession which she had just made to Robert.

With good reason, Robert no longer trusted Alice not to perform another U-turn. We can assume that he was about to set her up, and that Francis was in the know. It was Christmas Day and time for morning prayer in St Mary Magdalene's next door. Many of the villagers were gathered in the church. Robert went inside and returned with a number of villagers to his house. He stationed them outside underneath the window of the parlour, where they were invisible.

When Francis was aware that the parishioners were all in position, he spoke very loudly. Inventing a reason, he asked Alice to speak up too, in order that the neighbours outside would be able to hear all that passed between Alice and himself. Francis led her again to confess. This was the moment for which Robert had been waiting. He re-entered the parlour and called them both into the hall. When Alice emerged, accompanied by Francis, she was then confronted by all the neighbours, who, unbeknownst to her, had also heard her confession. Robert began now to read from the admission which Francis had written down. Alice tried to deny it. But the eavesdropping neighbours were having none of it. 'No,' they cried, 'it is now too late to deny anything. For we have heard all this with our own ears.' And they told her where they had been hiding. With fear in her heart, Alice knew that she was trapped.

John Samuel had by now got wind of these latest happenings, and arrived at the Throckmortons' in high dudgeon. Robert informed him that his wife had once again confessed, and that she would never have reneged in the first place had it not been for the pressure applied by him and his daughter.

'Did you say that, you bitch?' he demanded of Alice.

He would have struck her there and then had others not moved between them rapidly. Alice, seeing her enraged spouse bearing ominously down on her, collapsed in a swoon. Whether actual or pretended is not clear. But Elizabeth Throckmorton was sufficiently concerned to call for brandy to be brought for Alice's revival.

'If you leave her alone for a while,' said one of those present who was familiar with her ways, 'she will soon recover.'

This dramatic interchange between Alice, Robert, Francis, and the villagers is very important strategically for the text. For it is intended to demonstrate that Alice Samuel was cunning and devious in her series of confessions and denials in the presence of Robert and others. She is portrayed as a woman who confesses truly when she can do so with impunity, but just as quickly denies it when she believes that the confession will do her public harm. This is a woman who, if it becomes necessary, will fall into a counterfeit swoon, to avoid what is implied as a false allegation against her husband that he and Agnes forced her to renege. No sympathy is to be spared for Alice.

We can infer that, after Alice's death, there was a groundswell of opinion against Robert Throckmorton for having bullied her into all this. The text must persuade us that this is no simple soul able to be persuaded to say anything, but a manipulative and crafty woman whose true nature is compatible with her guilt in bewitching the children. 'These circumstances about her confession are therefore,' we read, 'the more expressly set down, although they be not so pertinent to the matter. Nor indeed would they have been declared at all, had it not been reported by some in the country, and those that thought themselves wise, that this Mother Samuel now in question was an old simple woman, and that one might make her by fair words confess what they would' (sig.H.1.r).

In the battle between her family and the Throckmortons, Alice had tried to please everyone. In the end, she satisfied no one. And so to Buckden Alice and her daughter Agnes were now to be despatched.

It is unclear why Alice's daughter, Agnes, should also be sent to Buckden at this point. There was a hint early on in the text that she was implicated in sorcery. She had certainly been unhelpful to the Throckmortons' case, and the text presents her as furtive and oppositional. But no serious charges against her had yet been made by the children.

Nevertheless, there was a general belief at the time that witchcraft ran in families. This was not an issue of heredity. Rather, witchcraft was thought of as a family business, and rather like a trade. Agnes was sent along with her mother on the grounds of suspicion alone.

ix.

In Courts Sacred and Secular

A lice had in fact been sent by Robert Throckmorton to a Church court for formal examination. Ecclesiastical courts were well established in England by 1300. And they were to remain a highly significant alternative system to the secular courts until well after the Reformation. They dealt with serious crime, as Chaucer's *Friar's Tale* makes clear:

> In my own district once there used to be
> A fine archdeacon one of high degree,
> Who boldly did the execution due
> On fornication and on witchcraft too
> Bawdry, adultery and defamation
> Breaches of wills and contracts, spoliations
> Of church endowments, failure in the rents
> And tithes and disregard of sacraments,
> All these and many other kinds of crime
> That need have no rehearsal at this time,
> Usury, simony too. But he could boast
> That lechery was what he punished most.[27]

Alice appeared before the Bishop of Lincoln, William Wickham, the next day, which was 26 December 1592. Given his attendance, we can assume that she had been sent to an episcopal court of audience. In the diocese of Lincoln, this stood right at the top of the hierarchy of courts ecclesiastical. It was the bishop's personal court. It was informal. It was swift. And it examined only the most serious offences.[28]

We have no very precise details of Alice's appearance before the bishop. There is no suggestion that she was resistant. On the contrary; she was again compliant. Perhaps she hoped that this would mitigate the punishment handed down to her. She may again have come to believe in her own guilt. She was now actively manufacturing her own memories as her 'inquisitors' led her along the path of confession. This was a route she seemed prepared to take willingly. But, willing or not, as the questioning focused on her familiars, Alice entrapped herself further.

> The Examination of Alice Samuel of Warboys, in the County of Huntingdon, Taken at Buckden before the Right Reverend Father in God, William, by God's Permission Bishop of Lincoln, the 26th of December 1592.

> Being asked whether a dun chicken did ever suck on her chin, and how often, the said examinant says that it sucked twice and no more since Christmas Eve last. Being asked whether it was a natural chicken, she says that it was not. She knows that it was not a natural chicken because, when it came to her chin, she scarcely felt it. But when she wiped it off with her hand, her chin bled. She says further that the said dun chicken first came to her and sucked on her chin before it came to Master Throckmorton's house, and that the ill and the trouble that has come to Master Throckmorton's children has come by means of the said dun chicken. The chicken, she knows, is now both gone from them and from her. And further, she says that Master Throckmorton and Master Doctor Dorington will bring further information of such things as she has not yet declared. (sig.H.1.r)

We can assume that the bishop subsequently referred her to a secular court to determine whether or not she would be committed for trial. For, on 29 December, she appeared before William Wickham again, now in his capacity as a Justice of the Peace, together with two other JPs, Francis Cromwell and Richard Tryce. Alice was hardly likely to get a sympathetic hearing in this court: Francis was Henry Cromwell's brother.

Alice had confessed already to feeding her familiars. Now, in front of a secular court, she richly embellished her story further. Whether she did so as a result of prompting by court officials, we cannot tell. She told of the gift of the spirits from a man called Langland. We do not know if it was noticed that the name 'Langland' belonged to an earlier Bishop of Lincoln, Henry VIII's confessor John Langland. We can, and no doubt we are intended to, read it solely as a confirmation of her pact with the Devil. Three months later, on 5 April 1593 – the afternoon on which she was found guilty – Alice admitted that this man, then called William Langley, had carnal knowledge of her body, when she received the spirits from him. For some, '[i]t was the Devil in man's likeness' (sig.O.3.r).

Alice was weighed down by six spirits, all in the appearance of brown chickens, and all of whom had taken up residence in her belly. We may recall that the spirits appeared to the children most often in the form of a brown chicken. At this point, the world of the nursery, the demonic, and the courts of the land intersect. The tragic and the comic overlap one another.

The Examination of Alice Samuel of Warboys in the County of Huntington, Taken at Buckden the Twenty-Ninth day of December 1592, before the Reverend Father in God, William, by God's permission Bishop of Lincoln, Francis Cromwell, and Richard Tryce, Esquires, Justices of her Majesty's Peace within the aforesaid County.

I have never done any hurt to any, except to the children in question.

How do you know that the dun chicken is gone from the children?

It is because the dun chicken, along with the rest of the spirits have now come into me. And they are now in the bottom of my belly. They make me so full that I am likely to burst. This morning they caused me to be so full that I could scarcely lace my coat. On the way here, they weighed so much that the horse on which I rode fell down and wasn't able to carry me.

The upright man about whom I have confessed to Master Throckmorton, told me that Master Throckmorton was a hard man and would trouble me much. For this reason, he said that he would give me six spirits that would vex and torment his children. And so he did. When the spirits were outside my body, I used to reward them by often letting them suck my blood. They used to suck my blood before I sent them off anywhere.

Whatever the children of Master Throckmorton spoke in their fits proved true, and was true. Whenever the children said that they saw the spirits, then the spirits were there. And I saw them too. Often I gave them a quiet wink or a nod. And then they presently sealed up the children's mouths, so that they couldn't speak until they came out of the children again. And then the children would wipe their eyes and would be well again.

I was taught by a man who came to my house. I don't know where he lives, or what his name was. But he told me that if I called the six spirits they would come. So I did. And they appeared in the likeness of dun chickens. Their names were as follows. First Pluck, second Catch. The third was called White. I would call them by their names and they would come.

I sent two of them to Master Robert Throckmorton of Warboys and his wife. But they came back again, and told me that God wouldn't allow them to prevail. So I sent the spirits to the children of the said Master Throckmorton, by means of which they have been so strangely tormented, as has been seen by the neighbours and country.

What I heard the children say in their fits was true. And it happened as they said it would.

What was the name of the upright man who gave you the devils?

I do not know.

Alice was persuaded then to go into another room and demand that her spirits tell her his name. There, in a loud voice, she cried three times, 'Oh, you Devil. I charge you in the name of the Father, the Son, and the Holy Ghost, that you tell me the name of the upright man who gave me the Devils.' She returned. 'My spirits tell me that his name is Langland.'
'Where does he live?'
'I do not know,' she said.
She was persuaded again to go into the other room and demand that her spirits tell her where the said Langland dwelt. Again, in a loud voice, she said three times, 'Oh Devil, I charge you in the name of the Father, the Son, and the Holy Ghost, tell me where the said Langland dwells.' Then she returned once more. 'He has no dwelling,' she reported. Again she went to enquire where Langland was at that moment. 'My spirits tell me that he went on a voyage beyond the seas,' she eventually reported back.
Was Alice quite self-consciously complicit in a drama being improvised by her inquisitors? Or are we witnessing a form of demonic Munchausen syndrome, in which Alice led her interrogators into a world of her own imaginings? What seems clear is that Alice was no longer capable of stepping out of the role that had been created for her, that of the witch in control of her familiars.
The Justices of the Peace also had their parts to play. They had to decide, on the basis of the examination or confession, whether

the matter should proceed to trial and, if necessary, to bind Alice and Agnes over for trial as well. So, after these confessions were made, Alice and Agnes were sent to Huntingdon. There they were locked in the dank and dark cellar which then served as the Huntingdonshire county gaol (see Plates 17 and 18). And there they too were to wait for the assizes sessions day on 9 January of the following year.

But thus far there has been no mention of the bewitching to death of Lady Susan Cromwell. Both in Warboys and in Buckden, Alice has confessed only to doing harm to the children. At the worst, she may have expected only to be imprisoned for a year. Her body would be punished, for she would be regularly pilloried. But capital punishment was as yet far from her mind.

Part Three

Agnes Accused:

1 January 1953 to 3 April
the Same Year

i.

Agnes on Bail

Although Agnes was incarcerated along with her mother, there was no evidence against her. We can surmise that this became clear to the Justices of the Peace on the morning of 9 January, the sessions day in Huntingdon, but that no decision was then made on what to do next with her. For we read that, around lunchtime, Robert Throckmorton requested the court to release her on bail into his custody. Robert appears determined that Agnes too will be made to suffer the penalty for witchcraft. He wished to take her back with him to his house in Warboys 'to see, if it might please God, whether any such evidence of guiltiness would appear against her, as had before appeared in the children against the Mother' (sig.H.2.v). We can assume that Robert's request was an unusual one. For, we are told, the Justices were uncertain whether, in the case of witchcraft accusations, the accused was able to be bailed. However, by three o'clock that afternoon, bail was approved.

Evening was setting in as they began the seven-mile journey back to Warboys. Agnes was doubtless relieved no longer to be languishing in the Huntingdon gaol. Elizabethan prisons were notably unpleasant places in which to reside for any length of time. Almost anything would have been preferable to the dark, dank, and insanitary cellar in which she and her mother, chained to the central pillar supporting the vaulted roof, had been kept since before the New Year. It was with relief, but, we may suppose, also with some apprehension at what awaited her there, that she set out with Robert Throckmorton for her home town.

The time of her release from gaol is important for, back at Warboys, events continued to unfold. We might have expected that, granted Alice's charge to the children, and their return to health, their seizures would have been at an end. But around noon, shortly before lunch, Mary, Jane, and Grace fell into their customary fits of lameness, blindness, deafness, and 'absence of feeling'. Robert, the youngest child of the Throckmortons, begins to play his minor role in the story. Christened on 30 June 1583, and now nine and a half years old, only he can communicate with Jane, and only she with Mary and Grace.

For this part of the story, we may assume that we are relying on evidence that was later given by Francis Dorington at the trial.

ii.

A Priest's Tale

The Report of Master Doctor Dorington of that which happened at Warboys, on Tuesday which was the Sessions Day at Huntingdon, the Ninth of January.

Immediately after lunch, I went to see them with a colleague of mine from Cambridge. I found all three of them in their fits. At the time, the fits seemed not so much grievous as merry. Each of them repeated often these words, 'I am glad, I am glad, none as glad as I.' I asked their brother Robert to ask them why they were so glad. And Jane answered, 'We will know good news within these two hours. I wish these two hours were passed.' The other two sisters affirmed the same. Mary and Jane were whispering secretly in each other's ears. Often, in our hearing, they said, 'I wonder how she should know that thing. I am sure no-one in this house told her. Therefore it cannot be but that the spirits told her.'

I asked Robert again to ask of Jane, and Jane of Mary and Grace, when they would come out of this fit. They all answered, 'Now by and by. And then we will be well, and we will all go out of this parlour into the hall. And returning from there quickly back here again, we will soon enter into another fit like this. And then you will hear news. For by that time the two hours will almost be spent. Yet after we have told the news, we will have a happy fit. But it will be short.'

All these things which they foretold proved most true. For they came out of their fit perfectly well, they arose from their stools themselves, and all three of them went first out of the great parlour into another room, to see how their Mother was who, then being not well, was staying in her bed. Soon, they went from there into the hall to see their sister Elizabeth who was then sitting by the fire. While there, they were asked by one of their kinswomen in the house not to return any more into the parlour. But, not withstanding that advice, they all three needed to go into the parlour.

No sooner had they entered that room, but each of them fell into their former fits, lame, blind, and deaf, so that they had to be carried to their stools by the fireside. Once there they began to say again, 'I am glad, I am glad, there is none as glad as I am.' And being asked why they were so happy, all three answered that Agnes Samuel would be brought to their Father's house from Huntingdon. 'We will not hear Agnes Samuel in our fits as we did her Mother,' they said, 'because our Father will not trouble us with any more questions. The spirit is telling us this.' Being asked one after the other, they all said these words.

And then they all together fell into extreme fits, bending their bodies backwards, their heads and feet almost meeting together, their bellies being highest, with great groaning. But, thanks be to God, this didn't last long. Then, rubbing their eyes two or three times, they seemed as if they were waking out of a sleep. And so they became as perfectly well as ever before. Jane was uttering words to the spirit which itself, so it would seem, was saying, 'We are gone.' Then Mistress Jane answered, 'Farewell and be hanged.'

All those of us who were there gave thanks to God. I asked them all how they were, and they said, 'Very well, we thank God.' 'How did you feel for the past two hours?' I asked them. They said that they had been in a sleep. I knew that they had eaten, for I had found them all at lunch merry and pleasant. Yet they answered, 'We have not dined, and yet we are not hungry.'[1]

Had Agnes known of all this, she might have preferred to stay in gaol.

iii.

A Devil Comes to Joan

For the first three or four days after Agnes had come to the Throckmortons' house, the children were well. Robert and Elizabeth were hopeful that the nightmare was over. But the children soon fell into fits again and were as badly afflicted as they had been while Mother Samuel was with them.

And now the spirits began to accuse Agnes as much as they had accused her mother. Mother Samuel had sent the spirits to them with Agnes, they claimed. Soon after Agnes had returned to Warboys,[2] Joan, the oldest daughter, also returned home. She had been staying with her uncle, Gilbert Pickering, at Titchmarsh Grove since December of the previous year.

Joan now becomes the most prominent of the possessed girls in the story. Of the five children, she is the most skilled and accomplished 'performer'. Like her sisters, she has long conversations with the spirit in which she continually swaps roles, playing both herself and the Devil. For her story, from 9 February 1593 and on into March, we return to quite detailed diary notes.

After Joan returned from Titchmarsh, her condition deteriorated. Several weeks afterwards, late in January, the pain in her legs became so severe that she was unable to walk or sit but could only lie in bed or else on cushions by the fireside. On 9 February 1593, towards evening, the spirit came to her. As was her custom, Joan spoke very familiarly and disdainfully with it, demanding of it whence it came, and what news it brought. The spirit refused to divulge its provenance. But it did say that she would soon have very extreme fits, worse than she had ever had before, torments during which she would retain all her senses and remember afterwards what had happened. 'I neither fear you nor care for you,' she said. 'For God is on my side and will protect me from you.' 'The Thing' departed, and she continued in her fit the better part of the night until she went to bed.

The next day, Saturday 10 February, Joan was lying by the fireside, groaning. Suddenly, her nose began to bleed copiously. Joan was genuinely surprised.

'I pray that God sends me good news after this,' she said, 'for it is unusual for me to bleed. Even years ago, I didn't bleed as much as this.'

Joan attributed her nosebleed to Mother Samuel. To counter Mother Samuel's magic, she said that she would hurl the bloodied handkerchief into the fire. It seemed to those gathered there that the spirit then came to her. For, smiling to herself and looking around, she said, 'What in God's name is this that comes tumbling towards me. It rolls like a football. I think it is some puppet-player. It is much like his Dame's knitted cap.'

It would be strange had Joan not heard of Mother Samuel's confession to the Bishop of Lincoln. Alice, we recall, had named three of her six spirits as Pluck, Catch, and White. Alice had 'personalised' her spirits, and the children picked up on it. Joan now added a new name to the list – Blue.

'What is your name, I pray you?' she enquired.

It would seem that the spirit answered 'Blue'. For soon she said, 'Master Blue, you are welcome. I have never seen you before. I didn't think that my nose was bleeding for nothing. What news have you brought?' And, as previously, it told her that she would be tormented worse than on any prior occasion.

'What are you saying,' she asked, 'that I will be tormented worse than ever before, and that I will have fits in which I will see, hear, and know everybody? Indeed. That is a new trick. I don't think any of my sisters were so treated. But I don't care about you. Do your worst.'

Joan was silent for a while, as if listening to something said by the spirit. Then she asked about Agnes Samuel.

'She has had too much liberty lately,' said Joan, 'for she has been in the kitchen talking with her spirits. She asked Blue, so he told me, not to let me have any such extreme fits in which I would speak, and hear, and know everybody. But he answered that he would torment me like that, and not give up until he had brought his Dame to her end.'

Agnes was now for the first time seriously implicated in sorcery. Called into the room, she was accused by Joan. For the children previously, their tormentor was 'the Thing' or 'the Spirit'. But Joan has learned some elementary demonology along the way. She was the first of the possessed expressly to demonise the spirits.

'Your Devils will no longer be at your command,' she said. 'It won't be any better with us until both you and your mother are hanged.'

Agnes admitted to having been in the kitchen alone, but denied that she had been talking with any spirits, or even knew of such things.

'Do not deny it,' said Joan. 'It is surely so. The spirits would not lie to me.'

Soon after this, Joan came out of her fit, complaining of suffering great pains in her legs. Asked if she remembered anything that had taken place, she replied that she had been asleep. And she was puzzled why her handkerchief should have been so bloodied. She was certain that someone had taken it from her and bloodied it before giving it back to her. It was her last amnesiac fit. For, later that night, she fell into the fit that Blue had threatened, and which was followed by total recall.

iv.

Joan's Fit, Saturday 10 February 1593

That night, as her Father and Mother rose from supper, she fell into the fit which before Master Blue had threatened her with. For she was most grievously wrung. And she twitched in every part of her body. Sometimes she would thrust forth her arms so straight and so stiff, that it was not possible to bend. Sometimes again she would so wrest and writhe them clean backwards that no man or woman was able to do the like by their natural strength. She herself cried out very pitifully, sometimes about her stomach, saying that she was very sick, and wanted to vomit. Sometimes she cried out about her head, and at some other times about her belly. And there was never a part or member of her free from extreme pain.

She herself was ever calling on God to think of her, and deliver her. Sometimes it would so stop her breath, and hold it so long, that when she could recover it again, she fetched a marvellously deep and loud groan. And being oftentimes asked in this fit by many that stood by how she did, she answered that she was marvellously sick and full of pain, affirming that she both heard and saw all that were present. In this woeful state, she continued the space of half an hour and more, to the great grief of the beholders, for this is one of the first fits that either she or her sisters had, having their perfect senses.

Now suddenly as she was thus complaining, she fell into her senseless fit, having her mouth also shut up. And now is she deprived of all manner of sense again. Remaining thus quietly a little space, she fetched a great groan, whereupon her mouth was opened. And she spoke saying,
'Here is a rule indeed. I perceive that you are as good as your word with me. From where do you now come? And what news do you bring now, I pray you?'
'You must yet be worse handled than all this,' the Thing replied.
'God is above the Devil,' she said. 'Do what you can, for you will not be able to hurt me. But tell me, why do you punish me

worse than all my sisters, with me having my fits when I can know everybody?'

The Thing answered, 'Because you told tales of our Dame.'
'Who is your Dame?'
'Nan Samuel,' it answered, 'Agnes.'

And this you must understand, in all their manner of talking together, that the children would first repeat the Spirit's answer, before they would ask any further question of them.

'Then,' said Joan, 'if Nan Samuel be your Dame, I will tell more tales of her yet. And I hope to tell such a tale of her one day, that she shall not be able to answer it, nor you for her.'

The Thing answered that he would then punish her more for it. She said that she cared not for that. Then the Thing said,
'When was Smack with you?' This Smack was another of the spirits' names.
Says she, 'I know no such fellow as Smack.'
'Yes,' says the Thing, 'you do. And he it is that tells you all these things. But I will beat him for it.'
'Do your worst to him or to me, for I care not for you. Farewell,' she says.
'Do you bid me farewell?' asks the Thing.
Says she, 'Fare you well and be hanged.'
For you will have the truth as she spoke it.
'And come again,' says she, 'when you are sent for.'

Soon after this, she came out of her fit. And she was very sick, and full of pain in her legs.

V.

Demoniacs on Display

After lunch the next day, which was Sunday 11 February, a visitor arrived in Warboys. He was a cousin of Robert Throckmorton from nearby Brampton, also called Robert. We can assume that, having heard about the children, he had come prepared at the very least to be entertained, and perhaps at best stupefied and amazed. He was not to be disappointed. For he had been there only a short while before Elizabeth fell into one of her customary disturbances. Robert was keen to impress his guest.

'Would you like to see a wonder, cousin?' he asked.

'Have you any greater wonders than to see this sight?' the latter replied.

'I have wonders just as great. For you will see this child brought out of this state in which she now is at the pronouncing of certain words by a maid in this house.'

'That I would like to see,' said Robert's cousin, 'for I am sorry to see this sight.'

Agnes was called for. It is no great surprise that she was instructed to repeat words similar to those which had incriminated her mother. And we may infer that she had been forced to do so many times since she had returned to Warboys from Huntingdon. One of the Throckmorton sisters had foretold a fortnight earlier that, whenever Agnes said these words, they, the girls, would soon become well. For Robert Throckmorton, Agnes's procurement had become literally a parlour trick – a diversion – for the amusement of his guests.

'I charge you, Devil,' commanded Agnes at Robert's request, 'in the name of the God of Heaven and Earth as I hate you, and am no witch, nor guilty in this matter, to depart from this child, and allow her to come forth out of her fit.' There was at first no response from Elizabeth.

'I charge you, you Devil,' said Agnes, again at Robert's request, 'as I love you, and have authority over you, and am a witch, and guilty of this matter, that you allow this child to be now well.'

No sooner had she spoken these words than the child wiped her eyes and was as well as any girl in the village. While Robert Throckmorton from Brampton conversed about the matter with Agnes, Jane also fell suddenly into a seizure. The same words said by Agnes rescued her too from her fit.

Agnes was demonstrably able to control the spirits as her mother had done. She was now correspondingly incriminated by the children. There is no hint in the text that Agnes was bullied into this position against her will. Had she been so, it would have been in the interests of the text to inform us explicitly. We can plausibly assume that she was compliant. As Alice had done, she probably acquiesced in the hope that co-operation on her part, while likely to implicate her, would also stand her in good stead were she to go to trial. It was a high-stakes gamble. And, in the light of the powerful forces ranged against her, it was one that she was unlikely to win.

vi.

Familiar Fights

oan's seizures and contortions continued that Sunday night. They were the same as the night before. Tortured in every part of her body, she suffered the still greater torment of having the use of all her senses. Then, all at once, she fell into insensibility, groaned piteously, and exclaimed, 'Where do you come from, Master Smack?'

Joan's spirits were unpredictably vicious and malevolent. And violence now seemed to be breaking out among themselves. Smack replied that he came from fighting.

'From fighting,' said Joan. 'With whom, I pray you?'

'With Pluck,' the spirit replied.

'Where did you fight, I pray you?'

'In old Mother Samuel's bakery,' he retorted, 'with great cowlstaffs.'

'And who got the mastery, I pray you?' Smack explained that he had broken Pluck's head. 'I wish he'd broken your neck too,' she said.

'Is that all the thanks I get for my labour?' he asked.

'Why do you look for thanks at my hand? I wish you were all strung up next to each other, and your Dame too. For you are all worthless. But it's no matter. It's not good to curse you, for God, I trust, will defend me from you all.'

As Smack was taking his leave, Joan asked him when he would come again.

'On Wednesday night,' he said.

No sooner had Smack gone than Pluck came to her. The onlookers heard Joan ask, 'Where do you come from, Pluck, with your head hanging down like that?' And he answered her as Smack had done.

Agnes, like her mother before her, had made it known publicly that she believed the children were dissembling. It was important for the Throckmortons that she, like Alice, should accept that the children were genuinely bewitched. Joan's fits provided the opportunity they sought.

On Monday 12 February Joan had been unwell for the whole day. In the afternoon she fell again into extreme distress, throughout the duration of which – half an hour or more – she was entirely conscious of what was happening. Agnes, like the others present, was deeply concerned and prayed heartily for her. 'The grievousness of that sight would have moved any stony heart to pity' (sig.I.2.v) – even, the text implies, the heart of the one who was the cause of it. Agnes was asked whether or not Joan's condition was wantonness. But now, we read, she could not deny that it was the work of some supernatural agent in the afflicted girl.

That evening, after supper, Joan was again in torment. Another of the spirits identified by Alice Samuel – Catch – had seemingly invaded her. 'Where have you just come from, limping like that?' asked the beleaguered Joan. 'I hope you have met your match.'

Catch replied that he and Smack had been in combat, and that on this occasion Smack had broken his leg. 'That Smack is a shrewd fellow,' she said. 'I wish I could see him once. Pluck came last night with his head broken, and now he has broken your leg. I hope that he will break both of your necks before he has done with you.' Catch replied threateningly that he would get even with his adversary before he was done. It was at this point that Joan said, 'Put out your other leg. Let me see if I can break it.' 'You cannot hit me,' said Catch. 'Can't I?' she exclaimed. 'Let me try.'

It was then as if the spirit put out its leg, for she lifted up her stick and suddenly hit the ground hard.

'You haven't hurt me,' mocked the spirit.

'Haven't I?' she retorted. 'No, but I would if I could, for then I would make some of you come home shorter.'

She seemed to strike at the spirit many times with her stick, but he seemed to jump over her stick just as often, 'like a monkey'.

The next day, Tuesday, after the evening meal, it was Blue who entered into her.

'Are you now come with your arm in a sling?' she asked him. 'Who have you met with, I wonder?'

'You know well enough,' replied Blue.

'Do I? How would I know?'

'Smack and I were fighting, and he has broken my arm.'

'That Smack is a stout fellow,' she said. 'I hope that he'll break all your necks, because you punish me without reason. I wish that I could meet him just once.'

'We'll be even with him one day,' said Blue.

'Why,' asked Joan, 'what will you do?'

'We will all fall upon him and beat him,' replied Blue.

'Probably, he cares for none of you, for he has broken Pluck's head, Catch's leg, and your arm. Now you have something to do. You can go and heal your arm.'

'Yes,' said the spirit, 'when my arm is whole, we will beat Smack.'

After supper the following night, Joan again fell into her senseless fit. As before, she groaned deeply. Smack had arrived.

'Who sent for you, Master Smack?' she asked. The demon answered that he had come according to the promise he had made to her on Sunday night.

'Likely you've kept your promise,' she said, 'but I would rather you would keep away, and come when I send for you. What news do you bring?'

'I told you last Sunday night that I had been fighting. But I have had many battles since.'

'Yes, so it seems,' she said. 'For Pluck, Catch, and Blue were here, and they all came to me maimed.'

'Yes,' he said, 'I have met with them all.'

'I'm surprised that you could beat them. They are very big, and you're just a little one.'

'I am good enough for two of the best of them together,' he said.

'I've got news for you,' said Joan.

'What is that?'

'They will all, at one time, fall upon you and beat you.'

'I don't care about that that,' he said. 'I will beat any two of the best of them.'

'And who will beat the other two? she enquired. 'There is one that has been spoken of many times. He carries the name of "Hardname". For his name has eight letters. And every letter stands for a word. But what his name is we don't know. We only know "Hardname"'

'My cousin Smack will help me to beat the other two,' he said.

'Will your cousin Smack help you?' she asked. 'Is there kindred among Devils? I have never heard before that Devils were cousins. God keep me from relatives like that.'

'You will have no more fits like those you have had,' the spirit finally said.

'That's good,' replied Joan. 'But you can do nothing but lie.'

'Don't you believe me?'

'No. Will I believe the Devil who is the Father of all Lies?'

'But you will find it true,' he said.

'If I do, then I will believe you,' she rejoined, 'but not before. I pray God it is true. But whether it is or not, I don't care a fig for you.'

'No? Won't you thank me?'

'Thank you?' she cried. 'Hang you and all your fellows. I won't believe you further than I can see you. Nor do I care about any of you all.'

Like her sisters, Joan used the opportunity to resist the temptations of the devils, and establish her pious credentials. And the authors of the story leave us in no doubt that she is under the immediate protection of God. Like Jesus in the wilderness, she resists:

> This Smack has often gone about to win her favour, making her very fair promises to her that he would do anything for her, if she would love him. But it has pleased God by the work of his good spirit that she has always withstood him, denying him, and defying him to the utmost. And she wished all evil to light upon him and his fellows for so tormenting her and her sisters without cause, always desiring the assistance of God's Holy Spirit to preserve her and her sisters from such temptations. (sig.I.4.r)

This gave Joan a further chance to implicate Agnes. Smack was co-operative. Joan looked to the spirit for advice on scratching Agnes.

'You have told me many times,' said Joan to Smack, 'that I would scratch Agnes Samuel. Tell me now when I will scratch her.'

'You should scratch her before the assizes,' replied Smack.

'What?' she said. 'And will she stand before the judges with a scratched face? I want to scratch her, for I cannot stand her nowadays. It makes me sick to look at her.'

'You will have no more fits after the assizes,' maintained the spirit in parting.

'I am very glad of that,' said Joan.

'But if you do, then woe to Agnes Samuel, for I will bring her to her end.'

Joan came out of her fit, and in a much better state than she was usually.

Four nights later, on the evening of Sunday 18 February, Smack came back.[3] Joan and two of her sisters were having seizures. All of a sudden, Smack entered Joan.

'Have you come again?' the girl asked him. 'I had thought that you would come no more and that we were well rid of you. But where have you been?'

'My cousin Smack and I have been fighting with Pluck and Catch,' he replied. 'We have beaten them both so much that they dare not come to you any more.'

Finally, Joan asked when she would scratch Agnes Samuel. The demon told her that, if she scratched Agnes now, the latter's face would be healed before the assizes. Joan promised to keep her nails ready for her target.

Joan's seeming hatred of Agnes now reached new levels of intensity. The demise of Lady Cromwell as a result of bewitchment was for the first time announced by Smack. Agnes was cited as the cause. Lady Cromwell had now been dead for around seven months. But this, as far as we know, is the first time the Samuels had been accused of bringing about her death.

'She was also consenting to the death of the Lady Cromwell,' Smack announced.

'I thought so,' said Joan.

'Yes,' the spirit continued, 'and to prove this to be true, whenever any stranger comes into the house, you will fall into your fit. And if then Agnes Samuel will come to you and say, "As I am a witch, and consenting to the death of Lady Cromwell, so I charge you to depart, and to let her come out of her fit," you will be presently well' (sig.I.4.v). Joan repeated Smack's words, and they were set down in writing. Now that the death of Lady Cromwell from witchcraft had been laid on the table, alongside the allegation against Agnes and Alice as being the cause, Joan recognised the inevitable penalty.

'Then I hope,' she said, 'she will be hanged as well as her Mother, and that Sir Henry Cromwell will see to it.'

It was not until the following Friday that an opportunity to put Agnes to the test presented itself to Joan and Smack. Smack related to Joan a conversation he had had with Agnes. He told Joan that Agnes had begged him that, if he loved her, Joan should have no more fits.

'Even though I don't love her,' said Smack, 'you will have no more fits this week, unless some strangers come, if you will get up early in the morning.'

'If rising early will prevent my fit, then I will get up early tomorrow morning. But why must I have my fits if strangers come?' she asked.

'To bring her to shame,' replied Smack.

'But when did you talk to her?'

'Just now, in the parish room.'

'She will deny it if she's asked,' said Joan.

'Well, she would, wouldn't she? But you must have a week of very bad fits,' said the spirit, 'before the assizes come.'

'Must I? Who for?' asked Joan.

'Agnes will have it so,' came the reply.

'Let me know when that day will be.'

'You will know a week from tonight,' said Smack, 'and what kind of fit it will be.'

Two days later, on Sunday 25 February, Robert Throckmorton of Brampton made a return visit. He was the first person to have visited since the previous Friday. Soon after his arrival, as expected, Joan had a seizure. Soon Smack arrived too and entered her. Joan asked the spirit why she was having her fit then when he had promised that she would not suffer another until the following Friday. The demon reminded her that she would have a fit in order to prove that Agnes was a witch if strangers were to come to the house. While she sat talking with Smack, Jane too showed signs of an impending seizure. Suddenly Joan said, 'Jane, the Thing tells me that you will soon have a very bad fit.'

No sooner had Joan spoken than her sister was assailed grievously, groaning and crying out in torment and pain. Robert Throckmorton, the children's father, called for Agnes to be brought in and asked her to hold Jane. The child struggled in Agnes's arms. Joan spoke. 'Be of good comfort, sister Jane,' she said, 'for the Thing says that Nan Samuel is weary of holding you, and therefore you will be well.'

Soon after that, Jane's struggles ceased, and she returned to the dormant state in which she had been beforehand.

Robert told his cousin of the prediction about the arrival of strangers. Robert Throckmorton, his curiosity aroused, asked for a demonstration. Agnes, now fully aware of the danger, did her best to resist. But, unable or unwilling to refuse to do as Robert wished, she stumbled over the words, refusing to allow the 'magic formula' to work its effect: 'Either she could not, or else she would not speak them plainly. But she would always say, "Consenting to our death of our Lady Cromwell." And she would not speak the words plainly, even after repeating them over three or four times' (sig.K.1.v).

Joan intervened. Joan was unhappy that Agnes appeared to be getting away with it on the grounds of linguistic incompetence.

She believed such inadequacy constituted passive resistance on Agnes's part. So, apparently, did the spirit.

'There is something telling me,' she said, 'that she will not speak the words aright.'

In the end, Agnes did speak the words. And Joan emerged from her seizure. Using the same charge, another of the girls was similarly brought out of her fit.

That Agnes was able to control the spirits was further reinforced the next day. Elizabeth, although in her fit, was asked to say grace at dinner. Halfway through, her mouth was closed up so that she could not finish the invocation. As we have seen, it was common for the children to react violently on religious occasions. But Agnes was now recognised as both cause and cure. She was told by Robert Throckmorton to charge the spirit to open Elizabeth's mouth again so that she might finish the prayer. Agnes's charge was effective.

The inability of the children to say grace was a common facet of their condition. And Robert Throckmorton held Agnes responsible for shutting up their mouths. The author of the text at this point, probably Robert Throckmorton himself, hints strongly that Agnes was not among the brightest of young women. Or perhaps he is suggesting instead that, since she was a witch, she absolutely refused to recite religious verse. For he did try to teach a short grace of two or three lines to her. And the children also tried numerous times one day to instruct her. But she could not do it. Was she unwilling or unable? We cannot tell. The answer, like so much of the Warboys story, remains ambiguous and mysterious.

vii.

Mary Draws First Blood

Although Mary was the third of the sisters originally to have become sick, she appears to have been one of the least afflicted, and has thus far played only a supporting role. And we can infer from the text that, up until this point, the child – although ill – had not shown the vindictiveness more characteristic of Jane and Joan. But it was Mary who now initiated the scratching of Agnes.

It was now Thursday 1 March, and Mary had not suffered any seizures since the assizes day, 9 January. At nine o'clock that morning, in one of the upstairs rooms, she is reported to have fallen into a 'great quaking and trembling' (sig.K.1.r). Recovering a little soon afterwards, she said, presumably to one of the spirits within her, 'Is it true? Is this the day in which I must scratch the young witch. I am heartily glad of it for I will certainly pay her in full for myself and my sisters.'

Two of the children's uncles and a number of others were present: Henry Pickering, the Cambridge scholar who, we recall, had had the argument with Agnes's mother by the Warboys pond; and Edward Pickering, an older brother to Elizabeth Throckmorton, the children's mother, by a little over a year.[4] The two Pickerings had Agnes brought into the room.

'Are you come, you young witch, who has done all this mischief?' Mary said.

Agnes was amazed, for she was unused to hearing hard words from this child. She was persuaded to carry Mary downstairs. Very quietly, as Agnes bent down to pick her up, she allowed herself to be taken up into Agnes's arms. She clasped her hands about her neck. But no sooner had Agnes begun to lift Mary up than the child attacked. She began to scratch Agnes so eagerly, and so fiercely, that all were astonished.

'I will scratch you, you young witch,' she exclaimed, 'and pay you in full for punishing me and my sisters. The Thing tells me that I would have been well, and never would have had my fits any more but for you.'

Agnes was entirely dumbfounded. She broke down in tears, weeping pitifully. Yet she did not move her head away, allowing the child to continue scratching her. Agnes, like her mother, now appeared completely defeated by it all. But there was no mercy forthcoming from Mary.

'No,' she said, 'I know you cry, but the spirit said that I wouldn't hear you, because I shouldn't pity you.'

Agnes's failure to move her head away from the child's ripping fingernails was now interpreted as supernatural intervention by the spirit.

'He it is that holds you now so that you cannot get away from me.'

This attack amounted to a serious assault on Agnes. The text says that the child scratched Agnes's face until the skin came off, the width of a shilling. When Mary came out of her fit, and saw the damage which she had done to Agnes's face, she collapsed in tears. Did Mary have a sudden and deep regret for her behaviour? Or was she, having realised that she had been behaving in a way of which she was genuinely unaware, genuinely shocked and horrified by what she had done. She had, we read, a mild disposition. And others were no doubt genuinely surprised by the sudden and unexpected viciousness of her actions: '[I]t appeared to be altogether besides her nature' (sig.K.2.v). What we can say for sure is that Mary had had enough. Her role in this drama was about to end.

Friday 2 March, and Mary was now in contact with Smack.

'I am glad, and marvellously so,' said Mary.

But she was unable – or unwilling – to say why she was so glad. She spoke then as if to someone who stood next to her.

'But I know you will lie to me as you have often done.'

'No,' said the Thing, 'I didn't use to lie.'

'No trouble,' she replied. 'Who are you?'

'Smack,' the Thing answered.

'What,' she asked, 'are you that Smack that used to come to my sister Joan and tell her so many things?'

'Yes,' he said, 'but I never told your sister Joan any lies before, and I'm not lying now to you. After dinner, you will come out of your fit and never have any more because you have scratched Agnes Samuel.'

Mary informed her sisters of this conversation. They wished that Smack would say the same to them. As had been predicted, after the midday meal, Mary emerged from her seizure. She was never troubled by the spirits again.

viii.

Joan, Smack and Catch

I f Mary's possession had finally come to an end, Joan meanwhile was still negotiating with the spirits about her own torments. For that same morning, Friday 2 March, Joan too had fallen into a fit.[5] This was the day on which Smack had told her previously that she would be instructed when her week of seizures would begin. It is Smack who appears to have come to her that morning while she was still in bed. For Joan announced to her sisters, who were suffering their own torments, that she had some news and was getting out of bed to go downstairs to tell of it. The news in question, as we later discover, is that Smack has told her she won't be afflicted by a week of seizures.

When she had been downstairs for a short while, and sitting by the fireplace in the parlour, Joan spoke as if to someone next to her. It was not Smack but Catch who was present.

'I will not lower myself to look at you,' Joan said. 'You never come without bringing some bad news with you. I was sick the last time you were here. I wonder who sent for you this time.'

'You were really sick the last time I was here,' Catch answered. 'But now you will be much worse.'

'Do your worst,' she declared angrily. 'God will preserve me. I'm not afraid of you. I wonder how your leg is. I think Smack spoke with you when he broke your leg.'

'Do not tell Smack that I was here, I beg you,' he said.

'Do you beg me? I don't know that Smack,' she lied, 'but if I did, I would surely tell him so that he'd break your neck too.'

'You know him well enough, for you made him break my leg. But I wouldn't want him to know for anything that I was here. I'll make you pay for all of the next week if you tell him.'

'Will you?' she said. 'I'll bet you anything you like that I won't be sick this week if I don't want to. That I do know.'

'Yes,' he replied, 'I know that Smack was with you this morning. But do what you like, the both of you, you will have a sick week.

And you will find that you will be so sick this next week, that your body will be sore all the week after. For I will thrash you as well as Smack has thrashed me.'

'Why then,' she asked, 'are you having your revenge on me and not on Smack?'

'I don't dare fight with him,' he answered. 'He's too tough for me.'

After a short silence, she asked her sisters, who were similarly in their fits, 'Do you see Catch who was talking with me just now?'

'No,' they replied.

'Why then,' said Joan, 'he's probably gone, for I don't see him either.'

Then she began to talk very quietly with them, as if she wished no one to overhear them:

> Smack was with me this morning when I was in bed. And he told me that next week will be a really sick week for me which he couldn't help. But he did tell me that he had so thrashed Pluck that he will never come to me again. And if he does, he will kill him. And then he said to me that if I go to some friend's house and stay there all week, I will be fine and escape this sick week. But I told him that I didn't have a friend's house to go to, and there was none that I would go to, whatever he did to me. He wanted me to go to Sommersham.[6] I wonder how he knows about Sommersham. He must know his way around the whole county. I told him that I wouldn't once set foot out of the door for him, whatever he did to me. He'll be back tonight soon after supper.

Word of Agnes's power over the spirits had got around. Before Smack returned, another group of visitors arrived at the manor, anxious to see Agnes summon Joan out of her torments with the charge 'As I am a witch and consented to the death of the Lady Cromwell'. By the time supper came Joan had again gone into her supernatural netherworld.

After supper, as the company were sitting around the fire, and just as Joan had predicted, Smack came to her again. The two of them talked about the seizures that she was due to have during the following week. The demon told her that, unless she went away from home, he couldn't do anything about it.

'I will not go away,' she said. 'Do your worst.'

'When was Catch with you?' Smack asked.

'He was here today,' she replied. 'He threatened to punish me with really sick fits because, he said, I had caused you to break his leg. I hope that you'll break his neck too, and that somebody will break yours. You are all of no account.'

'I'll thrash him for it. I promise you that he will never come again by the time I've finished with him.'

'When will my fits begin, and when will they end?' asked Joan.

'On Monday morning next they will begin,' he replied, 'and end the following Monday, in the morning.'

'It will be a whole week, then?'

'Yes,' he replied, 'and your body will be sore for a whole week afterwards.'

During the next two days, Saturday and Sunday, Joan suffered many fits. But Agnes brought her out of them all with the usual charge. Monday 5 March was the first day of the week of severe fits. They continued for a week, as expected.

ix.

Elizabeth's Exhortation

I t was not only Joan who was troubled during this week. Elizabeth too was severely tormented. Elizabeth, we may recall, had played a significant part in the early stages of the possession, especially during her stay at her uncle Gilbert's in 1589. She was now almost fourteen years old.

It was Saturday 10 March 1593, and Elizabeth was about to incriminate Agnes further. As Elizabeth sat at her supper, she gave the appearance of wanting to talk to something that stood on the table. She was unable to speak a word, for her mouth had been closed up. She began to weep bitterly, though she was unable to say why she did so. Agnes was instructed to hold her, which she did. Grace, the youngest of the sisters, fell into a worse seizure than Elizabeth. Agnes was told to put down Elizabeth and pick up Grace. Elizabeth, furious at being neglected, took her revenge on Agnes.

'Now I can see the young witch,' she said, 'which I never could before.'

Unlike Joan or Jane, Elizabeth in her fits had never before been especially vindictive, either to Agnes or to her mother, Alice. Now she upped the ante.

'My sister Joan's Devil,' she said to Agnes, 'told me just now as I was having supper that I must scratch the young witch.'

And with that she quickly slipped from the bench on which she was sitting, fell upon her knees, grabbed Agnes by her free hand, and scratched it fiercely.

'It is you that has bewitched me and all my sisters,' she said. 'I would have been well a long time ago if not for you. Oh you young witch, fie upon you, fie upon you, who ever heard of a young witch before?'

So vehemently did she scratch Agnes that she soon exhausted herself. When she had caught her breath she fell upon Agnes again, claiming that it was Joan's devil who 'didn't use to lie' (or Smack) who made her scratch her.

'I don't want to scratch you,' she said. 'And it was against my wishes to do it. But the Devil makes me scratch you, stretching out my arms and bending my fingers. Otherwise, I wouldn't. But I have to. And all my sisters must too, even if they are unwilling like I am.'

All this time Agnes continued to hold Grace in her arms, not once trying to withdraw her hand from Elizabeth's grasp. But she cried out piteously to God, asking him to take care of her. One of the spectators asked Agnes to state honestly whether or not she thought that the child scratched her of her own free will. Was it wantonness in the child or was she under the control of another?

This amounted to a no-win situation for Agnes. To have accused any of the girls of wantonness would have exacerbated the rage of the child (or the devil within her). To have denied that the child was culpable was to accept the authenticity of possession (and thus her own control of the spirits). Agnes must have thought long and hard. She plumped for what must have seemed the lesser of two evils.

'I don't think so,' said Agnes. 'No,' she continued, 'I know that she didn't. It is not *her* desire to scratch me like this.' Elizabeth was appeased by this response. Agnes had chosen correctly, at least for the moment. For the second time, Elizabeth grew weary of scratching her.

Since no threat was made to the authenticity of her possession, Elizabeth felt able to be charitable. For, suddenly, she put out both her hands and cried, 'Look here. The Devil says that I must now scratch you no more.'

Then, a number of times, while still murmuring to her, she rubbed her hand on Agnes's hand, which was bleeding a little. When the scratching had ended, Elizabeth began to weep. Tears fell from her eyes and, crying bitterly, she said, 'I didn't want to scratch you, but the Devil made me. And he forced me whether I wanted to or not. If only you hadn't deserved to be treated in such a way.'

Elizabeth, like her sisters, was prone to demonstrations of her own piety. She began vehemently to exclaim and desire that Agnes would amend, 'the like was never heard to come out of a child's mouth' (sig.L.1.r). She was now, it seems, possessed by the Spirit of God.

'Oh that you had grace to repent of your wickedness that your soul might be saved. For you have forsaken your God and given your self to the Devil.' Elizabeth had learned her demonology well. She is remembering the confession of Alice.

Oh if you knew what a precious thing your soul is, you would never then have parted so lightly with it. You need to pray night and day to get God's favour again. Otherwise, your soul will be damned in hellfire for ever.

You often pray at home here, when we pray, and likewise at church. But you pray in vain, because you don't pray with your heart. But I will pray for you with all my heart. And I will forgive you. And I will ask all my sisters and all my friends to forgive you if you will confess your fault. But you have a hard heart, and the Devil holds your heart and won't allow you to confess it. But you must confess it, whether you want to or not, when your time is come. But oh, that you would confess it now, so that your soul might be saved.

'My sister Joan's Devil is standing here in front of me.' Then, pointing with her finger to the spot she continued. It tells me that, in spite of you, you will one day confess it, or else you will be hanged. For we will not be well until you confess it, or are hanged. But if even now you will confess it, we'll soon be well. Now, therefore, defy the Devil and confess it so that God may forgive you and that your soul may be saved.

If you would think of the torments of Hell, and that your soul must burn in hellfire unless you do confess and repent, then you wouldn't stand so stiffly in denial of it all like you do. But you are a wicked child, and you have been a witch for this past four or five years or more. You have done more than harm to me and my sisters. For you have killed my Lady Cromwell and more. The Devil that stands here tells me so. And you would have killed our sister Joan in this her sick week. But God would not let you.

What a wicked heart you have, that nothing will satisfy you but our deaths. You, and your Father, were the reason why your Mother denied that which once she confessed. She was doing alright. And she would never have gone back on her words had not you and your Father persuaded her. And if your Mother's soul is damned, you and your Father must answer for it.

Your Mother had confessed a truth, and was sorry for her wickedness. Everybody had forgiven her, and would have prayed for her. Oh that she had never gone home that her soul might have been saved.

X.

The Accusation of
John Samuel

We know nothing of Agnes's reaction to all this. The text is silent on the matter. Perhaps its reticence reflects the silence of Agnes herself. We can well imagine her speechless in the face of this onslaught.

There was, of course, some truth in Elizabeth's words. Had Alice not retracted her first confession at the persuasion of Agnes and her unpleasant father, Robert Throckmorton's public honour would not have been brought into question. The situation might well not have escalated, Robert Throckmorton's standing might well have been saved by Alice's confession and repentance in the parish church. The spirits too might have felt it was time to end it all. But, like her father's honour, Elizabeth's reputation was also at stake. Alice's reversal of her confession had stopped the children letting the matter go too. As we have seen, Elizabeth had long ago accused Alice of bewitchment. She had been relentless in her pursuit of Agnes. And a new accusation was about to be made.

> Your Mother is a witch, your Father is a witch, and you are a witch. But of all three of you, you are the worst. Your Mother would never have done as much hurt as she has done but for you. The Devil has told me so. You wicked child! You are a wicked child. May the Lord give you grace to confess and to repent that your soul may be saved. Oh that your Father were now here. For the Devil now says that I should scratch him too. He is a witch and a wicked man. Oh that he were here that he might hear me now speak to him.

It seems not unreasonable to assume that Robert Throckmorton was far from unhappy to hear this. We read that he at once dispatched two of his relatives – his brother-in-law Henry Pickering (the Cambridge scholar), and his cousin-in-law John Pickering – to inveigle John Samuel to come to the house.[7] Those present were not confident that Samuel would be persuaded. He was, we are reminded, 'of so churlish a nature' (sig.L.1.v), and was ever drawn to the manor only with the greatest difficulty. And John Samuel does seem to have been one of those who actively resisted the Puritan mindset and programme which the Throckmortons represented. His detractors saw him dwelling (metaphorically, if not literally) on the dark outer fringes of the village, an ever-present threat to law and order, and social and religious propriety.[8]

So the Samuels and the Throckmortons were agents of the two sides of a conflict between 'Puritans', on the one hand, and those whom they saw as the ungodly, on the other hand. And the battle was joined between those who saw it as their role to live a godly life and their responsibility to impose this life on others, and those who, not surprisingly, resented their interference. But minding someone else's business *was* the business of Puritans. It was not only a social and political responsibility to do so but a religious one as well.

The Throckmortons would have placed the irascible and boorish John Samuel on the profane side of the holy ledger, like his wife and his daughter. And it was but a short step from seeing him standing on the wrong side of the line to seeing him as an active member of the army of Satan.

Henry and John Pickering had hardly gone twenty yards from the house when they saw John Samuel advancing quickly towards them. Agreeing to let him go past them without addressing him, they turned round and followed him back to the manor house. All three had entered the hall and were about to go into the parlour where Elizabeth knelt. Although she is said not to have been able to see him, her clairvoyance served her well: 'He has come, he has come. I will go and scratch him.' And she crawled on her knees towards the parlour door. Francis Dorington, preventing her, called for John Samuel to be conducted into the room. When Samuel entered, Elizabeth attempted once again to crawl towards him, saying the while 'I must scratch him, I must scratch him'.

Suddenly she desisted. This was not a man to be trifled with, and perhaps, looking at him then, she realised it herself. 'I must not scratch him,' she said. 'Look here.' And she showed her fingers, now clenched into the palms of her hands. 'If he had been here a moment ago, the Devil says I should have scratched him. But now I mustn't.'

Robert Throckmorton demanded to know why John had come to the house. The latter's response was that he been told that his daughter was sick and so he had come.

'Who was it who told you this?' Throckmorton asked, demanding that he should tell the truth and not lie.

'I won't tell you,' he replied, 'however much you urge me.'

Eventually, somewhat relenting, Samuel told them that his brother's daughter had come to his house and told him that she had seen Dr Dorington and a servant of Robert looking for him. He, thinking it had to do with his daughter, arrived to make enquiries. This seems a plausible explanation. But no one in the room accepted it. The situation was now extremely volatile, teetering on the edge of violence. Elizabeth may have ceased crawling towards Samuel to scratch him. She was keeping her distance. But she had not ceased her accusations against him.

'You are a wicked man,' she cried, 'and a witch. If it wasn't for you and your daughter, your wife's soul might have been saved. You must answer for it before God one day.'

And she repeated many of the speeches which she had directed previously at Agnes, exhorting him to prayer, and to ask God's forgiveness.

Alice and Agnes may have been frightened and intimidated by the threat of hell fire and eternal damnation. John Samuel was a different proposition. So vigorous and contemptuous was his response that Elizabeth could not be heard for his shouting. He called Elizabeth and all of them there liars for accusing him of sorcery, and he charged her also with being a fake, trained in her deception by others. He refused to be silent until compelled to be quiet by the exhortations of Robert. Meanwhile, Elizabeth's pious urgings to both John and Agnes continued for the next hour and a half.

Behind the text, we can hear the words of John Samuel shouting for all to hear that this was a conspiracy hatched by the Throckmortons and their kin against him. The charge amounted to a renewed slur on Robert Throckmorton's honour and integrity which the latter could not allow to stand unchallenged. But this time, Throckmorton had a new weapon in his arsenal. Alice and Agnes had shown that they could control spirits with their words. John Samuel had to be forced to do the same. Unsurprisingly, he refused.

'I will not,' he said, 'and neither will anyone make me say them, not for anything.'

'Then seeing that you came to this house unasked,' Robert replied, 'you won't leave it until you have, even if you're here for the week.'

And in order to encourage him, Francis Dorington and several others of those present repeated the charge which previously Agnes had been directed to say.

John Samuel remained obdurate. Only when it dawned on him that Robert was genuinely determined to keep him there by force until he repeated the exorcising charge did he decide to relent. Then he began to speak as instructed by Throckmorton.

'As I am a witch, and consenting to the death of the Lady Cromwell, so I charge the spirit now to depart from Mistress Elizabeth Throckmorton and to allow her to be well.'

No sooner had he spoken these words than, the spirit having gone, the child stood up restored to normality. She was amazed to see such a crowd gathered.

'Do you remember anything you said or did?' Elizabeth was asked.

'I don't remember anything,' she said. 'I have been asleep.'

And her eyes filled with tears when told what she had been doing just moments beforehand.

John Samuel strode angrily from the house. He could never be persuaded to come again and repeat the charge. The crowd dispersed. And Elizabeth went to bed, quite well.

xi.

The Bewitching of Elizabeth Pickering

Two days later, on the morning of Monday 12 March, Joan was due to recover from her week of sickness. The week had passed just as Smack the demon had predicted and as all had expected. The first day, Monday 5 March, the child was aching all over. All that day, and every day that followed for the whole week, she cried out in pain. Unable to eat, she lost the use of her legs and her hands were cold and numb. The worst pain of all was in her head. Not sleeping, she did nothing but cry out and groan all night. No one else in the house could get any rest for the disturbance and commotion.

Besides these ongoing physical afflictions, Joan suffered fits every day and night of such severity that no one who saw her thought that she could survive them. Sometimes she was comatose, seeming not to breathe for fifteen minutes at a stretch. At other times she screamed continuously for up to four or five hours. As Smack had prophesied, she had the use of her senses throughout. Unless she was in a swoon, and her breathing had seemed to cease, she was able to answer questions, although she reported later that, even when she could not speak, she could still hear. She could not bear to be in the presence of Agnes Samuel, or even to hear her name. The longer Agnes was in her vicinity the worse Joan's torments became.

On the Monday morning she recovered, although – as expected – her pains endured, as if, she said, she had been beaten. Though the seizures and throbbing continued, this was still a week of relative freedom from sickness. Then, during the early evening of 19 March, after supper had finished, Joan entered into a trance. Smack had appeared.

'I trust God will one day revenge me on you and all your company,' she cried out to him, 'for punishing me and my sisters like this.'

'Why,' he said, 'have you had a sick week of it?'

'It's no business of yours,' she replied.

'Well, I told you,' he said, 'that I couldn't do anything about it unless you went to some friend's house.'

'You go where you want and do what you can, I will not stir a foot out of doors for your pleasure. I know you would kill me if you could. And you are using all the means you can to kill both me and my sisters. But I trust God will not allow you. But if he does, then I am nevertheless contented. For I would rather be dead than to live in this continual pain, and not able to stand or move.

'You have often told me,' Joan went on, 'that I would scratch the young witch before the assizes. Now tell me when it will be. I would enjoy scratching her. Lately, I can't stand her. Whatever the circumstances, I think God has set my heart against her. I cannot eat my food if she is standing in front of me, it so upsets my stomach. And yet I can't tell why. But tell me,' she said, 'on what day will I scratch her?'

'You will scratch her two or three days before the assizes,' the spirit told her.

'Tell me on which day it will be, for I will never believe you.'

'It will be on the Monday before the assizes,' replied Smack.[9]

'Well,' she said, 'make sure it is. For I will keep my nails long for her. I will scratch one side of her face for me, and the other for my aunt Pickering.'

This is the first that we have heard of the bewitchment of aunt Pickering. She is identified as the wife of John Pickering of Ellington. As noted above, he is probably a cousin of Elizabeth Throckmorton, the children's mother. The Warboys Parish Registers record the marriage of a John Pickering to an Elizabeth Cervington on 15 November 1591. John and Elizabeth, we may recall, are the parents of the young Gilbert Pickering, christened on 17 September 1592. It was Alice Samuel's visit to the manor house to see the young mother which had re-ignited the demon possessions, when Jane again fell into a seizure at the sight of Alice.

Once again, Elizabeth is resident in the house, perhaps because she is in ill health. She has been 'grievously tormented with pain and ulcers on her legs' (sig.L.4.r), so badly it seems that she has been unable to walk. When did Elizabeth Cervington become possessed? She is here described as 'one of the twelve that were bewitched' (sig.L.4.r). This is the first mention of her as possessed and as one of the twelve. In late 1589 Joan had named the twelve who were to be enchanted as herself, her sisters, and seven female servants. Of course, in the circumstances the text was rushed to the printer, and this may well be a slip of the quill. But, if the Warboys text was correct at *that* point, it would suggest that Elizabeth was then one of the servants who was later to marry into the family, and who was periodically one of the possessed since that time.

There is a suggestion to this effect from Joan less than a week after this first accusation against Agnes of having bewitched Elizabeth Pickering. Then Joan remarks that Elizabeth would by then have been well had Agnes not bewitched her *again* after her mother had confessed. In any case, as we will see, one of the confessions which Joan hopes that Agnes will make at the assizes is that she has bewitched Mistress Pickering 'since her Mother confessed' (sig.M.3.r). It would undoubtedly have made for a better case against Agnes if a person previously free from possession had become so infected after Alice had been gaoled and Agnes had come to reside on bail at the Throckmortons'. Consistency in the text can be found only if we assume that Elizabeth Cervington, originally a servant, later one of the family, originally evinced some early signs of possession, and a fresh set of symptoms now appeared after the imprisonment of Alice.

If it is the case that Elizabeth Pickering again fell sick after Alice had been gaoled, this is further evidence of the opportunism of the Throckmortons, who by this time were seeking out all avenues to incriminate Agnes. For there is no suggestion that Elizabeth had suffered any fits like those of the children. The symptoms described are not suggestive of demonic possession. Rather, they admit of a variety of explanations beyond that of bewitchment and infestation by Smack and his gang. But the crucial point is that any misfortune which befalls those in the Throckmortons' circle has now become attributable to the Samuels. All the evidence points towards it. And no evidence can gainsay the belief of Robert Throckmorton and his confederates in the Samuels' guilt. Their conviction has become a matter of faith, impervious to proof against it, and all proofs compatible with it.

Meanwhile, Joan and Smack continued to discuss the scratching of Agnes.

'Well,' Joan went on, 'whenever it is, I will really lay it on so that all the world may see that she is a witch.'

'Those that think otherwise about her are deceived,' said Smack, 'and I'll prove it.'

'How will you do that?' asked Joan.

'By forcing you to scratch her.'

'Will you force me? Then I won't scratch her.'

'Oh yes you will,' he responded.

'I want to scratch her,' she said, 'but I wouldn't if I didn't have to.'

'You must scratch her as hard as your two sisters have. And your other sisters have to as well.'

When the conversation between Joan and Smack had ceased, Joan called for Agnes. What before had been the certain proof of Agnes's guilt had now become a routine administration. Joan told Agnes that she could not emerge from her seizure until the latter has charged the spirit to go. Agnes obliged, and Joan quickly became well.

xii.

Joan Tightens the Noose

Sunday 25 March. Joan and Smack were about to further tighten the noose around Agnes's neck. All Agnes's actions would be read retrospectively as evidence of her witchcraft, even those in which she was attempting to protect her mother from harm or persecution. Joan had again fallen into a stupor at the end of supper. Although Smack had absented himself since the previous Monday night, it seemed to the spectators that he had returned. Though Joan was not speaking out loud, it seemed by her face and her gestures that she was talking to someone. For she was turning her face away and shaking her head as if unwilling to listen to an interlocutor. Suddenly the girl exclaimed: 'Go on, then; if what you say is true, let's see what you'll do.'

Agnes was summoned on cue.

'Smack says that you must say these words,' Joan informed Agnes. '"As I am a witch and would have bewitched Mistress Joan Throckmorton to death in her last great week of sickness, so I charge the spirit to depart and allow her to be well." After you have spoken them, I will come out of my fit. But I will fall into it again and have many more fits tonight. But I will come out of them through your speeches.'

Agnes intoned the charge and, as soon as she had done so, Joan recovered. Another seizure quickly came. Joan started to report on the spirit's demands again.

'The Thing says that you must say, "As I am a witch, and have bewitched Mistress Pickering of Ellington since my Mother has confessed, so I charge the spirit to depart and allow her to be well." The spirit says that my aunt Pickering would have been well before this time, had you not bewitched her again since your Mother confessed. Alas, good aunt Pickering, what harm have you done to any of them that they should treat you like this?'

Joan began to weep bitterly. Those who stood by wept too. When she had mastered her emotion, she asked Agnes to say the charge to release her. Again, Agnes complied. And, again, Joan recovered. But the respite was only a brief one.

'The spirit says that you must say, "As I would have bewitched Mistress Joan Throckmorton to lameness, since I could not bewitch her to death as I wished to do in her last week of great sickness, so I charge the spirit to depart and allow her to be well." Then I will be well, and soon fall into my fit again.'

Agnes said these words as she was instructed. Joan recovered but, as predicted, was soon in yet another fit. Agnes was then accused not only of bewitching Elizabeth Throckmorton but of bewitching all the sisters again since the time of her mother's confession. Joan addressed Agnes once more: 'The spirit says that you have bewitched all of my sisters over again since your mother confessed or else they would have now been well.'

Agnes was now ordered to charge the spirit to depart from Joan, once for each of the bewitched sisters, beginning with Mary. Joan then had four successive seizures, and came out of them as the result of four charges made in the names of her sisters. Then she said, 'The spirit says that now I must also fight and struggle whenever you say "God" or "Jesus" or mention any good work. Though I cannot hear you, the spirit can. And he will make me struggle.'

Robert Throckmorton took the opportunity to ask Agnes to charge the spirit in the name of God to answer certain questions and not to lie. Agnes complied, and enjoined the spirit to be truthful. Smack said to Joan, 'The young witch charges me to tell the truth in certain questions which she will ask me.'

'Yes,' Joan replied, 'and see that you do tell the truth and don't lie about anything.'

'I don't tell as many lies as the young witch does,' he retorted.

Robert then asked Agnes to compel the spirit to reveal in which part of her body she would be scratched. The spirit told Joan that she would scratch Agnes on the face, on the right cheek for herself, and on the other for Elizabeth Pickering.

'I will surely scratch her left cheek well for my aunt Pickering if it will do her any good,' she said, 'whatever I do for myself.'

'Yes,' said Smack, 'and the young witch would do well to take it patiently for you will have your pennyworth before you have done.'

Agnes was asked to enquire of the spirit whether her mother would publicly confess at the assizes all that she had already confessed on other occasions.

'The old witch will confess all again at the assizes,' prophesied Smack, 'as long as she has no evil counsel. And she will also confess that her daughter is a worse witch than she. For when the old witch had bewitched the Lady Cromwell, and would have un-witched her again and couldn't, she put it to her husband and asked him to help her. And when he couldn't, she put it to this young witch her daughter. And when she couldn't help her either, then she advised her Mother to kill her.'

Prior to this, any involvement of Agnes and John in the death of Lady Cromwell was only inferred from the children's reactions to the charges which Agnes and John had been forced to make to the spirits so that they would depart. But, at this point, Joan has given a full explanation of their involvement in the aristocrat's death. All the Samuels are complicit. But Agnes has now been accused as the instigator.

'And to prove that all this is true,' the spirit said to Joan, 'whenever any strangers come to the house before the assizes, you will fall into your fit. And you will have three fits and will come out of them after three charges by the young witch. The first charge that she must use is "As I am a witch and a worse witch than my Mother in consenting to the death of the Lady Cromwell, I charge the spirit to depart, and you to be well". The second is "As I have bewitched Mistress Pickering of Ellington since my Mother confessed". And the third is "As I would have bewitched Mistress Joan Throckmorton to death in her last week of great sickness"'.

Agnes then used all three of these charges to the spirit. And on each occasion Joan came out of her fit, before lapsing into it again. Robert no doubt wondered if Agnes could be brought to say these charges before the court. For he realised that her public incrimination would be dependent on Joan being in her fits at the time. So Agnes was asked to find out from the spirit whether Joan would have her fits before the judge at the assizes were she to be carried there.

'The young witch would know, whether she will have her fits before the judge at the assizes,' Smack said to Joan. And Joan reinforced the message by repeating his words to all present.

Then Agnes was compelled to ask of the spirit whether Joan would have any more fits *after* the assizes. The spirit told Joan that she would not suffer any more seizures, and that neither Agnes, nor her mother, nor any of their kin would be able to harm them after that day. Agnes enquired if this guarantee would apply to all the sisters. Smack refused to answer, saying that Jane's own spirit would reveal this information. Agnes then asked for the names of all the spirits. Alice Samuel had already confessed to having six spirits on 26 and 29 December, of whom three were called Pluck, Catch, and White. Joan had added four more names – Blue on 10 February, Smack on 11 February, while Hardname and another Smack – the original Smack's cousin – were added on 13 February. The spirit now increased the company of spirits by a further two – a further Smack, also a cousin, and Callico – to nine in total.

According to the original Smack, these were all variously dispersed among the children: Joan had the original Smack, Mary had his cousin Smack, Elizabeth had the third Smack, Jane had Blue, Grace had White, and Alice had Hardname still with her in the gaol. Smack did not know what had happened to Pluck, Catch, or Callico.

'Did my mother reward them with anything or not?' Agnes was made to ask.

'She rewarded them every day,' said Smack, 'with blood from her chin. Once, she desired God to show some sign of her being a witch, and her chin bled of itself which proves it.'

Agnes had been forced to this point to ask the questions, the answers to which condemn her. In the absence of John Samuel, Joan took over the questioning from Agnes. It seems clear that she wished Smack to make it apparent that, quite independently of Agnes and Alice, John Samuel has committed acts of maleficia.

'Is John Samuel a witch?' asked Joan.

'He is,' said Smack, 'and he will be a worse one than either this young witch or the old witch her Mother when these two are hanged. For all the spirits will then go to him, and he will do more hurt than any of them has done yet. He has already bewitched a man and a woman. If you want to prove it, get the young witch to say "I charge the Devil to depart from Joan Throckmorton now as my Father has bewitched two people" and you'll soon be well.'

Agnes did as she was told, and Joan was well – for a moment. Soon she was in her fit again.

'Who were the two people bewitched by John Samuel?' asked Joan.

'I won't tell unless the young witch goes out of the room,' said the spirit. 'And let her be watched so that she doesn't hear when she is gone.'

Agnes left the room. Then Smack said, 'It was Chappel and his wife.'

The Chappels were next-door neighbours of the Samuels, but that is all we know of them. There were Chappels who had lived in Warboys during the period. The year 1557 was a bad one for plague in Warboys. We know from the parish records that 118 parishioners suffered and died from it in that year. Among them was a Joane Chappel, buried on 8 October.

What is clear is that between the Chappels and John Samuel there had been a history of enmity, and Smack was aware of it. Both the Chappels, he said, had been much troubled with 'bleach' – that is, a skin disease like leprosy. And the husband had had several seizures, which suggested that he was bewitched.

'John Samuel once tried to break Chappel's neck,' the spirit went on, 'when they met each other on a narrow causeway across the bog.' We can envisage an argument between the two enemies as to who should give way. A struggle ensued. In order to avoid being thrown by Samuel onto the stones, Chappel cast himself into the bog. This story would certainly have been commonly known in the village. Tales about John Samuel's short fuse and hair-trigger capacity for violence would have been much talked of. On this occasion, as Chappel later remarked when verifying the spirit's account, 'I was marvellously soiled, and would have been in real danger had not another been there to help me.'

Joan then continued to build the case against Agnes. Having been brought back into the room, she was required to ask the spirit, 'Will Mistress Joan be well on the way to the assizes, and will she be better at the assizes than at home?'

'She will be better there than at home,' replied Smack. 'But it will be worse for the young witch if Mistress Joan does go. She will be well all the way until she has arrived and goes into her room. And then she will fall into a fit.

'You will have three fits on the assizes day,' the spirit then told Joan, 'and the young witch must bring you out of them by three charges. The first must be "As I am a witch and a worse witch than my Mother in bewitching the Lady Cromwell to death". The second must be "As I am a witch and a worse witch than my Mother and have bewitched Mistress Pickering of Ellington". And the third must be "As I am a witch and a worse witch than my Mother and would have bewitched Mistress Joan Throckmorton to death in her last week of great sickness".

'All this is true,' said Smack, 'and will be proved true later. As a sign of it, you will be very well all day tomorrow and, unless a stranger comes, you will not have a fit; let the young witch do what she can. But if a stranger does come, then you must have three fits to prove her a witch. And each time any strangers come, you will have

them. But you must remember to cut your nails when you have scratched the young witch.'

'Why do I have to cut my nails?' asked Joan.

'Because,' he said, 'the young witch's blood will stick under your nails. And you must burn her blood, lest you be worse afterwards.'

'Well you remind me of it in case I forget,' said Joan, no doubt with sincerity.

'I will,' said the spirit as he departed.

'I mustn't come out of my fit unless Nan Samuel helps me out of it by one of her charges,' said Joan.

Agnes obliged, and Joan went to bed well. No strangers came to the house on the following day, which mercifully passed without incident.

But the next day, Tuesday 27 March, a stranger did knock on the door. John Dorington had arrived from London. He arrived at the manor house with his brother Francis Dorington, the vicar. John Dorington was a Justice of the Peace. He was to play a part in the trial of the Samuels. Although doubtless a stranger to Joan, he was no stranger to Robert Throckmorton. He and Robert had served together in the army that had been raised to fight the Spanish Armada under Sir Henry Cromwell.[10]

As predicted, Joan fell into one of her contortions. As a visitor, the reaction of a demoniac to sacred words had the value of novelty for John Dorington. Agnes was asked to recite the Lord's Prayer and the Creed. And, whenever she said the words 'God', or 'Jesus Christ', or 'the Holy Ghost', Joan reacted so fiercely that she could barely remain sitting on her stool. Eventually, Agnes summoned her out of her fits on three occasions by repeating the three charges that the spirit had outlined the Sunday before.

More spectators arrived on the following Thursday, 29 March. This time, the newcomers were Henry Cromwell, the son of Sir Henry, and one of his men. At the time of their arrival, Joan was well. But within fifteen minutes both she and her sister Jane fell into their fits, and, as Smack had predicted two days earlier, they were severely tormented whenever Agnes cried out 'God' or 'Christ Jesus'. As before, Joan was brought out of her fits by the charges said by Agnes.

Joan was becoming something of a local celebrity. Word was spreading, for, we are told, many strangers came to the house that week. The drama was entering its final acts, and a curious and expectant audience was gathering for entertainment and edification. This betokened no good for the Samuel family.

xiii.

Agnes Attacked

Monday 2 April 1593. It was now only two days before the assizes. This was the day on which, as Smack had predicted on 19 March, Joan was set to scratch Agnes.

Joan fell into a demonic seizure a little before supper that evening. As soon as the grace had been said following the meal, Joan advanced to the side of the table where Agnes was sitting and suddenly launched an attack on her. Gripping Agnes's head under one of her arms, she first scratched the right side of her face. When she had done her grisly work, she said, 'Now I must scratch the left side for my aunt Pickering.' Blood poured down both sides of Agnes's face.

We derive no sense from the text that Agnes resisted any of these attacks. On the contrary. Only once, as we will see, on Friday 16 March, did she go on the offensive. But then it was to no avail. Was her passivity the consequence of having given up all hope? Or did it amount to a strategic decision on her part that co-operation would, in the end, see her released, or at least in line to receive a lesser sentence? As we recall, Smack had suggested on 25 March that Agnes would do well to take her scratching patiently. And she may well have concluded that passivity was where her best interests lay. But we have heard too of her tears of anguish.

This time too, Agnes remained passive. 'The maid stood stone still' (sig.M.3.v), the text informs us. She made no attempt to get away from Joan. But she cried very pitifully, 'Lord, be merciful unto me.' Hope, if there was any left, appeared to be giving way to despair.

When Joan had finished her scratching, she sat down on her stool. Despite the lack of resistance from Agnes, the girl acted as if she were exhausted. She gasped for breath, and trembled like a leaf. This signified a spiritual struggle, of her having done battle, not with Agnes but with darker, more dangerous and spiritual powers. Joan called for scissors to cut her nails, but lacked the strength to do it. Dr Dorington's wife, Mary, took the scissors and cut her nails on her behalf. As she did so, Joan kept the pared remains. When Mary had finished, the girl threw them into the fire and called for water to wash her hands. And when she had finished her ablutions she hurled the water into the fire also. The blood of a witch, gathered under her nails and on her hands, was dangerous and needed to be disposed of carefully.

Joan fell upon her knees and asked Agnes to come and kneel by her. They said the Lord's Prayer together, and then the Creed. Agnes would get it wrong many times, and the onlookers would help her out. But it appeared to those present that Joan couldn't hear Agnes, for Joan didn't wait for her when she stumbled over the words. She ended her prayers before Agnes was halfway there.

Francis Dorington then took a prayer book and read certain prayers which he thought would be helpful. When he had finished, Joan again began exhorting Agnes to repent of her witchcraft. As she did so, the girl began to weep. She sobbed so greatly she could hardly speak though her tears.

'I didn't want to scratch you,' she said, 'but the spirit forced me to do it.'

Suddenly, Elizabeth Throckmorton advanced on Agnes. Elizabeth, we recall, had been the first to scratch Agnes on 10 March. She had also been the first to accuse John Samuel on that same day, though she was too frightened of him to scratch him. Again, having fallen into a fit, she grabbed Agnes by the hand, saying 'I must also scratch you'. She was dragged away from Agnes, not ceasing to try to scratch her until she was too exhausted to struggle further.

'Will nobody help me?' she asked, repeating her question several times.

'Will I help you, sister Elizabeth?' said Joan, still in her fit.

'Yes,' said Elizabeth, 'for God's sake.'

Joan went over to Agnes and, taking one of her hands, held it up to Elizabeth. She scratched Agnes's hand until the blood flowed. Elizabeth is reported to have been overjoyed at having drawn blood. She too cut her nails, washed her hands, and threw water and clippings into the fire.

Agnes was again to help Joan out of her fit three times by the three charges to the spirit to depart. Another charge was added: 'As I am a witch and have bewitched Elizabeth Throckmorton since my Mother confessed, so I charge the spirit to depart and allow her to be well.' And Elizabeth too emerged from her seizure.

xiv.

A Tormented Jane
Torments Agnes

Jane had been regularly suffering fits since at least the beginning of March, if not since the week before. Of all the sisters, Jane had been the most severely tormented, a fact that was attributed to her having been the first to accuse Mother Samuel. Jane was alarmingly and histrionically self-destructive. Claiming that it was the Devil who was tempting her, she had often tried to throw herself into the fire, or else drown herself. Only the prompt action of those present kept her from doing so. On some occasions, she had attempted to cut her own throat with a knife. On others, having got a knife from its sheath, she had thrown it away. She would say that while the spirit was tempting her to kill herself she was resisting, and wanting the Lord to strengthen her against temptation.

The Warboys text notes that she never made an attempt to injure herself while she was alone but only when there were others present to restrain her from doing herself real harm. The same was true of the other sisters when their behaviour was likely to be injurious. This happy coincidence required an explanation, and one that did not necessitate the suggestion that the girls were themselves complicit in ensuring that they did themselves no serious harm.

One explanation was that it was the goodness and providence of God that ensured that their behaviour, being *genuinely* self-destructive, occurred only when there were others present to rescue them from harm. The other was that their behaviour was in reality only *apparently* self-destructive, 'some secret illusion and mockery of the Devil to deceive the bystanders' (sig.M.4.v). The Devil, after all, was a consummate conjuror. In this case, their destructive urges were not real but only seemingly so. And the question of why God allowed them to have truly destructive impulses only when in the company of others was neatly side-stepped. It was a question which, the text declared, 'cannot be determined among men' (sig.M.4.v). In either case God's Providence was in play and he 'deserves the glory' (sig.M.4.v).

It was this ambiguity at the heart of things – that the same event could be read as evidence of God or Satan, together with the capacity of the Devil to mimic the good – that made all acts by those bewitched and all acts by those accused of bewitchment evidence of such sorcery, and no acts proof against it.

It was also on this Friday 16 March 1593 that Jane was to scratch Agnes. Jane was the next girl to scratch Agnes after Elizabeth had done so on 10 March, and before Joan did the same on 2 April. Jane had been regularly enduring her worst attacks before or after meals. On this day, as she sat having lunch, it seemed to others present that something sat on the table and was conversing with her about Agnes Samuel. For a while, Jane sat there as if listening. She was looking back with a sad face to Agnes, who stood behind her, and shaking her head as if in great sorrow.

Jane had often been told by her sisters that the spirit had informed them that she would scratch Agnes before the assizes. And she in turn had always replied that she would not succumb, let the Devil do what he could against her. She had also been directly informed by the spirit himself that she would scratch Agnes. She had often reported this. But, just as often, she claimed always to have defied him.

That evening, at suppertime, Jane soon fell into a severe fit, bowing and bending her body. Her hands shook so much that she could not hold steady the knife with which she tried to slash her arms. When this attack had blown itself out, the spirit seemed to speak to her again. Jane regarded Agnes as before, showing even greater signs of sorrow. Quite suddenly, she stood up from the table, and moved to its far end. She fixed Alice with a baleful stare. It was recognised that she was unable to speak, her mouth having been locked up by the spirit. Agnes was asked to enquire how she was. 'The worse for you, you young witch,' said Jane, turning her face aside as if she could not bear to look at her. It was the first time Jane had called her 'witch'. She continued to question her as she had been instructed. But Jane, covering the ear that was closer to Agnes, said that she couldn't stand to see or hear her. When Agnes was told to ask her what the matter was, she replied, 'The spirit says that I have to scratch you.'

'When do you have to scratch me?' Agnes asked.

But Jane's mouth was again sealed by the spirit, so that she could not respond. She began then to weep, 'most lamentably' (sig.N.1.v). Yet her sorrow was mixed with rage towards Agnes, her teeth clenched 'as if the evil spirit had been whetting and kindling her fury against the maid' (sig.N.1.v). Fifteen minutes later, Agnes was persuaded to ask Jane again when she would scratch her. Able to hear, but unable to speak, Jane responded in sign language to Agnes's questions, holding one finger upwards to mean 'yes', pointing it downwards to mean 'no'. It was ascertained that she intended to scratch Agnes after supper, as soon as grace had been said. In response to Agnes's question about where she would be scratched, Jane indicated by sign that it would be on her right hand, the opposite to that which Elizabeth had scratched earlier in the week.

For the next half an hour, the girl wept pitifully while occasionally rushing angrily towards Agnes from where she sat, as though she would scratch her before the announced time. On one occasion, she assaulted her so fiercely it was as if she wished to pull the flesh on her hands from the bones. Yet she was scarcely able to mark Agnes's skin.

'The spirit that stands next to me tells me,' said Jane, 'that Pluck holds your heart and your hand and will not allow the blood to come.'

In the meantime, sent for by Robert Throckmorton, a small crowd had gathered. Francis Dorington asked those present to pray with him. During prayers, Jane remained quiet. But, as soon as the prayers had ended, she launched herself once more at Agnes. With tears coursing down her cheeks, she screamed, 'I don't want to scratch you, but the spirit is making me, saying that I have to scratch you, just as much as my sisters have done, and as my sister Joan must do before the assizes.'

When Jane first began to scratch Agnes, the latter moved to get away from the child. But Jane followed her on her knees, saying, 'I must draw blood from you. I must have my pennies' worth from you. I know that you are crying. The spirit has told me that I would not be able to hear you so that I cannot pity you.'

When at last she was tired and out of breath, she stopped scratching. She wiped off Agnes's blood from her hands.

Francis Dorington began then to try to compel Agnes towards a confession. 'God,' he said, 'would surely not allow you to be accused by these wicked spirits, and scratched by these innocent children against their wills, if you weren't consenting to, or at least concealing some knowledge of, these wicked practices to which your Mother has confessed.'

Agnes denied it all. Compliant she may have been. But, unlike her mother, she was not going to be drawn into a false confession. She went on the attack herself.

'If I am guilty of these matters,' she said, 'I pray God may send some sign upon me so that all will know if I am.'

Soon after uttering these words, her nose began to bleed profusely. No doubt the temptation was strong to see this as a sign sent by God of her guilt. But it was known that she had already had four nosebleeds that day. And, fortunately for Agnes, she had said on each occasion that she hoped that these nosebleeds did not foreshadow any evil that might afflict her. Since there was no reason for God to have sent the earlier nosebleeds, it was difficult to certify him as the direct cause of this latest one.

Probably to Agnes's intense relief, the group's attention shifted to Jane when she began now to speak again. With Agnes resistant, Jane focused on her absent father. On 10 March Elizabeth had accused John Samuel. *She* was too scared of him to scratch him. But Jane now took up the challenge herself. 'The Thing that stands by me,' she said, 'tells me that I must not come out of this fit until the maid's Father comes and says what I tell him.'

'What will you say?' Agnes was told to ask her.

Jane made no immediate reply. Again, she had become deaf. Eventually she spoke, as if to the spirit. 'What? Has her Father come into the reckoning again? Will I never come out of my fit until he says the words "Even as I am a witch and consented to the death of the Lady Cromwell, I charge the spirit to depart and Mistress Jane to be well". I always thought he was as bad as any of them. He looks so evil.'

Robert Throckmorton asked Henry Pickering, the children's uncle, and two others to go and see if they could at last persuade John Samuel to come. Point-blank, he refused. Every day, until the assizes, Robert despatched someone to plead with him to relent. He even went round himself. But John Samuel remained adamant in his decision. This was a trap into which he had no intention of walking.

Two days later, on the morning of Sunday 18 March, the spirit came again to Jane. We can assume that Jane was well aware that John Samuel had twice refused to visit. So she applied still greater pressure to Agnes. And Agnes learned for the first time that, for her, there was now no way out.

'The Thing says that I should not both see and hear the young witch and the Thing all at the same time. It tells me that I must be tormented, like my sister Joan, whenever the young witch says the word "God". It says that I must not come out of my fit, not this week nor the next, nor perhaps ever, until one of these three things comes to pass. Either your Father must come and speak these words to me

"Even as I am a witch and have consented to the death of the Lady Cromwell". Or you must confess that you are a witch and have bewitched me and my sisters. Or else you must be hanged.'

This must have been the fateful day on which Agnes realised that resistance to these dreadful events was futile, and that in compliance and co-operation lay her best hope.

'Will you come out of your fit whenever and wherever my Father speaks these words?' Agnes was asked to enquire. Correspondingly, Jane asked the same of the spirit.

'She will,' he replied. And so he departed.

Jane persisted in her condition. Sometimes she would sit all day depressed, speaking to nobody or wanting any company. At other times she turned light-hearted and happy, playing with her sisters for the better part of the day, yet not hearing or seeing a soul. When anyone passed by her, she would say, 'There goes a coloured gown. I wonder how it moves on its own.' Or else she would cry, 'Over there is a pair of socks, or a hat, a pair of shoes, or a cloak. But I can't see anything else.' If anyone showed her their hand with a ring on it, she would say, 'There's a ring hanging in the air. I wonder how it hangs with nobody holding it.'

Mealtimes were exceedingly difficult. All of a sudden, Jane would be struck dumb. Agnes had to come and put a knife between the girl's lips, at which point she would be able to take food again. This recurred five or six times during a meal and for the whole period of three weeks before the assizes. In fact, Jane was to remain in her torments until 4 April, when she appeared before Justice Fenner in the Huntingdon court.

XV.

The Play of the Possessed

How are we to understand the behaviour of the Throckmorton children over this period of three years? Were they genuinely possessed? Were they suffering from collective mental illness? Were they faking it?

To their contemporaries, it must have seemed that the girls were genuinely possessed by capricious demons. Contemporary medicine had proved ineffectual. And the girls clearly showed many of the signs of possession. They exhibited paranormal strength together with bouts of extreme physical rigidity. They cried and gnashed their teeth. They were violent both to themselves and others. At times, they lost the use of their senses, not being able to hear, speak, or see. They had difficulties in eating. They clairvoyantly knew what was happening elsewhere. They had visions of spirits and spectres. They spent long periods in trances. They reacted violently and aggressively to prayer and Bible reading. They stayed 'in character' for long periods of time, apparently communicating with the various spirits who had taken up residence within them.

The predisposition to believe that they were possessed was certainly present among many of the spectators, at least as much as the will to persuade themselves and others was present in the children. Not that many of the witnesses to their possession would have needed much persuasion. For the children were consummate 'performers'. And, like many other demoniacs of the time, they learned 'on the job', as it were. Their demonic repertoire became increasingly sophisticated and developed during the period of their seizures. It must have been well nigh impossible, given the verisimilitude of their performances, for those who saw them to think that this was all a charade. That they were frauds was a charge made only by the Samuels. And the spirits in the children punished the latter for their doubts.

So the Throckmorton girls fulfilled most if not all of the early modern criteria for being possessed by the Devil. Indeed, so central was their story to early modern English understandings of possession that they were crucial in its construction. They set the benchmark against which possession and bewitchment were measured subsequently. In this sense, they were *genuinely* possessed.

Were they liars and dissemblers? From the perspective of *The Witches of Warboys*, the answer clearly is 'no'. To prove the authenticity of their possession and the guilt of the Samuels was the clear intention of the book. But what about behind the text? The answer to that question is more complex.

In the case of the Throckmorton children, as with other contemporary demoniacs, the line between simulated and non-simulated behaviour is hard to draw. The girls are, at some times, both associated with and dissociated from their actions at particular moments. At other times, they move from what seems uncalculated to cunningly predetermined behaviour. At some times they seem genuinely oblivious to their actions. When they hear what they have done, they regret their behaviour. But at other times they appear actively and cruelly to revel in it. They learned from each other and from those around them how to be 'possessed'. They were certainly fakes at times. But they were too good at it to be merely consummate actors.

Were they ill? Even for their contemporaries, the answer was both 'yes' and 'no'. In the context of early modern England, the line between possession and a variety of 'natural' illnesses – epilepsy, melancholy, worms, 'the Mother' – was hard to draw. And it was difficult to distinguish between the ill, the possessed, and the charlatan. This was in part because symptoms overlapped. But it was also because, in Elizabethan England, the three categories also interconnected, and the three modes of explanation were not necessarily incompatible. The Devil could be involved not only in genuine possession but also in illness and charlatanry. To diagnose the one was not to exclude the others.

From the perspective of the twenty-first century, we are not inclined to think the possibility of 'possession'. Nor are we generally prone to seeing the realm of the demonic as a possible cause, direct or indirect, of ill health or fakery. The demonic is not a category of explanation open to most of us who operate within a Western framework not determined by the supernatural.

We can conclude that, though there were elements of the fraudulent in their activities, the children were more than mere fakes. A judgement as to how much more than mere fakes they were is a difficult one to make. If we wished to begin to formulate an answer to this question, we should probably look to the discourse of 'mental health' and 'mental illness'. And we should ask where to situate the girls on the continuum from the one to the other.

Any conclusions drawn about their mental health will also have ramifications for the extent to which we might wish to hold the children morally responsible for their actions, and their accusations. Were they mad or bad? And at what point can the former excuse the latter? Regardless of their mental state, the moral culpability of the children depends too on the extent to which we see children generally as moral beings, and at what age we believe moral and immoral acts to be attributable to them.

The moral guilt of the children is also mitigated by the responsibility of the adults in this story. And the guilt of the Throckmortons, their relatives, and friends may be mitigated too by the fact that they were not acting out of ill intent towards their neighbours the Samuels, but were driven by concern for the good of their children. The children were the leading actors in this drama. But their parents and relatives, the villagers of Warboys, the religious and legal authorities, even the Samuels themselves, all contributed to the outcome. These are complex issues now, and were made more difficult then by the context of sorcery and Satanism in which they were imbedded.

All had roles in this poignant drama of village life. And the roles of all those who participated were played out, improvised, developed, embellished, and refined over a long period of time within the format of a loosely constructed script – of sorcery, witchcraft, and Satanic possession known to all. So the facts and the fictitious, the authentic and the fake, overlapped indistinguishably in a 'real-life' drama. This was a deadly morality play, one which created its own reality for the children, the Throckmorton family and friends, and the Samuels.

xvi.

A Capital Crime

As the date for her return to Huntingdon for trial approached, Agnes must have wondered if her situation could possibly get any worse. She was certainly in a more precarious position than when she had returned from Huntingdon to the manor house in Warboys. At that time, she was implicated in her mother's bewitchment of the children, though there was no evidence to that effect. Now, along with her father and mother, she was not only held to be culpable for the bewitchment of the children, but was seen as the prime mover in the death of Lady Cromwell.

The Samuels were supposed to have been in control of the spirits. But, ironically, the children (or the spirits in them) had outwitted their supposed puppet masters at every turn.

And now they faced a death sentence. This looked like the final curtain for the yeoman family caught up in an escalating conflict that had now assumed its own momentum. Was there any way out – any possible way of escape? Or was this truly the end of the road?

Part Four

The Trial:

4 April to 6 April 1593

i.

John Samuel's Day in Court

On the morning of Wednesday 4 April 1593, Joan and Jane Throckmorton made their way to Huntingdon. We can assume that, riding along with them, travelled their parents. Agnes went along too. Witnesses who were to appear against the Samuels probably made the journey at the same time – Francis Dorington, Gilbert Pickering of Titchmarsh Grove, Robert Throckmorton of Brampton, and John and Henry Pickering. It seems probable that John Samuel was taken into custody also and made the journey to Huntingdon on that same day.

It is difficult from the materials that have survived to reconstruct the trial of the Samuels. The chronology of the events in the text is confused. And, while in early modern England there were clear procedures laid down in principle, in practice there was much variation.[1]

Unlike Alice and Agnes, John had not yet had a day in court. But, by the afternoon of 4 April, John was being examined for committal to trial. Jane was present too, and was in a trance. Both were appearing before Judge Edward Fenner. He had been appointed a judge of the King's Bench in 1590. This was to be the case for which he is most remembered by posterity.

Appearing in the court, and now in a fit, Jane was asked many questions. The Devil would not, however, allow her to speak. Even though her eyes were open, and her father, her relatives, and family friends were in the court, she gave no sign at all of recognising any of them.

John Samuel was present in the lower bar with other prisoners. Edward Fenner had been forewarned that, were John Samuel to speak certain words, then Jane would come out of her seizure. So, at the judge's request, Samuel was moved from the lower to the upper bar, near the clerk of the court, and close to Jane.

'Is there any means by which you can bring Jane out of her fit?' John was asked by the judge.

'No,' he replied.

'I want you to say these words,' he said: '"as I am a witch and did consent to the death of the Lady Cromwell, so I charge the Devil to allow Mistress Jane to come out of her fit".'

'I will not say them,' replied John Samuel.

In order to give him encouragement, the judge himself then said the words to Jane. And, at his request, Francis Dorington and others present did likewise. Still he refused. Many prayers were then said by the judge and others in an attempt to bring relief to Jane. But she remained in her trance-like state. At the judge's request, John Samuel agreed to pray for her. Whenever he said 'God' or 'Jesus Christ', the child's head, shoulders, and arms shook severely, worse than before. Justice Fenner's patience eventually ran out.

'If you will not say the words of the charm,' he said sternly, 'the court will hold you guilty of the crimes of which you are accused.'

Thus, in the end and under much duress, John Samuel said in a loud voice, 'As I am a witch and did consent to the death of the Lady Cromwell, so I charge the Devil to allow Mistress Jane to come out of her fit.'

These words were no sooner spoken than Jane wiped her eyes and came out of her fit. Seeing her father, she knelt down and asked his blessing. And she curtsied to her uncles who were standing nearby.

'Oh Lord, Father,' she cried, 'where am I?'

Alluding to the passage in the Old Testament in which Saul, troubled by an evil spirit, received comfort when David played his harp,[2] the judge said, 'She is now well, but not with the music of David's harp.'

John Samuel, we may assume, was bound over for trial and lodged in the gaol, within the cell next to his wife that was reserved for men.

ii.

Joan, the Judges and the Justices

O n their arrival in Huntingdon the Throckmortons had lodged at the Crown Inn, which was close to the gaol, and next to the Church of St Mary. Joan had seemed to be well on the way there. But, within half an hour of entering her room in the inn, she fell into a trance. She was soon being visited by the curious locals. She sat so quietly they could not believe anything was wrong with her.

Agnes too was there, and those present turned their attention to her. If the bewitched would not perform properly, maybe the witch would. She was asked about her faith and her service of God. She answered that she served God like others did. But, at the mention of the word 'God', Joan reacted violently. The crowd brought her over closer to Agnes. They asked Agnes to say the Lord's Prayer and the Creed. But, before she was halfway through, they stopped her. Joan had become severely tormented and afflicted. They were all amazed – and convinced – of her supernatural affliction. They continued talking with Agnes. And, whenever she said 'God' or 'Jesus Christ', Joan reacted startlingly. When Agnes cried 'Oh God of Heaven and Earth, help me', or 'Jesus Christ, the Son of God, be merciful unto me', Joan's torments were doubled. The onlookers were fascinated and horrified.

One gentleman there present tried another experiment. He persuaded Agnes to say to Joan 'My God help you', or '*My* God preserve and deliver you', or 'The God whom I serve defend you and be merciful unto you'. This was similar to the unsuccessful attempt of Henry Pickering to get Alice to confess to worshipping another god by the Warboys pond. Henry, we may suspect, is at it again. But, on this occasion, he had Joan to provide the proof. And, this time, the Devil in Joan did not respond violently. The demon in Joan was not to be troubled or concerned by the mention of his own master rather than his divine nemesis. The experiment, we read, was tried a hundred times that day. In all, five hundred men observed it.

That evening, after the court had finished its business for the day, Joan received a visit from Judge Edward Fenner. He too was staying at the Crown. Along with a number of Justices of the Peace and other gentlemen, he met Joan in the garden. After some conversation between her and the judge she fell into a fit. Her eyes were closed, her shoulders were shaking, and her arms were stretched out. Unable to stand, she was assisted by her father into an arbour, followed by the judge and the rest of the group. There she was severely tormented. All prayed for her release, but to no avail.

Robert had enquired of the spirit on 25 March whether Joan would have her fits before the judge at the assizes were she carried there. So far the spirit had been proved right. Robert took the opportunity to incriminate Agnes before the judge. He indicated to Fenner that Agnes was able to relieve Joan's torments. Judge Fenner had Agnes brought forward. Robert informed the judge of the charge which would release Agnes from her fit: 'As I am a witch, and a worse witch than my Mother, and did consent to the death of the Lady Cromwell, so I charge the Devil to let Mistress Joan Throckmorton now come out of her fit.' To test the charge, Edward Fenner himself, Robert Throckmorton, Francis Dorington, and others all said it. It had no effect. The judge and others then prayed for Joan's release. Again, no effect was to be seen.

Agnes was then commanded by the judge to pray to God to ease Joan's sufferings. Whenever Agnes said the words 'God' or 'Jesus Christ', Joan's sufferings were increased. Then Agnes was commanded to say 'As I am not a witch, neither did consent to the death of the Lady Cromwell, so I charge the Devil to let Mistress Joan now come out of her fit'. The spirit in Joan was unmoved. Finally, Agnes was commanded to say 'As I am a witch and a worse witch than my Mother, and did consent to the death of the Lady Cromwell, so I charge the Devil to let Mistress Joan Throckmorton come out of her fit now'. No sooner had Agnes spoken these words than Joan, wiping her eyes, came out of her trance and made a deep curtsy to the judge. Assuming the presence within Joan of an evil spirit, this was no doubt impressive evidence of Agnes's power over demons.

Fifteen minutes later, Joan again had a seizure, shaking one leg after the other, then one arm after the other, and then her head and shoulders. All those present were distressed and prayed without result for her release. Agnes was again forced to repeat another charm: 'As I am a witch and would have bewitched Mistress Joan Throckmorton to death in her great week of sickness, so I charge you Devil to let Mistress Joan now come out of her fit.' Joan was soon well again.

'Where have you been?' Justice Fenner asked Joan.

'I have been asleep,' she replied.

'I pray that God send you no more such sleeps,' said the judge.

Soon afterward, Joan again fell into another fit, with 'a most terrible and strange kind of sneezing, and other violent actions'. All were moved to pray to God to save her, fearing that her head would burst or her eyes fall out of their sockets. The judge moved quickly and commanded Agnes to say a third charge: 'As I am a witch and did bewitch Mistress Pickering of Ellington since my Mother's confession, so I charge you Devil to let Mistress Joan come out of her fit now.'

Joan was soon as untroubled as she had ever been in her life. It was as Smack had predicted on 25 March. She would have her fits before the judge and she would have no more after the assizes.

iii.

A Trial of Witches

On Thursday 5 April, before eight o'clock in the morning, the grand jury assembled for the formal proceedings. It was the grand jury's duty to examine all the evidence up to that point and determine if the matter should proceed to trial. It met privately. The indictments, the formal record of the charges against the Samuels, were made and presented to the jury members.[3] In this case three charges were levelled. The Samuels were all indicted for bewitching Lady Cromwell to death, contrary to God's laws and the statute against witchcraft made in 1563. The remaining two indictments concerned their having bewitched Mistress Jane Throckmorton and others, contrary to the same statute.

The confessions which Alice had already made would have been read to the jury. Witnesses were then called. As far as we know, none appeared for the defence of the Samuels. And all those who appeared against them were either Throckmortons (Robert and his cousin Robert from Brampton) or were relatives and friends (Francis Dorington, whose brother John was also sitting on the bench, Gilbert Pickering of Titchmarsh Grove, John and Henry Pickering, and Thomas Nut, vicar of Ellington from 1575–1594, and a graduate of Peterhouse College, Cambridge).[4]

The grand jury did not delay. The indictments were formally marked as 'true bills'. And Alice, Agnes, and John were handed over for trial.

The formal court proceedings in front of Edward Fenner began at eight. The brevity of the proceedings before the grand jury gave the impression of 'rubber-stamping'. This could not be said of the trial itself. All the evidence presented to the grand jury was read out to the judge and 'the jury of life and death', including the two confessions already made by Alice. Court business lasted for five hours.

A guilty verdict was inevitable. The children had been convincingly bewitched for a long time, and some were still in a desperate state. There was strong testimony from a large number of respectable local gentry and clergy which authenticated the children and underlined the complicity of the Samuels. There was supernatural evidence too – the spirits responded to orders from the Samuels to cease tormenting the children, although only on those occasions on which the Samuels admitted to being witches. And Alice Samuel had confessed to sorcery on at least five separate occasions: twice to Robert, once in church, once to a Church court, and once to a committal court.

All in all, it was more than reasonable for the jury to have concluded that the children were indeed bewitched. It was also far from unreasonable for its members to conclude that Alice was guilty. And, although Agnes and John had not themselves confessed, it was feasible to conclude that her husband and daughter had colluded with her, all the way down the line.

For us, the question is, granting the impossibility of the charges being true, and thus the consequent irrelevance and weakness of any supposed evidence for them, how could the Samuels have been found guilty? For the jury, the question was, granting the possibility of the charges being true, and the consequent relevance and strength of the evidence for them, how could they have been found innocent? Was it unreasonable and unjust to have found them guilty? What is 'reasonable' and what is 'just' depend on the criteria of reason and justice employed. And these differ within different cultural contexts. In this context, a guilty verdict was neither unreasonable nor unjust.

The Samuels were not permitted to present a defence. But it is difficult in any case to imagine what kind of defence could have been presented. The 'bewitchment' performance of the Throckmorton girls was far too convincing for the charge of 'wantonness in the children' to stick. And, if in late 1589 the Samuels had no reason to wish the Throckmortons harm, and therefore no reason to bewitch the children, relations between the families had been stretched to the absolute limits during the intervening years. The Samuels had not wished the Throckmortons ill to begin with. But they could easily have been forgiven for not wishing them well later on. And, of course, Alice *had* confessed, perhaps had even come to believe that, in some way or another, she really was responsible for the children's misfortunes and afflictions.

It may not have been, from our later perspective, a fair trial. But it was not a mere show trial, and the text is determined to persuade us of it:

So many of these proofs, presumptions, circumstances, and reasons contained in this book, was at large delivered, as that time would afford, which was five hours, without intermission or interruption, until both the Judge, Justices, and Jury said openly that the cause was most apparent: their consciences were well satisfied that the said witches were guilty, and had deserved death. (sig.O.1.r)

John Samuel was his characteristically ungracious self. He cursed his wife. 'A plague of God light on you,' he said, 'for you are she that has brought us all to this, and we may thank you for it' (sig. O.2.v). But he did have a point. For neither he nor his daughter Agnes had confessed to anything. And it was his wife's initial confession of witchcraft shortly before Christmas the year before that had seen not only Alice Samuel but also her daughter and husband formally charged with witchcraft for the bewitching to death of Lady Cromwell, the wife of Sir Henry Cromwell, and the bewitching of the children of Sir Robert Throckmorton and others. And her several confessions already made would have been enough to convince any jury.

After five hours of evidence, the judge had had enough. We cannot be certain if he directed the jury to find the Samuels guilty. This was not uncommon practice. What we are told is that the judge, the justices on the bench, and the jury openly declared that their consciences were well satisfied, that the said witches were guilty, and that they deserved to die for their crimes.

For witchcraft trials of the period, five hours was a considerable time. Doubtless, with Cromwell and Throckmorton reputations on the line, it was in their families' interests to ensure that justice was not only done but seen to be done. But that it had gone on for so long was, at least in part, the result of unexpected witnesses who wanted their day in court – Robert Poulter, vicar of Brampton, Robert Throckmorton of Brampton again, and the Huntingdon gaoler. They were all convinced that the Samuels had spread their vindictiveness – and their maleficia – well beyond Warboys manor and Ramsey Abbey.

iv.

Witnesses for the Prosecution

The Evidence of Robert Poulter, Vicar and Curate of Brampton.

One of my parishioners, John Langley, is still lying very ill in his bed. He told me that, one day, he was at Huntingdon at the Sign of the Crown. In the hearing of old Mother Samuel, he forbade Master Knowles of Brampton to give her any food for she was an old witch. That afternoon, as he went from Huntingdon to Brampton, although he had a good horse under him, it died on the way. Within two days, by the Providence of God, he escaped death two or three times. Though it pleased God not to allow the Devil to have the mastery of his body at that time, yet he soon after lost as many good and well cattle worth, to all men's judgments, twenty marks. Not long after, he himself was extremely ill.

John Langley is said to have died that night.

Robert Throckmorton of Brampton had already given evidence to the grand jury on the children's behalf. But he also had his own story to tell.

The Evidence of Robert Throckmorton of Brampton.

At Huntingdon and in other places I spoke very rudely to Mother Samuel. On a Friday ten days later, I had one of my two year old beasts die. The next week after, on the Friday, I had a yearling calf die, and the following Sunday another calf of the same herd and a similar age. In the following week, on the Friday, I had a hog die, and the next Sunday a sow with ten pigs sucking on her side. I was given advice that, whatever died next, I should make a hole in the ground and burn it. In the fourth week, on a Friday, I had a very good cow worth four marks die. My servants made a hole in the ground and placed the cow in it. They threw wood on her and burnt her. After that, all the cattle did well.

Robert Throckmorton's suspicion of witchcraft was correct. The counter-magic had worked. Mother Samuel, we read, confessed that night to bewitching the cattle.

The scratching of Agnes and Alice by the children had been a dismal failure. The girls had been allowed to scratch them by their parents in spite of the latter's misgivings. And it had not worked. But in one case, that of the gaoler's manservant, it did.

The Evidence of the Gaoler of Huntingdon.

A manservant of mine found Mother Samuel very unruly while she was a prisoner. So he chained her to a bedpost. Not long after this, he felt sick. In all respects, he acted just like the children. His bodied heaved up and down, and his arms, legs and head shook. He had more strength than any two men. He cried out against Mother Samuel saying that she bewitched him. He remained extremely ill like this until he died five or six days later.

Not long after his death, one of my sons fell ill. He acted for the most part like my manservant had. It was obvious that he was bewitched. I went into the prison and brought Mother Samuel to my son's bedside. I held her there until my son had scratched her. Soon after, my son recovered.

Sentence of death was passed on all three of the Samuels.

The jury having delivered its verdict, Judge Edward Fenner asked John Samuel if he had any reasons to give why a death sentence should not be put into effect. When he realised that there was nothing to be done that could save him, he asked God to have mercy on his soul.

The judge then asked Alice the same question. She 'pleaded the belly', as we have seen, to no avail. He then asked Agnes in her turn if she had anything to say. As was common at the time, other prisoners were standing in the dock waiting to receive their sentences. To Agnes, one of these whispered: 'Say that you also are with child.' It must have been tempting. But the cost would have been very high. A determination by women of the period to defend their reputation, particularly in matters of sexual morality, was typical of the times. To be called a 'whore' was the most common grounds for suing for defamation in the Church courts of York in the 1590s.[5] Sexual reputation was not to be given away lightly. And she would have known that it was unlikely to succeed. So it is not surprising that the cost of attempting to save her life, or at least attempting to postpone her death, at the expense of her reputation was too great a price to pay for Agnes Samuel. In that light, her reply can the more readily be understood. 'No,' she said, 'I will not do that. It shall never be said that I was both a witch and a whore.'

Agnes and her parents were remanded to be hanged the following day.

Both Agnes and John would go to their deaths without admitting their guilt. Alice had never confessed to having bewitched Lady Cromwell to death. And, on the morning of her execution, she was again to refuse to do so. But her resolve not to confess to the murder of Susan Cromwell did not last long.

V.

An Execution of Witches

The next day, Friday 5 April 1593, was the day of their executions. All three were visited in prison by a number of godly men. Among them was John Dorington, Justice of the County of Huntingdon, and brother to Francis Dorington, the vicar of the parish of Warboys. Their motives were no doubt well intentioned. They were there to persuade all three that it was desirable that, at the point of execution, they should confess to their misdeeds to witness that justice had been done.

But they were motivated also by their desire that those about to be executed should leave this earth reconciled to God, and to their fate. In so doing they would be reconciled too with that community whose lives they had disrupted and whose laws they had broken. So it was no doubt a disappointment to them that Mother Samuel, in spite of her previous confessions, denied bewitching Lady Cromwell, and this in spite of her husband's beseeching her to confess the truth: '[O]ne way or another,' he said, 'you did it' (sig.O.3.r). And it was no doubt a disappointment too that John and Agnes Samuel do not appear to have been willing to die a 'good death'.

It was but a ten-minute walk from the Huntingdon gaol to Mill Common, the place of public execution (see Plate 19). We can see the gallows in the fields in the map of Huntingdon drawn by John Speed in 1611 (see Plate 20). Their execution was a public one. At least forty people were present.

Faced with the prospect of imminent death, with the noose around her neck and standing on a ladder about to be kicked out from under her, Mother Samuel changed her mind yet again. Asked by the presiding clergyman, Master Doctor Chamberlin, she confessed to having bewitched Lady Cromwell to death and to having bewitched the children of Robert Throckmorton. Asked whether her husband was an accessory to the death of Lady Cromwell, she said that he was. Asked if her husband was a witch or had any skill in witchcraft, she said that he did. This was her only act of malice against a man who, many may have agreed, deserved it. But she would not implicate her daughter. Even at the point of death, she tried to save Agnes: 'She would in no way confess anything, but fought by all means to clear her' (sig.O.3.v).

Master Doctor Chamberlin asked Alice Samuel to recite the Lord's Prayer and the Creed. She no doubt saw it as an apt preparation for her death. She recited the Lord's Prayer until she came to say 'But deliver us from evil'. Over these words, she stumbled. In her recital of the Creed she left much out, and did not say that she believed in the Holy Catholic Church. Some may have seen her inability as a result of her simplicity, some as the consequence of her terror. For the authorities at least, her stumbling performance provided indirect evidence of her guilt. For a witch was deemed incapable of saying the Creed or the Lord's Prayer without faltering. Her prayers both redeemed and condemned her.

The Confession of the old Woman Alice Samuel to certain Questions asked of her by Master Doctor Chamberlin, at the Time and Place of her Execution, being upon the Ladder.

'What were the names of those spirits with which you bewitched?'

'They were called Pluck, Catch, and White,' she replied, repeating them again and again.

'Did you bewitch the Lady Cromwell to death or not?'

'I did,' she replied.

'With which of your spirits did you bewitch the Lady to death?'

'With Catch,' she said.

'Why did you do it?' Chamberlin asked her.

'Because the Lady had some of my hair and hair-lace burned. Catch wanted me to have my revenge of her. I told him to go and do what he wanted.'

'What did Catch say when he returned?'

'He said that he had had his revenge,' she replied. And she confessed again her responsibility for Lady Cromwell's death.

'Upon my death, I am guilty of it.'

'Did you bewitch Master Throckmorton's children?' she was asked.

'Yes,' she replied.

'With which of your spirits did you do it?'

'With Pluck,' she said.

'What did you tell him to do?' Chamberlin asked her.

'I told him to go and torment them, but not to hurt them.'

'For how long will they be tormented?'

'I cannot tell. I haven't seen Pluck since last Christmas.'

'What did you do with White?'

'I never used him to do harm,' she said. 'I sent him to sea. He sucked on my chin. But I never rewarded the other two. I had these spirits from Langley. I don't know where he lives.'

'Was your husband privy to the death of the Lady Cromwell?' she was asked.

'He was,' she said.

'Is he a witch, and does he have skills in witchcraft?'

'Yes, and he can both bewitch and un-bewitch.'

John Samuel remained determined to confess nothing. And, like his wife, he denied that his daughter Agnes had any involvement in sorcery. He went to his death without admitting to anything, or acknowledging culpability of any sort.

As did Agnes. As she stood upon the ladder awaiting her death, she was asked by Master Doctor Chamberlin to confess. She refused. Untutored she may have been, but she was not willing to confess to a crime of which she was utterly innocent.

Epilogue

i.

The Witch's Mark

For Michael Dalton's *The Countrey Justice*, the keeping of familiars was the first proof of witchcraft. The second was the witch's mark. Witches, he wrote, have 'some big or little teat upon their body, where he sucks them. And besides their sucking, the Devil leaves other marks upon their body, sometimes like a blue spot, or red spot, like a flea-biting... And these Devil's marks be insensible, and being pricked will not bleed, and be often in their secretest parts, and therefore require diligent and careful search.'[1]

In 1566, in the trial of Mother Agnes Waterhouse, the marks of the accused were examined at the request of the Queen's attorney: 'And then the gaoler lifted up her headscarf on her head and there was divers spots in her face and one on her nose. Then said the Queen's Attorney, "In good faith, Agnes, when did he suck of your blood last?" "By my faith, my Lord," said she, "not this fortnight."'[2]

Later, juries of women were on occasion empanelled during trials to search for witch's marks that were believed to be found in the genital area. Alice Samuel was to play her part in the development of this idea. Even in 1593, we can read *The Witches of Warboys* as early evidence of the transition of the witch's mark from the face to the genital parts. It occurs in the second last paragraph of the work.

In the case of Alice Samuel, a jury was not formed during the trial to examine her. But, after her execution, the gaoler stripped Alice, her daughter, and her husband of their clothes, and found upon the naked body of Alice a small lump of flesh, 'sticking out as if it had been a teat to the length of half an inch' (sig.O.3.v). Initially, the gaoler and his wife intended to say nothing, 'because it was adjoining to so secret a place which was not decent to be seen' (sigs. O.3.v–O.4.r). The mark was on Alice's upper thigh.

Eventually, deciding not to conceal it, and covering Alice's private parts, they displayed it to the forty people present. The gaoler's wife squeezed the teat. From it there came 'beesenings' – a mixture of yellow milk and water, then a liquid like clear milk, and finally blood. There is no hint in the text that this is the place at which Alice fed her familiars. But, with its teat-like nature, and the emission of milk and blood – the two principal foods of familiars – there is little doubt that its readers would have thought of it as such.[3] With its proximity to the genitals, those of a more Continental demonological mindset would have seen it as further evidence of demonic sexuality.

The story of Alice Samuel thus ends with the visible evidence on her dead body of her witchcraft, both in the English and the Continental mode. It must have brought, if not joy, at least satisfaction to the Throckmortons. For them, no doubt, this mark was the final evidence of her guilt. It was a powerful sign too of their moral rectitude, and of their Puritan piety.

ii.

In Good Estate and Perfect Health

From the day of the execution onwards, the Throckmorton children were hale. They 'have all of them been', we read, 'in as good estate and as perfect health as ever from their birth' (sig.O.4.r). We know little of their later lives. We catch mere glimpses of them marrying into Huntingdonshire and Bedfordshire families and, we can only assume, leading relatively normal adult lives.

After the executions, Robert Throckmorton and his family were to leave Warboys. Within five years he was back in Ellington, the village in which he may have been brought up. It is tempting to think that the villagers of Warboys ultimately came to believe that an old and fairly simple woman had confessed to crimes for which she was innocent, and that she, her daughter, and her husband – and not the Throckmorton children – were the real victims in this case. The Throckmortons, no longer welcome in Warboys, moved on. The Samuels' relatives too may have left Warboys. The Warboys Parish Registers continue until 1662. But we find no mention of any Samuels after the burial of a Francis Samuel on 9 April 1592.

The goods of the Samuels became the property of Sir Henry Cromwell. Perhaps unwilling to profit from the deaths of such criminals, he gave the £40 from their sale to sponsor an annual sermon to be preached on 25 March in All Saints Church in Huntingdon. To be delivered by a Doctor or Bachelor of Divinity from Queens' College, Cambridge, Sir Henry's old college, it was intended 'to inveigh and preach against sorcery'.[4] The preacher was to receive forty shillings, of which it was intended that ten shillings should be distributed to the poor, and part of the Huntingdon corporation to be treated to dinner. The last All Saints annual sermon was preached by the Reverend C.G. Gorham in 1812.

A collection of four of these sermons from the years 1792–1795 was published under the title *The Inantity* [sic] *and Mischief of vulgar Superstitions*. Two hundred years later, and the sermon was no longer serving its intended purpose as an incentive against sorcery.

'The sin of Witchcraft,' declared the editor, M.J. Naylor, 'has long ceased to be the theme of their annual discourses, nor has the subject ever been mentioned, except to explode, and deprecate the lamentable effects of, such miserable delusions.'[5]

'The sin of Witchcraft' had brought to an end the lives of Alice, Agnes, and John Samuel. It is not without irony that their estate went to fund sermons that, two hundred years later, if the sins of witchcraft and sorcery were mentioned at all, saw them as nothing but 'miserable delusions'.

> And thus ye haue the Storie of these three Witches of Warboyse, so plainly and briefly, as may be deliuered vnto you Gods blessed Name be euermore praised for the same. Amen.

Notes

NOTES TO PROLOGUE

1   Statute 5 Eliz. I, cap.15. See Sharpe, James, *Witchcraft in Early Modern England* (London: Longman, 2001), p.99.

2   Arber, Edward, *A Transcript of the Registers of the Company of Stationers of London; 1554–1640 A.D.* (London: privately printed, 1875), ii.299.

3   According to Herbert Norris, there is an edition published in November 1589 held in the Bodleian entitled *A true and particular observation of a notable piece of Witchcraft, practiced by John Samuel the Father, Alice Samuel the Mother and Agnes Samuel the Daughter, of Warboise in the Countie of Huntington, Upon five Daughters of Robert Throckmorton of the same towne and Countie Esquire, and certaine other maid-servants to the number of twelve, in the whole, all of them being in one house.* This is in fact the subtitle that occurs after 'to the Reader' in the 1593 B.M. edition (sig.A.3.r). Norris is incorrect in his assumption that this is a 1589 version of the text. See Norris, Herbert E., 'The Witches of Warboys: Bibliographical Note', *Notes and Queries*, Series 12, 8 April 1916, pp.283–284, 15 April 1916, pp.304–305.

    The Bodleian contains three copies of the text. One is the same as the British Library version, although it is missing sigs.A.1–2, B.1, B.4, O.3–4. It is therefore missing its first several pages, its first page having the title referred to above by Norris. Norris cannot have looked at this text. Had he done so he would have realised that, since the text contains (virtually) the whole story up to 1593, the date of 1589 could not have been correct.

    This copy was in fact bequeathed to the Bodleian by Richard Gough. The catalogue of the books thus bequeathed includes a title '*A true and particular observation of a notable piece of Witchcraft, practiced by John Samuel the Father, Alice Samuel the Mother and Agnes Samuel the Daughter, of Warboise in the Countie of Huntington, Upon five Daughters of Robert Throckmorton of the same towne and Countie Esquire, and certaine other maid-servants to the number of twelve, in the whole, all of them being in one house, November 1589.* Thus Norris was in fact led astray by the incorrect title in this catalogue (see anon., *A Catalogue of the Books relating to British Topography... bequeathed to the Bodleian Library in the year MDCCXCIX, by Richard Gough* [Oxford, 1814]).

    The remaining two copies in the Bodleian are slightly differently paginated versions of the British Library copy, with occasional variants in spelling, paragraph format, and typographical style. The British Library version has been 'Printed by the Widdowe Orwin, for Thomas Man, and John

Winnington'. These two Bodleian copies read only 'Printed for Thomas Man and John Winnington'. Apart from these minor differences, the two texts are identical. For various typographical reasons, it can reasonably be concluded that the British Library version is the earlier one. The Norris Museum version is the same as that in the British Museum.

    For a full discussion, see Almond, Philip C., '"The Witches of Warboys": A Bibliographical Note', *Notes and Queries* 52 (2005), pp.192–193.

4   See de Windt, Anne Reiber, 'Witchcraft and Conflicting Visions of the Ideal Village Community', *Journal of British Studies* 34 (1995), p.450.

5   See Brownlow, F.W., *Shakespeare, Harsnett, and the Devils of Denham* (Newark: University of Delaware Press, 1993).

6   Harsnett, Samuel, *A Discovery of the fraudulent Practices of John Darrel* (London, 1599), p.93. See also p.97.

NOTES TO PART ONE

1   The text follows the Julian calendar. In the main, it is remarkably accurate in its dating. I have remarked in the notes on any dating errors in the text. That the Julian calendar is followed is not a matter for surprise. The 'Christian' calendar follows the solar year of 365.25 days, with 365 days making up each year and an extra day added every fourth year to make up the lost quarter. Because the additional quarter day is not a complete quarter but only almost so, the Christian calendar had by the late sixteenth century got ahead of the solar year by ten days. In order to bring the Christian calendar into line with the solar year, Pope Gregory XII decreed that ten days be omitted from the month of October in 1582, the 4th of October to be followed by the 15th. This was accepted throughout Europe except in Russia, Sweden, and England. The Reformed calendar was finally adopted in England in 1752.

2   The necessity of infant baptism was a major source of doctrinal friction between Lutherans and Calvinists. See Nischan, Bodo, 'The Exorcism Controversy and Baptism in the Late Reformation,' *Sixteenth Century Journal* 18 (1987), pp.31–52.

3   The Warboys Parish Registers record the christenings of Joan, 23 May 1574; Mary, 3 July 1575 (buried 23 October 1575); Gabriel, 11 April 1577; Mary, 18 May 1578; Jane, 21 August 1580; Grace, 10 March 1581; Robert, 30 June 1583. Elizabeth was christened in Titchmarsh, Northamptonshire, on 19 July 1579. See Titchmarsh Parish Registers, Northamptonshire Record Office. With the exceptions of the first Mary (deceased) and Gabriel, all the other six children appear in the story.

4   Leaska, Mitchell A., *A Passionate Apprentice: The Early Journals, 1897–1909, Virginia Woolf* (London: Hogarth Press, 1990), pp.138–139.

5   See Owen, T.M.N., *The Church Bells of Huntingdonshire* (London: Jarrold and Sons, 1899). The five bells then present were recast in 1765. There was space for six bells, though, according to tradition, the sixth was lost in transit at sea. A sixth has since been added in honour of Queen Elizabeth II.

6   See Page, William, and Proby, Granville, *The Victoria History of the County of Huntingdon* (London: University of London, 1974), ii.13, 242–243.

7   See de Windt, 'Witchcraft and Conflicting Visions, pp.435–436.

8   Quoted in Wrightson, Keith, 'The Politics of the Parish in Early Modern England', in Fox, A., Griffiths, P., and Hindle, S., *The Experience of Authority in Early Modern England* (London: Macmillan, 1996), p.18.

9   See Sharpe, James, *Defamation and Sexual Slander in Early Modern England: The Church Courts at York* (York: University of York, 1980) pp.95–96; and Wrightson, Keith, *English Society, 1580–1680* (London: Hutchinson, 1982), pp.51–57.

10 See Thomas, Keith, 'Children in Early Modern Europe', in Avery, Gillian and Briggs, Julia, *Children and Their Books* (Oxford: Clarendon, 1989).

11 Quoted in Briggs, Katharine M., *The Anatomy of Puck* (London: Routledge and Kegan Paul, 1959), p.20.

12 See Otto, Rudolf, *The Idea of the Holy* (Oxford: Oxford University Press, 1958).

13 Lemnius, Levinas, *The Secret Miracles of Nature* (London, 1658), p.309.

14 Crooke, Helkiah, *Microcosmagraphia* (London, 1615), p.215.

15 Roper, Lyndal, *Witch Craze: Terror and Fantasy in Baroque Germany* (New Haven, CT: Yale University Press, 2004), p.160.

16 Roper, *Witch Craze*, p.177.

17 Summers, Montague (ed.), *The Discoverie of Witchcraft by Reginald Scot* (New York: Dover, 1972), p.31.

18 Wellcome Library, Western Ms. 537, ff.16–16v. Quoted in Rawcliffe, Carole, *Medicine and Society in Later Medieval England* (Phoenix Mill: Sutton Publishing, 1997), p.48.

19 Barrow, Philip, *The Methode of Physicke, conteyning the Causes, Signes, and Cures of Inward Diseases in Mans Body from the Head to the Foote* (London, 1583), preface.

20 Barrow, *The Methode of Physicke*, p.105.

21 Ibid.

22 See Barrow, *The Methode of Physicke*, p.31, 'Of the Falling Sickness, *De Epilepsia*'.

23 Ady, Thomas, *A Candle in the Dark* (London, 1656), p.115.

24 Quoted in Brownlow, *Shakespeare, Harsnett, and the Devils of Denham*, pp.308–309.

25 Fairfax, Edward, *Daemonologia: A Discourse on Witchcraft* (London: Muller, 1971), p.37.

26 Digby, Kenelm, *Of the Sympathetic Powder* (London, 1669), p.183.

27 See anon., *The most wonderful and true Storie, of a certaine Witch named Alse Gooderidge* (London, 1597).

28 Karlsen, Carol, *The Devil in the Shape of a Woman* (New York: Vintage Books, 1989), p.234.

29 Faulkner, Thomas C., Kiessling, Nicholas K., and Blair, Rhonda L., *Robert Burton: The Anatomy of Melancholy* (Oxford: Clarendon Press, 1989), i.135–136.

30 Halliwell, James O., *The Private Diary of John Dee* (London: Camden Society, 1842), pp.35–36.

31 Wood, Anthony A., *Athenae Oxoniensis*, 4 vols (London: F.C. and J. Rivington et al., 1813–1820), ii.163 (*Fasti Oxoniensis*). See also Venn, John, and Venn, J.A., *Alumni Cantabrigiensis*, 10 vols (Cambridge: Cambridge University Press, 1922–1954), 1.i.274; and Barber, Richard (ed.), *John Aubrey: Brief Lives. A Selection based upon Existing Contemporary Portraits* (London: Folio Society, 1975), p.62.

32 Barber, *John Aubrey: Brief Lives*, p.64.

33 Keynes, Geoffrey (ed.), *The Works of Sir Thomas Browne* (London: Faber and Faber, 1928), i.38–39.

34 See anon., *A Detection of damnable driftes, practiced by three Witches arraigned at Chelmisforde in Essex* (London, 1579), sigs.A.6.r–v.

35 Dalton, Michael, *The Countrey Justice: Containing the Practice of the Justices of the Peace out of their Sessions* (London, 1630), p.278.

36 See Dubois, C.G., 'Pathologie du Corps Spectral à la Renaissance', *Cahiers Elisabethians* 59 (2001), pp.45–58.

37 See Almond, Philip C., 'The Journey of the Soul in Seventeenth-Century English Platonism', *History of European Ideas* 13 (1991), pp.775–791.

38 Thomas, Keith, *Religion and the Decline of Magic* (Harmondsworth: Penguin, 1973), p.704.

39 Quoted by MacDonald, Michael, *Mystical Bedlam: Madness, Anxiety and Healing in Seventeenth-century England* (Cambridge: Cambridge University Press, 1983), p.207.

40 Anon., *A Detection of damnable driftes*, sig.C.8.r–v.

41 Summers, *The Discoverie of Witchcraft*, 'Epistle to Sir Thomas Scot'. I am indebted here to Gibson, Marion, 'Understanding Witchcraft? Accusers' Stories in Print in Early Modern England', in Clark, Stuart (ed.), *Languages of Witchcraft: Narrative, Ideology and Meaning in Early Modern Culture* (London: Macmillan, 2001), p.45.

42 See Darrell, John, *A true Narration of the strange and Grevous Vexation by the Devil, of 7. Persons in Lancashire* (England [?], 1600), p.14.

43 Anon., *The most wonderful and true Storie*, p.4.

44 See MacDonald, Michael (ed.), *Witchcraft and Hysteria in Elizabethan London: Edward Jordan and the Mary Glover Case* (London: Tavistock/Routledge, 1991), p.3; More, George, *A true Discourse concerning the certain Possession and Dispossession of 7 persons in one Family in Lancashire* (London, 1600), p.14.

45 See anon., *The Boy of Bilson* (London, 1622), p.46.

46 It was particularly crucial to the Salem trials a century later. For a balanced assessment of the role of spectral evidence at Salem, see Craker, Wendel D., 'Spectral Evidence, Non-Spectral Acts of Witchcraft, and Confession at Salem in 1692,' *Historical Journal* 40 (1997), pp.331–358. As in Salem, so in Warboys; it was Alice Samuel's alleged malevolent acts and her confession which were decisive.

47 The Warboys Registers records the birth of another Mary in July 1575. Her burial was noted in October of the same year.

48 Tatem, Moira, *The Witches of Warboys* (March: Cambridgeshire Libraries Publications, 1993), p.15, has Elizabeth born in 1576 and thus older than Mary. She was not aware of the record of Elizabeth's birth in the Titchmarsh

Parish Registers, which makes Elizabeth the third oldest sister, after Joan and Mary.

49 We do not know the ages of the servants, but we do know that they were all women, and we can assume they were in their teen years.

50 Anon., *The Witches of Northamptonshire* (London, 1612), sig.c.2.v. Quoted by Gibson, Marion, *Early Modern Witches: Witchcraft Cases in Contemporary Writing* (London: Routledge, 2000), p.167. The text was closely related here to James I's *Daemonologie* (Edinburgh, 1597), pp.80–81.

51 Rosen, Barbara (ed.), *Witchcraft* (London: Edward Arnold, 1969), pp.79–80.

52 Anon., *A breife Narration of the Possession, Dispossession, and, Repossession of William Sommers* (London, 1598), sig.B.3.v.

53 See anon., *A breife Narration of the Possession*, sigs.E.3.r–v.

54 See Bernard, Richard, *A Guide to Grand-jury Men* (London, 1627), pp.49–52.

55 See Sharpe, James, *The Bewitching of Anne Gunter: A Horrible and True Story of Football, Witchcraft, Murder and the King of England* (London: Profile Books, 1999).

56 Fisher, John, *The Copy of a Letter describing the wonderful Woorke of God in delivering a Mayden within the City of Chester, from an horrible kinde of torment and sicknes 16. of February 1564* (London, 1564), sig.A.6.r. Interestingly, there is no suggestion in this text of bewitchment, or of possession by the Devil, but only by a spirit.

57 See James I, *Daemonologie*, pp.70–71. The third criterion was the ability to speak various languages, though this could be dispensed with were the demoniac possessed with a dumb and blind spirit.

58 For Robert Throckmorton's family tree, see Throckmorton, C. Wickliffe, *A Genealogical and Historical Account of the Throckmorton Family* (Richmond, VA: Old Dominion Press, 1930), p.257.

59 Anon., *A Most Certain, Strange, and True Discovery of a Witch* (n.p., 1643), pp.5–6.

60 Ibid., p.7.

61 Anon., *A Rehearsall both straung and true, of hainous and horrible actes* (London, 1579), sigs.B.1.v–B.2.r.

62 B.R., *A most wicked Worke of a wretched Witch* (London, 1592), p.4.

63 Ibid., p.5

64 Anon., *The most wonderful and true Storie*, p.6.

65 Sharpe, James, *Instruments of Darkness: Witchcraft in England 1550–1750* (London: Hamish Hamilton, 1996), p.159.

66 Gaule, John, *Select Cases of Conscience touching Witches and Witchcrafts* (London, 1646), p.144.

67 Cooper, Thomas, *The Mystery of Witch-craft* (London, 1617), p.168.

68 Gifford, George, *A Dialogue Concerning Witches and Witchcraftes* (London, 1593), sig.E.4.r.

69 Almond, Philip C., *Demonic Possession and Exorcism in Early Modern England: Contemporary Texts and Their Cultural Contexts* (Cambridge: Cambridge University Press, 2004), p.161.

70 Cotta, John, *The Triall of Witch-craft* (London, 1616), p.77.

71 Anon., *The Boy of Bilson*, p.60.

72 See Jollie, Thomas, *The Surey Demoniack* (London, 1697), pp.3, 23.

73 Bernard, *A Guide to Grand-jury Men*, p.193.

74 See Perkins, William, *A Discourse of the damned Art of Witchcraft as it is revealed in the Scriptures, and manifest by true Experience* (Cambridge, 1608), p.206.

75 See anon., *A true and fearfull Vexation of one Alexander Nyndge* (London, 1615).

76 Quoted by Macfarlane, Alan, *Witchcraft in Tudor and Stuart England: A Regional and Comparative Study* (London: Routledge, 1999), p.121.

77 See W.W., *A true and just Recorde, of the Information, Examination and Confession of all the Witches, taken at S. Oses in the Countie of Essex* (London, 1582), sigs.E.1.r–v. I owe the reference to Macfarlane, *Witchcraft in Tudor and Stuart England*.

78 Perkins, *A Discourse of the damned Art of Witchcraft*, pp.177–178.

79 Bernard, *A Guide to Grand-jury Men*, p.129.

80 Ibid., p.130.

81 Ibid. See also Cooper, *The Mystery of Witch-craft*, pp.211ff.

82 Bernard, *A Guide to Grand-jury Men*, p.130.

83 More, *A true Discourse*, p.14.

84 Ibid., p.21.

85 See Belgion, Helen, *Titchmarsh, Past and Present* (Kettering: printed by the author, 1979); and Sheils, William J., *The Puritans in the Diocese of Peterborough, 1558–1610* (Northampton: Northamptonshire Record Society, 1979), pp.12, 40, 46.

86 Harsnett, *A Discovery of the fraudulent Practices of John Darrel*, p.288.

87 Dalton, *The Countrey Justice*, p.273.

88 Anon., *The Examination and Confession of certaine Wytches at Chensforde in the Countie of Essex, before the Quenes majesties Judges, the xxvi. Daye of July. Anno. 1566.* (n.p., 1566), sig.B.1.r.

89 One of the three was Elizabeth Francis again. She had escaped punishment in 1566.

90 See anon., *A Detection of damnable driftes*, sig.A.6.v.

91 W.W., *A true and just Recorde*, sig.A.3.v.

92 Ibid, sig.B.2.r.

93 See Sharpe, *Instruments of Darkness*, p.72.

94 Anon., *The Apprehension and Confession of three notorious Witches, arreigned and by Justice condemned and executed at Chelmes-forde, in the Countye of Essex* (London, 1589), sig.B.1.v.

95 Anon., *The Examination of John Walsh… upon certayne Interrogatories touchyng Wytchcrafte and Sorcerye* (London, 1566), sig.A.5.r.

96 Ibid.

97 Ibid., sig.A.6.r.

98 Purkiss, Diane, *Troublesome Things: A History of Fairies and Fairy Stories* (London: Penguin, 2001), p.152. I am also indebted in the following to Emma Wilby, 'The Witch's Familiar and the Fairy in Early Modern England and Scotland', *Folklore* 111 (2000), pp.283–305.

99 Anon., *The Examination and Confession of certaine Wytches*, sig.A.8.v.

100 Ibid., sigs.A.6.v, B.1.r.

101 Anon., *A Rehearsall both straung and true*, sig.A.2.v.

102 Potts, Thomas, *The Wonderfull Discoverie of Witches in the County of Lancaster* (London, 1613), sig.B.2.v.

103 Bynum, Caroline Walker, *Holy Feast and Holy Food: The Religious Significance of Food to Medieval Women* (Berkeley: University of California Press, 1988), p.193.

104 MacDonald, *Witchcraft and Hysteria in Elizabethan London*, p.4.

105 Anon., *Wonderfull Newes from the North. Or, a true Relation of the sad and grievous Torments, inflicted upon the bodies of three children* (London, 1650), p.3.

106 See Bynum, *Holy Feast and Holy Food*, ch.6.

107 The Oliver Cromwell of the English Revolution was the grandson of Sir Henry Cromwell, and the son of one of Sir Henry's younger sons, Robert. Susan Weeks was his second wife. He was first married to Joan Warren, daughter of Sir Ralph Warren, Mayor of London. She was buried on 12 October 1584 having borne eleven children. See All Saints, Huntingdon, Parish Registers.

108 See Darby, H.C., *The Draining of the Fens* (Cambridge: Cambridge University Press, 1956), p.16.

109 Edelen, Georges (ed.), *The Description of England by William Harrison* (Ithaca, NY: Cornell University Press, 1968), pp.94ff.

110 The Christian name is difficult to read. 'Susan' is the most likely.

111 Goodwin, Philip, *The Mystery of Dreames* (London, 1658), p.15.

112 See Crawford, Patricia, 'Women's Dreams in Early Modern England', *History Workshop Journal* 49 (2000), p.133; and MacDonald, *Mystical Bedlam*.

113 Hill, Thomas, *The Most Pleasaunte Arte of the Interpretacion of Dreames* (London, 1576), epistle dedicatory.

114 Artemidorus, *The Interpretation of Dreames, Digested into five books* (London, 1644), p.75.

115 See Venn, and Venn, *Alumni Cantabrigiensis*, 1.iii.359. Henry's daughter Mary, was to marry Erasmus Dryden, and become the mother of the English dramatist John Dryden.

116 W.W., *A true and just Recorde*, sig.A.3.v.

117 Hutchinson, Francis, *An Historical Essay Concerning Witchcraft* (London, 1718), p.106.

118 Cotta, John, *The Infallible True and Assured Witch* (London, 1625), p.99.

NOTES TO PART TWO

1   Hunt, William, *The Puritan Moment: The Coming of Revolution in an English County* (Cambridge, MA: Harvard University Press, 1983), p.155.

2   Walsham, Alexandra, *Providence in Early Modern England* (Oxford: Oxford University Press, 1999), p.86.

3   See John 8.44.

4   De Windt, 'Witchcraft and Conflicting Visions', p.457.

5 See Walker, Daniel, P., *Unclean Spirits: Possession and Exorcism in France and England in the Late Sixteenth and Early Seventeenth Centuries* (London: Scolar, 1981), p.21.

6 See anon., *The most wonderful and true Storie*, p.34.

7 See anon., *The Disclosing of a late counterfeyted Possession by the Devyl in two Maydens within the Citie of London* (London, 1574), sig.A.4.v.

8 See Brownlow, *Shakespeare, Harsnett, and the Devils of Denham*, pp.243–253.

9 Robert Throckmorton's father Gabriel had married an Emma Lawrence.

10 Potts, *The Wonderfull Discoverie of Witches*, sig. B.3.v.

11 Anon., *The Examination of John Walsh*, sig.B.3.r.

12 See Oldham, James C., 'On Pleading the Belly: A History of the Jury of Matrons', *Criminal Justice History* 6 (1985), pp.1–64.

13 Summers, *The Discoverie of Witchcraft*, p.273.

14 Robbins, Rossell Hope, *The Encyclopedia of Witchcraft and Demonology* (New York: Crown, 1959), p.466.

15 Summers, Montague (ed.), *The Malleus Maleficarum of Heinrich Kramer and James Sprenger* (New York: Dover, 1971), p.109.

16 Quoted by Stephens, Walter, *Demon Lovers* (Chicago: University of Chicago Press, 2002), p.62. I am particularly indebted to Stephens for this discussion of demonic bodies.

17 See Summers, *The Malleus Maleficarum*, p.26.

18 Aquinas, Thomas, *Summa Theologica* 1.51.3, translated by Stephens, *Demon Lovers*, p.64.

19 More, Henry, *An Antidote against Atheism* (London, 1655), p.241.

20 Quoted by Sharpe, *Instruments of Darkness*, p.74.

21 Anon., *The Apprehension and Confession of three notorious Witches*, sig.A.3.r .

22 On maximisation and minimisation techniques in police interrogations, see Kassin, Saul M., and McNall, K., 'Police Interrogations and Confessions: Communicating Promises and Threats by Pragmatic Implication', *Law and Human Behaviour* 15 (1991), pp.233–251.

23 On this distinction, see Kassin, Saul, M., 'The Psychology of Confession Evidence', *American Psychologist* 52 (1997), pp.225–226.

24 On public penance, see Ingram, Martin, *Church Courts, Sex and Marriage in England, 1570–1640* (Cambridge: Cambridge University Press, 1987); and Emmison, F.G., *Elizabethan Life: Morals and the Church Courts* (Chelmsford: Essex County Council, 1973).

25 See Major, Kathleen, 'The Lincoln Diocesan Records', *Transactions of the Royal Historical Society*, 4th Series 22 (1940), pp.63–64; and Nathan, Debbie, and Snedeker, Michael, *Satan's Silence: Ritual Abuse and the Making of the Modern American Witch Hunt* (New York: Basic Books, 1995).

26 See de Windt, 'Witchcraft and Conflicting Visions', pp.444–446.

27 Coghill, N. (trans.), *The Canterbury Tales* (Harmondsworth: Penguin, 1977), p.311.

28 See Owen, Dorothy M., 'An Episcopal Audience Court', in Baker, J.H. (ed.), *Legal Records and the Historian* (London: Royal Historical Society, 1978), pp.140–149; and Thompson, A. Hamilton, *The English Clergy and Their Organization in the Later Middle Ages* (Oxford: Clarendon, 1947), pp.210–246.

NOTES TO PART THREE

1 I have not tried here to reconcile Dorington's claim that he arrived after lunch, and that he had found them all eating.

2 Boulton, Richard, *A Compleat History of Magick, Sorcery, and Witchcraft*, 2 vols (London, 1715) has a fairly complete version of the story. He reads 'Jane' rather than 'Joan' at this point. His confusion is caused by the fact that the spelling of 'Jane' and 'Joan' varies throughout this section, and often it can be determined only from other evidence internal to the text which of these sisters is being referred to.

3 The text incorrectly has Sunday 20 February. Granting it was a Sunday, 18 February was the correct date.

4 He was christened in Titchmarsh on 13 October 1560.

5 The text has 2 February. The context shows clearly that March is meant. In the text at this point, the reference is to 'Iaone'. I read this as 'Joan'.

6 Joan had probably spent some time there with a relative during the period when Robert had dispersed the children. Sommersham was a small village near Warboys. The only Pickering or Throckmorton to appear in the Sommersham Parish Registers is a Richard Pickering, son of Richard Pickering of Pidley, who was buried on 2 December 1599.

7 The text refers to John Pickering as one of the children's uncles. There is no record of a John Pickering, brother to Elizabeth, the children's mother. Nevertheless, the Titchmarsh Parish Records note the baptism of a John Pickering, son of Boniface Pickering, on 18 January 1559. Boniface was the brother of John Pickering, Elizabeth's father. The John Pickering in the story is thus Elizabeth's cousin, and only the children's uncle in an 'extended family' sense.

8 See Hunt, *The Puritan Moment*, ch.6.

9 That is, on Monday 2 April.

10 See Noble, W.M., *Huntingdonshire and the Spanish Armada* (London: E. Stock, 1896), p.35.

NOTES TO PART FOUR

1 See Cockburn, J.S., 'Trial by the Book? Fact and Theory in the Criminal Process 1558–1625', in Baker, *Legal Records and the Historian*, (London: Royal Historical Society, 1978) pp.60–79.

2 See 1 Samuel 16.23.

3 Under standard procedures, the grand jury, having decided the accused should proceed to trial, would mark the indictment as a true bill (*billa vera*). The matter would then be heard before a petty jury. In this case, the two juries appear to be conflated. The indictments are marked as true bills at the end of the formal trial by the 'jury of life and death', the petty jury, a role usually reserved for the grand jury before the formal trial. We cannot determine whether this is a regional variation on the ideal or incorrect reporting on the procedure by the author

of our text. Granting the involvement of Edward Fenner in the text, we can assume the former.

4   See Longden, Henry J., *Northamptonshire and Rutland Clergy from 1500* (Northampton: Northhamptonshire Record Society, 1938–1952), x.105.

5   See Sharpe, James, *Defamation and Sexual Slander.*

NOTES TO EPILOGUE

1   Dalton, *The Countrey Justice*, p.273.

2   Anon., *The Examination and Confession of certaine Wytches*, sigs. B.3.v–B.4.r.

3   In medieval physiology, there is no gap between maternal milk and menstrual blood. The child in the womb was thought to subsist on menstrual blood, which after birth turned into milk. So Alice's emission of both blood and milk is not surprising. See Bynum, Caroline Walker, *Fragmentation and Redemption: Essays on Gender and the Human Body in Medieval Religion* (New York: Zone, 1992), ch.6.

4   See Bede, Cuthbert, 'The Witches of Warboys and the Huntingdon Sermon against Witchcraft', *Notes and Queries* 12 (1879), pp.70–71.

5   Naylor, M.J., *The Inantity* [sic] *and Mischief of vulgar Superstitions. Four Sermons, Preached at All-Saints Church, Huntingdon* (London, 1795), p.vii.

Bibliography

\Ady, Thomas, *A Candle in the Dark* (London, 1656).

Akeroyd, Alan, and Clifford, Catherine, *Huntingdon: Eight Centuries of History* (Derby: Breeden Books, 2004).

Almond, Philip C., *Demonic Possession and Exorcism in Early Modern England: Contemporary Texts and Their Cultural Contexts* (Cambridge: Cambridge University Press, 2004).

———, 'The Journey of the Soul in Seventeenth-Century English Platonism', *History of European Ideas* 13 (1991), pp. 775–791.

———, '"The Witches of Warboys": A Bibliographical Note', *Notes and Queries* 52 (2005), pp.192–193.

Anon., *A breife Narration of the Possession, Dispossession, and, Repossession of William Sommers* (London, 1598).

———, *A Catalogue of the Books relating to British Topography... bequeathed to the Bodleian Library in the year MDCCXCIX, by Richard Gough* (Oxford, 1814).

———, *A Detection of damnable driftes, practiced by three Witches arraigned at Chelmisforde in Essex* (London, 1579).

———, *A Most Certain, Strange, and True Discovery of a Witch* (n.p., 1643).

———, *A Rehearsall both straung and true, of hainous and horrible actes* (London, 1579).

———, *A true and fearfull Vexation of one Alexander Nyndge* (London, 1615).

———, *The Apprehension and Confession of three notorious Witches, arreigned and by Justice condemned and executed at Chelmes-forde, in the Countye of Essex* (London, 1589).

———, *The Boy of Bilson* (London, 1622).

———, *The Disclosing of a late counterfeyted Possession by the Devyl in two Maydens within the Citie of London* (London, 1574).

———, *The Examination and Confession of certaine Wytches at Chensforde in the Countie of Essex, before the Quenes majesties Judges, the xxvi. Daye of July. Anno. 1566.* (n.p., 1566).

———, *The Examination of John Walsh... upon certayne Interrogatories touchyng Wytchcrafte and Sorcerye* (London, 1566).

———, *The most strange and admirable Discoverie of the three Witches of Warboys, arraigned, convicted, and executed at the last Assises at Huntington, for the bewitching of the five daughters of Robert Throckmorton Esquire, and divers other persons, with sundrie Divellish and grievous torments: And also for the bewitching of the Lady Crumwell, the like hath not been heard of in this age* (London, 1593).

———, *The most wonderful and true Storie, of a certaine Witch named Alse Gooderidge* (London, 1597).

————, *The Witches of Northamptonshire* (London, 1612).

————, *Wonderfull Newes from the North. Or, a true Relation of the sad and grievous Torments, inflicted upon the bodies of three children* (London, 1650).

Arber, Edward, *A Transcript of the Registers of the Company of Stationers of London; 1554–1640 A.D.* (London: privately printed, 1875).

Artemidorus, *The Interpretation of Dreames, Digested into five books* (London, 1644).

B.R., *A most wicked Worke of a wretched Witch* (London, 1592).

Barber, Richard (ed.), *John Aubrey: Brief Lives. A Selection based upon Existing Contemporary Portraits* (London: Folio Society, 1975).

Barrow, Philip, *The Methode of Physicke, conteyning the Causes, Signes, and Cures of Inward Diseases in Mans Body from the Head to the Foote* (London, 1583).

Bede, Cuthbert, 'The Witches of Warboys and the Huntingdon Sermon against Witchcraft', *Notes and Queries* 12 (1879), pp.70–71.

Bedells, J., 'The Gentry of Huntingdonshire', *Local Population Studies* 44 (1990), pp.30–40.

Belgion, Helen, *Titchmarsh, Past and Present* (Kettering: printed by the author, 1979).

Bernard, Richard, *A Guide to Grand-jury Men* (London, 1627).

Boulton, Richard, *A Compleat History of Magick, Sorcery, and Witchcraft*, 2 vols (London, 1715).

————, *The Possibility and Reality of Magick, Sorcery, and Witchcraft, demonstrated* (London, 1722).

Briggs, Katharine M., *The Anatomy of Puck* (London: Routledge and Kegan Paul, 1959).

Brownlow, F.W., *Shakespeare, Harsnett, and the Devils of Denham* (Newark: University of Delaware Press, 1993).

Bynum, Caroline Walker, *Fragmentation and Redemption: Essays on Gender and the Human Body in Medieval Religion* (New York: Zone, 1992).

————, *Holy Feast and Holy Food: The Religious Significance of Food to Medieval Women* (Berkeley: University of California Press, 1988).

Cockburn, J.S., 'Trial by the Book? Fact and Theory in the Criminal Process 1558–1625', in Baker, J.H. (ed.), *Legal Records and the Historian* (London: Royal Historical Society, 1978), pp.60–79.

Coghill, N. (trans), *The Canterbury Tales* (Harmondsworth: Penguin, 1977).

Cooper, Thomas, *The Mystery of Witch-craft* (London, 1617).

Cotta, John, *The Infallible True and Assured Witch* (London, 1625).

————, *The Triall of Witch-craft* (London, 1616).

Craker, Wendel D., 'Spectral Evidence, Non-Spectral Acts of Witchcraft, and Confession at Salem in 1692', *Historical Journal* 40 (1997), pp.331–358.

Crawford, Patricia, 'Women's Dreams in Early Modern England', *History Workshop Journal* 49 (2000), pp.129–141.

Crooke, Helkiah, *Microcosmagraphia* (London, 1615).

Dalton, Michael, *The Countrey Justice Containing the Practice of the Justices of the Peace out of their Sessions* (London, 1630).

Darby, H.C., *The Draining of the Fens* (Cambridge: Cambridge University Press, 1956).

Darrell, John, *A true Narration of the strange and Grevous Vexation by the Devil, of 7. Persons in Lancashire* (England [?], 1600).

De Windt, Anne Reiber, 'Witchcraft and Conflicting Visions of the Ideal Village Community', *Journal of British Studies* 34 (1995), pp.427–463.

———, 'Local Government in a Small Town: A Medieval Leet Jury and its Constituents', *Albion* 25 (1991), pp. 627–654.

Digby, Kenelm, *Of the Sympathetic Powder* (London, 1669).

Dubois, C.G., 'Pathologie du Corps Spectral à la Renaissance', *Cahiers Elisabethians* 59 (2001), pp.45–58.

Edelen, Georges (ed.), *The Description of England by William Harrison* (Ithaca, NY: Cornell University Press, 1968).

Eliade, Mircea, *Shamanism: Archaic Rites of Ecstasy* (London: Routledge and Kegan Paul), 1964.

Emmison, F.G., *Elizabethan Life: Morals and the Church Courts* (Chelmsford: Essex County Council, 1973).

Estes, Leland, 'The Medical Origins of the European Witch Craze', *Journal of Social History* 17(1984), pp.271–284.

Fairfax, Edward, *Daemonologia: A Discourse on Witchcraft* (London: Muller, 1971).

Faulkner, Thomas C., Kiessling, Nicholas K., and Blair, Rhonda L., *Robert Burton: The Anatomy of Melancholy* (Oxford: Clarendon Press, 1989).

Fisher, John, *The Copy of a Letter describing the wonderful Woorke of God in delivering a Mayden within the City of Chester, from an horrible kinde of torment and sicknes 16. of February 1564* (London, 1564).

Freeman-Greville, G.S.P., *The Islamic and Christian Calendars AD 622–2222 (AH 1–1650)* (Reading: Garnet, 1995).

Fuller, Thomas, *The History of the Worthies of England*, 2 vols. (London, 1811).

Gaule, John, *Select Cases of Conscience touching Witches and Witchcrafts* (London, 1646).

Gibson, Marion, *Early Modern Witches: Witchcraft Cases in Contemporary Writing* (London: Routledge, 2000).

———, 'Understanding Witchcraft? Accusers' Stories in Print in Early Modern England', in Clark, Stuart (ed.), *Languages of Witchcraft: Narrative, Ideology and Meaning in Early Modern Culture* (London: Macmillan, 2001), pp.41–54.

Gifford, George, *A Dialogue Concerning Witches and Witchcraftes* (London, 1593).

Grainge, William, *Daemonologia: A Discourse on Witchcraft as it was acted in the Family of Mr. Edward Fairfax, of Fuyston, in the County of York, in the year1621* (Harrogate: R.Ackrill, 1882).

Goodwin, Philip, *The Mystery of Dreames* (London, 1658).

Halliwell, James O., *The Private Diary of John Dee* (London: Camden Society, 1842).

Harsnett, Samuel, *A Discovery of the fraudulent Practices of John Darrel* (London, 1599).

Hill, Thomas, *The Most Pleasaunte Arte of the Interpretacion of Dreames* (London, 1576).

Hunt, William, *The Puritan Moment: The Coming of Revolution in an English County* (Cambridge, MA: Harvard University Press, 1983).

Hutchinson, Francis, *An Historical Essay Concerning Witchcraft* (London, 1718).

Ingram, Martin, *Church Courts, Sex and Marriage in England, 1570–1640* (Cambridge: Cambridge University Press, 1987).

James, King of England, *Daemonologie* (Edinburgh, 1597).

Jollie, Thomas, *The Surey Demoniack* (London, 1697).

Karlsen, Carol, *The Devil in the Shape of a Woman* (New York: Vintage Books, 1989).

Kassin, Saul, M., 'The Psychology of Confession Evidence', *American Psychologist* 52 (1997), pp.221–233.

Kassin, Saul M., and McNall, K., 'Police Interrogations and Confessions: Communicating Promises and Threats by Pragmatic Implication', *Law and Human Behaviour* 15 (1991), pp.233–251.

Keynes, Geoffrey (ed.), *The Works of Sir Thomas Browne* (London: Faber and Faber, 1928).

Leaska, Mitchell A., *A Passionate Apprentice: The Early Journals, 1897–1909, Virginia Woolf* (London: Hogarth Press, 1990).

Lemnius, Levinas, *The Secret Miracles of Nature* (London, 1658).

Longden, Henry J., *Northamptonshire and Rutland Clergy from 1500* (Northampton: Northamptonshire Record Society, 1938–1952).

MacDonald, Michael (ed.), *Mystical Bedlam: Madness, Anxiety and Healing in Seventeenth-century England* (Cambridge: Cambridge University Press, 1983).

———, *Witchcraft and Hysteria in Elizabethan London: Edward Jordan and the Mary Glover Case* (London: Tavistock/Routledge, 1991).

Macfarlane, Alan, *Witchcraft in Tudor and Stuart England: A Regional and Comparative Study* (London: Routledge, 1999).

Major, Kathleen, 'The Lincoln Diocesan Records', *Transactions of the Royal Historical Society*, 4th Series 22 (1940), pp.39–66.

More, George, *A true Discourse concerning the certain Possession and Dispossession of 7 persons in one Family in Lancashire* (London, 1600).

More, Henry, *An Antidote against Atheism* (London, 1655).

Nathan, Debbie, and Snedeker, Michael, *Satan's Silence: Ritual Abuse and the Making of the Modern American Witch Hunt* (New York: Basic Books, 1995).

Naylor, M.J., *The Inanity* [sic] *and Mischief of vulgar Superstitions. Four Sermons, Preached at All-Saints Church, Huntingdon* (London, 1795).

Nischan, Bodo, 'The Exorcism Controversy and Baptism in the Late Reformation,' *Sixteenth Century Journal* 18 (1987), pp. 31–52.

Noble, W.M., *Huntingdonshire and the Spanish Armada* (London: E. Stock, 1896).

Norris, Herbert E., 'The Witches of Warboys: Bibliographical Note', *Notes and Queries*, Series 12, 8 April 1916, pp.283–284, 15 April 1916, pp.304–305.

Oldham, James C., 'On Pleading the Belly: A History of the Jury of Matrons', *Criminal Justice History* 6 (1985), pp.1–64.

Otto, Rudolf, *The Idea of the Holy* (Oxford: Oxford University Press, 1958).

Owen, Dorothy M., 'An Episcopal Audience Court', in Baker, J.H. (ed.), *Legal Records and the Historian* (London: Royal Historical Society, 1978), pp.140–149.

Owen, T.M.N., *The Church Bells of Huntingdonshire* (London: Jarrold and Sons, 1899).

Page, William, and Proby, Granville, *The Victoria History of the County of Huntingdon*, 4 vols (London: University of London, 1974).

Perkins, William, *A Discourse of the damned Art of Witchcraft as it is revealed in the Scriptures, and manifest by true Experience* (Cambridge, 1608).

Potts, Thomas, *The Wonderfull Discoverie of Witches in the County of Lancaster* (London, 1613).

Purkiss, Diane, *The Witch in History: Early Modern and Twentieth-century Representations* (London: Routledge, 1996).

———, *Troublesome Things: A History of Fairies and Fairy Stories* (London: Penguin, 2001).

Rawcliffe, Carole, *Medicine and Society in Later Medieval England* (Phoenix Mill: Sutton Publishing, 1997).

Robbins, Rossell Hope, *The Encyclopedia of Witchcraft and Demonology* (New York: Crown, 1959).

Roper, Lyndal, *Witch Craze: Terror and Fantasy in Baroque Gemany* (New Haven, CT: Yale University Press, 2004).

Rosen, Barbara (ed.), *Witchcraft* (London: Edward Arnold, 1969).

Sharpe, James, *Defamation and Sexual Slander in Early Modern England: The Church Courts at York* (York: University of York, 1980).

———, *Early Modern England: A Social History 1550–1760* (London: Edward Arnold, 1987).

———, *Instruments of Darkness: Witchcraft in England 1550–1750* (London: Hamish Hamilton, 1996).

———, *The Bewitching of Anne Gunter: A Horrible and True Story of Football, Witchcraft, Murder and the King of England* (London: Profile Books, 1999).

———, *Witchcraft in Early Modern England* (London: Longman, 2001).

Sheils, William J., *The Puritans in the Diocese of Peterborough, 1558–1610* (Northampton: Northamptonshire Record Society, 1979).

Stephens, Walter, *Demon Lovers* (Chicago: University of Chicago Press, 2002).

Summers, Montague (ed.), *The Discoverie of Witchcraft by Reginald Scot* (New York: Dover, 1972).

——— (ed.), *The Malleus Maleficarum of Heinrich Kramer and James Sprenger* (New York: Dover, 1971).

Tatem, Moira, *The Witches of Warboys* (March: Cambridgeshire Libraries Publications, 1993).

Thomas, Keith, 'Children in Early Modern Europe', in Avery, Gillian and Briggs, Julia, *Children and Their Books* (Oxford: Clarendon, 1989), pp.45–77.

———, *Religion and the Decline of Magic* (Harmondsworth: Penguin, 1973).

Thompson, A. Hamilton, *The English Clergy and Their Organization in the Later Middle Ages* (Oxford: Clarendon, 1947).

Throckmorton, C. Wickliffe, *A Genealogical and Historical Account of the Throckmorton Family* (Richmond, VA: Old Dominion Press, 1930).

Unsworth, C.R., 'Witchcraft Beliefs and Criminal Procedures in Early Modern England', in Watkin, Tomas G. (ed.), *Legal Record and Historical Reality* (London & Ronceverte: Hambledon Press, 1989), pp.71–98.

Venn, John, and Venn, J.A., *Alumni Cantabrigiensis*, 10 vols (Cambridge: Cambridge University Press, 1922–1954).

W.W., *A true and just Recorde, of the Information, Examination and Confession of all the Witches, taken at S. Oses in the Countie of Essex* (London, 1582).

Walker, Daniel P., *Unclean Spirits: Possession and Exorcism in France and England in the Late Sixteenth and Early Seventeenth Centuries* (London: Scolar, 1981).

Walsham, Alexandra, *Providence in Early Modern England* (Oxford: Oxford University Press, 1999).

Wilby, Emma, 'The Witch's Familiar and the Fairy in Early Modern England and Scotland', *Folklore* 111 (2000), pp.283–305.

Wood, Anthony A., *Athenae Oxoniensis*, 4 vols (London: F.C. and J. Rivington et al., 1813–1820).

Wrightson, Keith, *English Society, 1580–1680* (London: Hutchinson, 1982).

———, 'The Politics of the Parish in Early Modern England', in Fox, A., Griffiths, P., and Hindle, S., *The Experience of Authority in Early Modern England* (London: Macmillan, 1996), pp.10–46.

Index of Persons

Index of Subjects